Also by Katie Hafner

The House at the Bridge: A Story of Modern Germany

*Cyberpunk: Outlaws and Hackers on the Computer
   Frontier* (with John Markoff)

Where Wizards Stay Up Late

The Origins of the Internet

Katie Hafner and **Matthew Lyon**

Simon & Schuster

SIMON & SCHUSTER
Rockefeller Center
1230 Avenue of the Americas
New York, NY 10020

Designed by Levavi & Levavi

Manufactured in the United States of America

10   9   8   7   6   5

Library of Congress Cataloging-in-Publication Data

Hafner, Katie.
    Where wizards stay up late : the origins of the Internet / Katie Hafner
    and Matthew Lyon.
        p.   cm.
    Includes index.
    1. Internet (Computer network).   I. Lyon, Matthew.   II. Title.
    TK5105.875.I57H338 1996
004.6'7—dc20   96-19533
                                                                                    CIP

ISBN 0-684-81201-0

To the memory of J. C. R. Licklider

Contents

Los Alamos' lights where wizards stay up late
(Stay in the car, forget the gate)
To save the world or end it, time will tell

—James Merrill,
"Under Libra: Weights and Measures,"
from *Braving the Elements*

Prologue

❏ September 1994

They came to Boston from as far away as London and Los Angeles, several dozen middle-aged men, reuniting for a fall weekend in 1994 to celebrate what they had done twenty-five years earlier. These were the scientists and engineers who had designed and built the ARPANET, the computer network that revolutionized communications and gave rise to the global Internet. They had worked in relative obscurity in the 1960s; a number of them had been only graduate students when they made significant contributions to the network. Others had been mentors. Most of them had never gained much recognition for the achievement.

Bolt Beranek and Newman, a computer company based in Cambridge, had been their center of gravity, had employed many of them, had built and operated the original ARPA network, then slipped into relative obscurity as the Internet grew like a teeming city around its earliest neighborhood. Now, a quarter-century after installing the first network node, BBN had invited all of the ARPANET pioneers to come together, hoping to heighten its own profile by throwing a lavish celebration marking the anniversary.

Many of those at the reunion hadn't seen one another or been in touch for years. As they filtered into the lobby of the Copley Plaza for a Friday afternoon press conference kicking off the celebration, they scanned the room for familiar faces.

Bob Taylor, the director of a corporate research facility in Silicon Valley, had come to the party for old times sake, but he was also on a personal mission to correct an inaccuracy of long standing. Rumors had persisted for years that the ARPANET had been built to protect national security in the face of a nuclear attack. It was a myth that had gone unchallenged long enough to become widely accepted as fact.

Taylor had been the young director of the office within the Defense Department's Advanced Research Projects Agency overseeing computer research, and he was the one who had started the ARPANET. The project had embodied the most peaceful intentions—to link computers at scientific laboratories across the country so that researchers might share computer resources. Taylor knew the ARPANET and its progeny, the Internet, had nothing to do with supporting or surviving war—never did. Yet he felt fairly alone in carrying that knowledge.

Lately, the mainstream press had picked up the grim myth of a nuclear survival scenario and had presented it as an established truth. When *Time* magazine committed the error, Taylor wrote a letter to the editor, but the magazine didn't print it. The effort to set the record straight was like chasing the wind; Taylor was beginning to feel like a crank.

Across the room at dinner that night at the Copley, Taylor spotted an elderly, heavyset man with a thick mustache. He recognized him immediately as the one person who could convincingly corroborate his story. It was his old boss, Charlie Herzfeld, who had been the director of ARPA when Taylor worked there. The two men had last seen each other years earlier, before anyone else cared about how the network began. Seeing Herzfeld now, Taylor was buoyed. He was back among the people who knew the real story. Now they'd straighten things out.

The Fastest Million Dollars

❏ February 1966

Bob Taylor usually drove to work, thirty minutes through the rolling countryside northeast of Washington, over the Potomac River to the Pentagon. There, in the morning, he'd pull into one of the vast parking lots and try to put his most-prized possession, a BMW 503, someplace he could remember. There were few if any security checkpoints at the entrances to the Pentagon in 1966. Taylor breezed in wearing his usual attire: sport coat, tie, button-down short-sleeve shirt, and slacks. Thirty thousand other people swarmed through the concourse level daily, in uniform and mufti alike, past the shops and up into the warrens of the enormous building.

Taylor's office was on the third floor, the most prestigious level in the Pentagon, near the offices of the secretary of defense and the director of the Advanced Research Projects Agency (ARPA). The offices of the highest-ranking officials in the Pentagon were in the outer, or E-ring. Their suites had views of the river and national monuments. Taylor's boss, Charles Herzfeld, the head of ARPA, was among those with a view, in room 3E160. The ARPA director rated the highest symbols of power meted out by the Department of Defense (DOD), right down to the official flags beside his desk. Taylor was director of the Information Processing Techniques Office (IPTO), just a corridor away, an unusually independent section of ARPA charged with supporting the nation's most advanced computer research-and-development projects.

The IPTO director's suite, where Taylor hung his coat from 1965 to 1969, was located in the D-ring. What his office lacked in a view was compensated for by its comfort and size. It was a plushly carpeted and richly furnished room with a big desk, a heavy oak conference table, glass-fronted bookcases, comfortable leather chairs, and all the other trappings of rank, which the Pentagon carefully measured out even down to the quality of the ashtrays. (Traveling on military business, Taylor carried the rank of one-star general.) On one wall of his office was a large map of the world; a framed temple rubbing from Thailand hung prominently on another.

Inside the suite, beside Taylor's office, was another door leading to a small space referred to as the terminal room. There, side by side, sat three computer terminals, each a different make, each connected to a separate mainframe computer running at three separate sites. There was a modified IBM Selectric typewriter terminal connected to a computer at the Massachusetts Institute of Technology in Cambridge. A Model 33 Teletype terminal, resembling a metal desk with a large noisy typewriter embedded in it, was linked to a computer at the University of California in Berkeley. And another Teletype terminal, a Model 35, was dedicated to a computer in Santa Monica, California, called, cryptically enough, the AN/FSQ 32XD1A, nicknamed the Q-32, a hulking machine built by IBM for the Strategic Air Command. Each of the terminals in Taylor's suite was an extension of a different computing environment—different programming languages, operating systems, and the like—within each of the distant mainframes. Each had a different log-in procedure; Taylor knew them all. But he found it irksome to have to remember which log-in procedure to use for which computer. And it was still more irksome, after he logged in, to be forced to remember which commands belonged to which computing environment. This was a particularly frustrating routine when he was in a hurry, which was most of the time.

The presence of three different computer terminals in Taylor's Pentagon office reflected IPTO's strong connection to the leading edge of the computer research community, resident in a few of the nation's top universities and technical centers. In all, there were some twenty principal investigators, supporting dozens of graduate students, working on numerous projects, all of them funded by Taylor's small office, which consisted of just Taylor and a secretary. Most of IPTO's $19 million budget was being sent to campus laboratories in Boston and Cambridge, or out to California, to support work that held the promise of making revolutionary advances in computing. Under ARPA's umbrella, a growing sense of community was emerging in computer research in the mid-1960s. Despite the wide variety of projects and computer systems, tight bonds were beginning to form among members of the computer community. Researchers saw each other at technical conferences and talked by phone; as early as 1964 some had even begun using a form of electronic mail to trade comments, within the very limited proximity of their mainframe computers.

Communicating with that community from the terminal room next to Taylor's office was a tedious process. The equipment was state of the art, but having a room cluttered with assorted computer terminals was like having a den cluttered with several television sets, each dedicated to a different channel. "It became obvious," Taylor said many years later, "that we ought to find a way to connect all these different machines."

❑ A Research Haven

That there even existed an agency within the Pentagon capable of supporting what some might consider esoteric academic research was a tribute to the wisdom of ARPA's earliest founders. The agency had been formed by President Dwight Eisenhower in the period of national crisis following the Soviet launch of the first *Sputnik* satellite in October 1957. The research agency was to be a fast-response mechanism closely tied to the president and secretary of defense, to ensure that Americans would never again be taken by surprise on the technological frontier. President Eisenhower saw ARPA fitting nicely into his strategy to stem the intense rivalries among branches of the military over research-and-development programs. The ARPA idea began with a man who was neither scientist nor soldier, but soap salesman.

At fifty-two, Neil McElroy was a newcomer to the defense establishment. He had never worked in government, had never lived in Washington, and had no military experience except in the national guard. For thirty-two years, he had climbed the corporate ladder at Procter & Gamble, the giant soap manufacturer in Cincinnati.

A Harvard graduate, McElroy took his first job at P&G slitting envelopes as a mail clerk in the advertising department for twenty-five dollars a week. It was supposed to be a summer job; he had intended to enter business school in the fall. But he stayed on and began peddling soap door-to-door. Soon he became promotion manager. From there, he worked his way up by pioneering the selling of soap on radio and television. The TV soap opera was McElroy's brainchild, about which he once said without apology, "The problem of improving literary taste is one for the schools. Soap operas sell lots of soap." By 1957, P&G was selling about a billion dollars' worth of Ivory, Oxydol, Joy, and Tide every year. He had perfected the strategy of promoting brand-name competition—as if there were real differences—between similar products made by the same company. And for the past nine years, tall, handsome "Mac" as he was known to most (or "Soapy Mac from Cinci-O" to some), had been the company's president—until Eisenhower recruited him for his cabinet.

On the evening of Friday, October 4, 1957, President Eisenhower's new nominee for secretary of defense, McElroy, was in Huntsville, Alabama. He had already been confirmed by the Senate and was touring military installations in advance of his swearing-in.

A large entourage of Pentagon staff was in tow for Mac's tour of Redstone Arsenal, home of the Army's rocket program. At about six o'clock in the evening in the officers' club, McElroy was talking to German émigré Wernher von Braun, the father of modern rocketry, when an aide rushed up and announced that the Russians had succeeded in launching a satellite into earth orbit. Now suddenly, even before taking office, McElroy found himself engulfed in a crisis of huge proportions. In one night, the Soviet achievement had reduced America's booming postwar confidence and optimism to widening fear and despair. Suddenly "the spectre of wholesale destruction," in the president's words, bore down on the American psyche.

Five days later McElroy was sworn in, with Washington fully consumed in controversy over the question of who had let the Soviets steal the march on American science and technology. Some people had predicted the Soviets would launch a satellite in observance of the International Geophysical Year. "Their earlier preaching in the wilderness was redeemed by the Soviet scientific spectaculars," one observer said. "It now took on the aura of revealed truth." "I told you so" became a status symbol. Genuine fear, ominous punditry, and harsh criticism flowed around the central issue of the new Soviet threat to national security. Hysterical prophecies of Soviet domination and the destruction of democracy were common. *Sputnik* was proof of Russia's ability to launch intercontinental ballistic missiles, the pessimists said, and it was just a matter of time before the Soviets would threaten the United States. The least-panicked Americans were resigned to disappointment over Russia's lead in the race to explore space.

Eisenhower hadn't wanted a seasoned military expert heading the Pentagon; he was one himself. The president distrusted the military-industrial complex and the fiefdoms of the armed services. His attitude toward them sometimes bordered on contempt.

By contrast, he loved the scientific community. He found scientists inspiring—their ideas, their culture, their values, and their value to the country—and he surrounded himself with the nation's best scientific minds. Eisenhower was the first president to host a White House dinner specifically to single out the scientific and engineering communities as guests of honor, just as the Kennedys would later play host to artists and musicians.

Hundreds of prominent American scientists directly served the Eisenhower administration on various panels. He referred to them proudly as "my scientists." Ike "liked to think of himself as one of us," observed Detlev W. Bronk, president of the National Academy of Sciences.

Two prominent scientists once had breakfast with the president, and as they were leaving Eisenhower remarked that the Republican National Committee was complaining that scientists close to the him were not out "whooping it up" sufficiently for the Republican Party.

"Don't you know, Mr. President?" replied one of the men with a smile. "All scientists are Democrats."

"I don't believe it," Eisenhower shot back. "But anyway, I like scientists for their science and not for their politics."

When the *Sputnik* crisis hit, Eisenhower pulled his scientists still more tightly into his circle. First, he held a number of private meetings with prominent scientists from outside the government. Eleven days after the news of the Soviet satellite, on October 15, 1957, Eisenhower sat down for a lengthy discussion with his Science Advisory Committee, a full contingent of the nation's best minds. Neither he nor any of them was as concerned about the actual significance of *Sputnik* as were those who were using the issue against Ike. For one thing, Eisenhower knew a great deal more than he could say publicly about the status of the Russian missile programs; he had seen the exquisitely detailed spy photographs made from a U-2 spy plane. He knew there was no missile gap. He also knew that the American military and its contractors had a vested interest in the Soviet threat. Still, he asked his science advisors for their estimation of Soviet capability. Eisenhower listened closely as they soberly assessed the meaning of the *Sputnik* launch. They told him the Russians had indeed gained impressive momentum. They said the United States would lose its scientific and technological lead unless it mobilized.

Many of the scientists around Eisenhower had been worrying

since the early 1950s that the government either misused or misunderstood modern science and technology. They urged Eisenhower to appoint a single high-level presidential science advisor, "a person he could live with easily," to help him make decisions involving technology. The launch of *Sputnik II* just a month after the first *Sputnik* increased the pressure. The first satellite, a 184-pound object the size of a basketball, was bad enough. Its fellow traveler weighed in at half a ton and was nearly the size of a Volkswagen Bug.

A few days after the news of *Sputnik II*, Eisenhower told the nation that he found his man for science in James R. Killian Jr., president of the Massachusetts Institute of Technology. Killian was a nonscientist who spoke effectively on behalf of science. On November 7, 1957, in the first of several addresses to reassure the American people and reduce panic, the president announced Killian's appointment as science advisor. It came late in the address but made front-page news the following day. The president had drawn links between science and defense, and said Killian would "follow through on the scientific improvement of our defense." The press dubbed Killian America's "Missile Czar."

During the October 15 meeting with his science advisors, the president had spoken of his concern over the management of research in government. "With great enthusiasm and determination the president wanted the scientists to tell him where scientific research belonged in the structure of the federal government," said Sherman Adams, the president's executive assistant. In addition, Eisenhower told them he had a fine man in Secretary of Defense McElroy and urged the scientists to meet with the new secretary, which they did that very day.

They found that Secretary McElroy had a similar appreciation for them. One aspect of his career at P&G that he was most proud of was the amount of money the company had devoted to research. He believed in the value of unfettered science, in its ability to produce remarkable, if not always predictable, results. McElroy and P&G had created a large "blue-sky" research laboratory, had funded it well, and rarely if ever pressured its scientists to justify their work. It was one of the first corporate research operations of its kind, one in which scientists were left to pursue almost anything and were well supported from the top.

Significant technological advances had come from a similar arrangement between universities and government during World War II: radar, nuclear weapons, and large calculating machines resulted from what Killian called "the freewheeling methods of outstanding academic scientists and engineers who had always been free of any inhibiting regimentation and organization."

In consultation with Killian, whose support was crucial, McElroy began discussing the idea of establishing an independent agency for research. Perhaps McElroy was aware that the U.S. Chamber of Commerce had floated the notion of creating a single research-and-development agency for the federal government during congressional hearings months before *Sputnik*. Such talk was in the air. The idea now emerged in discussions with an informal advisory committee of astute industrialists who met regularly with the secretary of defense.

In the days immediately following the Soviet launch, two men had been to see McElroy: eminent nuclear physicist Ernest O. Lawrence, and Charles Thomas, a former CEO of the Monsanto Chemical Company and an occasional advisor to the president. In a meeting lasting several hours, they discussed the idea of a strong advanced R&D agency that would report to the secretary, and both visitors urged McElroy to run with it. Physicist Herbert York, director of the Livermore Laboratory and close confidant to both Eisenhower and Killian, joined the conversations. At the same time, McElroy himself was consulting frequently with Killian and the president. In Killian's view, the traditional missions of the armed services had been outmoded by modern science and technology. Here was a way to move the Pentagon into the new age. One of the principal attractions of the research agency concept, in McElroy's mind, was the ability it would give him to manage the fierce competition within DOD over R&D programs and budgets. The competition was reaching absurd new heights. Army, Navy and Air Force commanders treated *Sputnik* like the starting gun in a new race, each vying against the other for the biggest share of R&D spending.

McElroy believed that a centralized agency for advanced research projects would reduce interservice rivalry by placing federal R&D budgets substantially under his own close supervision. Moreover, it would almost certainly appeal to the president, since the military's often selfish claims and special-interest hype usually met with disdain in the White House.

Eisenhower liked the secretary's proposal. While the administration had larger plans in store—the creation of the National Aeronautics and Space Administration (NASA), passage of a Defense Reorganization Act, establishment of the office of a Director of Defense Research and Engineering—those things would take time. The Advanced Research Projects Agency concept was a response the president could point to immediately. And it would give him an agile R&D agency he and his scientists could call on in the future.

On November 20, 1957, McElroy went to Capitol Hill for the first time as secretary. In the course of testifying about U.S. ballistic missile programs he mentioned that he had decided to set up a new "single manager" for all defense research. In the near term, he told Congress, the new agency would handle satellite and space R&D programs. The next day he circulated to the Joint Chiefs of Staff a draft charter and directive for the new agency, asking for their review and comments.

The military bristled at the implied criticism. It was one thing to have civilian science and technology *advisors,* but McElroy was now clearly invading their turf, planning to manage and operate a central office that would control defense R&D programs and future weapons projects. They were prepared to fight back. Secretary of the Air Force James Douglas wrote, "The Air Force appreciates that the proposals are suggestions." That is, message received, not accepted. The Army, Navy and Joint Chiefs of Staff returned the draft charter with numerous revisions. They fiddled deviously with language concerning the new agency's contracting authority, their revisions peppered with subversive word changes, crafty additions, and sly deletions all designed to weaken and confine the agency.

McElroy conceded a few minor points but made two things clear:

The agency's director would have contracting authority, and the scope of the agency's research was to be unlimited.

On January 7, 1958, Eisenhower sent a message to Congress requesting startup funds for the establishment of the Advanced Research Projects Agency. Two days later he drove the point home in his State of the Union Message. "I am not attempting today to pass judgment on the charges of harmful service rivalries. But one thing is sure. Whatever they are, America wants them stopped."

Eisenhower also affirmed "the need for single control in some of our most advanced development projects," then delivered his coup de grâce to the generals: "Another requirement of military organization is a clear subordination of the military services to the duly constituted civilian authority. This control must be real; not merely on the surface."

In early 1958, Roy Johnson, a vice president of General Electric, was appointed ARPA's first director; five days after the appointment, funding was approved by Congress (as a line item in an Air Force appropriations bill), and ARPA went into business.

In the post-*Sputnik* panic, the race for outer space cut a wide swath through American life, causing a new emphasis on science in the schools, worsening relations between Russia and the United States, and opening a floodgate for R&D spending. Washington's "external challenge" R&D spending rose from $5 billion per year to over $13 billion annually between 1959 and 1964. *Sputnik* launched a golden era for military science and technology. (By the mid-1960s, the nation's total R&D expenditures would account for 3 percent of the gross national product, a benchmark that was both a symbol of progress and a goal for other countries.)

All eyes were on ARPA when it opened its doors with a $520 million appropriation and a $2 billion budget plan. It was given direction over all U.S. space programs and all advanced strategic missile research. By 1959, a headquarters staff of about seventy people had been hired, a number that would remain fairly constant for years. These were mainly scientific project managers who analyzed and evaluated R&D proposals, supervising the work of hundreds of contractors.

Roy Johnson, ARPA's first director, was, like his boss, a business-man. At age fifty-two, he had been personally recruited by McElroy, who convinced him to leave a $160,000 job with General Electric and take an $18,000 job in Washington.

Not surprisingly, Johnson approached America's R&D agenda as a management problem. Management skills were his strong suit. His job, as he saw it, was to exhort people to do anything necessary to get the edge on the Soviets. He argued often and vigorously with rooms full of generals and admirals, and aggressively took on the Air Force. It soon became apparent that Johnson was a serious and vociferous advocate of a strong military presence in outer space.

But of course Killian and other scientists around Eisenhower had wanted someone well versed in scientific and technological issues running ARPA. Johnson had been instructed to hire a military flag officer as his deputy, and to select a chief scientist to round out his leadership team. The scientific post had almost gone to Wernher von Braun, until he insisted on bringing his whole team of a dozen associates with him to the Pentagon. So Herbert York, whom Killian had been keen on, was given the job and moved to ARPA from the Lawrence Livermore Laboratory. When he arrived on the third floor at the Pentagon, York promptly hung a large picture of the moon on his office wall. And right beside it he hung an empty frame. He told visitors it would soon be filled with the first picture of the back side of the moon.

The rest of ARPA's staff was recruited from industry's top-flight technical talent at places like Lockheed, Union Carbide, Convair, and other Pentagon contractors. The staff's days were spent sifting for gold in a torrential flow of unsolicited R&D proposals.

ARPA's success hinged on Johnson's extremely vocal posturing about America's role in outer space and his simplistic view of Soviet-American tensions. He mistakenly defined ARPA's mission almost entirely in military terms, outlining the kind of space projects he envisioned: global surveillance satellites, space defense interceptor vehicles, strategic orbital weapon systems, stationary communications satellites, manned space stations, and a moon base.

Eisenhower and his civilian scientists had moved ahead with the rest of their agenda, and by the late summer of 1958 the National Aeronautics and Space Administration had been enacted into law. Almost overnight, while Johnson drummed for a military presence in space, the space projects and missile programs were stripped away from ARPA and transferred over to NASA or back to the services, leaving ARPA's budget whittled to a measly $150 million. ARPA's portfolio was gutted, its staff left practically without any role. *Aviation Week* called the young agency "a dead cat hanging in the fruit closet."

Johnson resigned. Before leaving, however, he commissioned his staff to draft a paper weighing four alternatives: abolishing ARPA, expanding it, making no changes, or redefining its mission. His analysts threw themselves into building a case for the fourth alternative, and their tenacity alone saved the agency from sure oblivion. They fleshed out a set of goals to distance ARPA from the Pentagon by shifting the agency's focus to the nation's long-term "basic research" efforts. The services had never been interested in abstract research projects; their world was driven by near-term goals and cozy relationships with industrial contractors. The staff of ARPA saw an opportunity to redefine the agency as a group that would take on the really advanced "far-out" research.

Most important of all, ARPA staffers recognized the agency's biggest mistake yet: It had not been tapping the universities where much of the best scientific work was being done. The scientific community, predictably, rallied to the call for a reinvention of ARPA as a "high-risk, high-gain" research sponsor—the kind of R&D shop they had dreamed of all along. Their dream was realized; ARPA was given its new mission.

As ARPA's features took shape, one readily apparent characteristic of the agency was that its relatively small size allowed the personality of its director to permeate the organization. In time, the "ARPA style"—freewheeling, open to high risk, agile—would be vaunted. Other Washington bureaucrats came to envy ARPA's *modus operandi.* Eventually the agency attracted an elite corps of hard-charging R&D advocates from the finest universities and research laboratories, who set about building a community of the best technical and scientific minds in American research.

The agency's new basic research and special-project orientation was ideally suited to the atmospheric change in Washington caused by the election of John F. Kennedy. With vigor, Washington's bureaucracies responded to the Kennedy charisma. At the Pentagon, Robert S. McNamara, the new secretary of defense, led the shift away from the philosophy of "massive retaliation" in America's strategic posture, and toward a strategy of "flexible response" to international threats to American supremacy. Science was the New Frontier.

In early 1961 ARPA's second director, Brigadier General Austin W. Betts, resigned and was replaced by Jack P. Ruina, the first scientist to direct ARPA. Ruina came with strong academic credentials as well as some military background. Trained as an electrical engineer, he had been a university professor and had also served as a deputy assistant secretary of the Air Force. He was on good terms with members of the science advisory panels to the White House.

A golden era for ARPA was just beginning. Ruina brought a relaxed management style and decentralized structure to the agency. Details didn't interest him; finding great talent did. He believed in picking the best people and letting them pick the best technology. He felt strongly about giving his program directors free rein. His job, as he saw it, was to build as much support and funding as he could for whatever projects they selected. Ruina had a theory that truly talented people wouldn't normally choose to hang around long in a government bureaucracy but could be convinced to spend a year or two if offered enough flexibility and large enough budgets. Turnover didn't bother him. The agency, he believed, would benefit from frequent exposure to fresh views. In keeping with all that, he saw himself as a short-timer, too.

In time, Ruina raised ARPA's annual budget to $250 million. Projects in ballistic missile defense and nuclear test detection, couched in terms of basic research, were the top priorities. (There were also programs like behavioral research and command and control which, though interesting, fell below the level of Ruina's close attention.)

Then in May 1961 a computer, and a very large one at that, demanded his attention. A program in military command and control issues had been started at ARPA using emergency DOD funds. For the work, the Air Force had purchased the huge, expensive Q-32, a behemoth of a machine that was to act as the backup for the nation's air defense early-warning system. The machine had been installed at a facility in Santa Monica, California, at one of the Air Force's major contractors, System Development Corporation (SDC), where it was supposed to be used for operator training, and as a software development tool.

Then the Air Force had been forced to cut back, which left the Santa Monica firm begging for some way to keep its employees working with the computer. The Air Force, which had already sunk millions into the SDC contract, suddenly had an embarrassing white elephant on its hands in the form of one massive, ungainly computing machine.

❏ Licklider

The relationship between the military and computer establishments began with the modern computer industry itself. During World War II, in the midst of a perceived need for faster calculating ability than could be provided by the banks of mechanical calculators run by human operators, the military funded dozens of computing experiments. The Navy supported Howard Aiken, the Harvard mathematics professor who dreamed of building a large-scale calculator and ended up with the Mark I, a fifty-one-foot-long, eight-foot-tall switchboard that could perform arithmetical operations without the intervention of an operator. The Army also supported the famous Electronic Numerical Integrator And Calculator (ENIAC) project at the University of Pennsylvania. Later at MIT, first the Navy and then the Air Force supported a computer called Whirlwind.

In the early 1950s computing meant doing arithmetic fast.

Companies, especially banks, put their machines to work doing large-scale calculations. In 1953, International Business Machines Corporation (IBM), already the country's largest manufacturer of time clocks as well as electromechnical tabulating equipment, jumped into the business of making large electronic computers. These were business machines of the future. The IBM machines weren't necessarily better than the Univac (the successor to the ENIAC), but IBM's sales staff became legendary, and before too long sales of IBM's machines had surpassed those of the Univac.

Then, in the late 1950s, just as IBM was passing the billion-dollar-sales mark, Ken Olsen, an individualistic and outspoken engineer, left MIT's Lincoln Laboratory with $70,000 in venture capital to exploit commercially the technology developed around a new machine: the TX-2 at Lincoln Lab. He formed the Digital Equipment Corporation to manufacture and sell computer components, and then he built something radically different from what had existed before: a smaller computer called a minicomputer that interacted directly with the user. Olsen's idea for an interactive computer had come from a pioneering group of computer researchers at MIT. A different, slightly younger group there came up with another dramatic concept in computing that was beginning to catch on, particularly in academic institutions. They called it "time-sharing," and it had obvious appeal as an alternative to the slow and awkward traditional method of "batch" processing.

Batch processing was a cumbersome way of computing. For even the smallest programming task, it was necessary to have the relevant code punched onto program cards, which were then combined with "control cards" to take care of the computer's administrative functions. A computer operator fed the cards into the computer or onto magnetic tape for processing, one batch at a time. Depending on the length of the queue and the complexity of the programs and problems, the wait could be long. It was not unusual to wait a day or longer for results.

Time-sharing was, as the term suggests, a new method of giving many users interactive access to computers from individual terminals. The terminals allowed them to interact directly with the mainframe computer. The revolutionary aspect of time-sharing was that it eliminated much of the tedious waiting that characterized batch-process computing. Time-sharing gave users terminals that allowed them to interact directly with the computer and obtain their results immediately. "We really believed that it was a better way to operate," recalled Fernando Corbató, an MIT computer scientist. "I suppose if somebody had said, 'I will give you a free machine,' we might have said, 'We do not need time-sharing.'" But computers in those days were huge things. They took up large rooms and required continual maintenance because there were so many components. "They were just not a casual thing," Corbató went on. "You did not normally think of having a personal machine in those days—exclusive use maybe, but not a personal one. So we really saw a need to try to change that. We were frustrated." The appreciation of time-sharing was directly proportional to the amount of direct access one had to the computer. And usually that meant that the more you programmed, the better you understood the value of direct access.

What time-sharing could not do was eliminate the necessity of coordinating competing demands on the machine by different users. By its nature, time-sharing encouraged users to work as if they had the entire machine at their command, when in fact they had only a fraction of the total computing power. Distribution of costs among a number of users meant that the more users the better. Of course, too many users bogged down the machine, since a high percentage of the machine's resources were allocated to coordinating the commands of multiple users. As the number of users increased, more of the computer's resources were dedicated to the coordination function, which reduced actual usable processing time. If programmers had to do very small jobs (such as tightening code or minor debugging of a program), they didn't need a powerful machine. But when it came time to run the programs in full, many of which used a lot of machine resources, it became apparent that users were still in competition with one another for computing time. As soon as a large program requiring a lot of calculations entered the mix of jobs being done on-line, everyone's work slowed down.

• • •

When the Air Force passed the Q-32 on to ARPA in 1961, Ruina didn't have anyone to administer the contract. Ruina had in mind a job with the potential for expansion far beyond the single contract that happened to be pressing at the moment: Computers, as they related to command and control, might one day provide high-speed, reliable information upon which to base critical military decisions. That potential, largely unfulfilled, seemed endlessly promising.

Coincidentally, Ruina also was looking for someone who could direct a new program in behavioral sciences that DOD wanted ARPA to run. By the fall of 1962, Ruina had found the candidate who could fill both posts, an eminent psychologist named J. C. R. Licklider.

Licklider was an obvious choice to head a behavioral sciences office, but a psychologist wasn't an obvious choice to oversee a government office focused on developing leading-edge computer technology. Yet Licklider's broad, interdisciplinary interests suited him well for the job. Licklider had done some serious dabbling in computers. "He used to tell me how he liked to spend a lot of time at a computer console," Ruina recalled. "He said he would get hung up on it and become sort of addicted." Licklider was far more than just a computer enthusiast, however. For several years, he had been touting a radical and visionary notion: that computers weren't just adding machines. Computers had the potential to act as extensions of the whole human being, as tools that could amplify the range of human intelligence and expand the reach of our analytical powers.

Joseph Carl Robnett Licklider was born in St. Louis in 1915. An only and much-beloved child, he spent his early years nurturing a fascination with model airplanes. He knew he wanted to be a scientist, but he was unfocused through most of his college days at Washington University. He switched concentrations several times, from chemistry to physics to the fine arts and, finally, to psychology. When he graduated in 1937 he held undergraduate degrees in psychology, mathematics, and physics. For a master's thesis in psychology, he decided to test the popular slogan "Get more sleep, it's good for you" on a population of rats. As he approached his

Ph.D., Licklider's interests narrowed toward psychoacoustics, the psychophysiology of the auditory system.

For his doctoral dissertation, Licklider studied the auditory cortex of cats, and when he moved to Swarthmore College, he worked on the puzzle of sound localization, attempting to analyze the brain's ability to determine a sound's distance and direction. If you close your eyes and ask someone to snap his fingers, your brain will tell you approximately where the snap is coming from and how far away it is. The puzzle of sound localization is also illustrated by the "cocktail party" phenomenon: In a crowded room where several conversations are taking place within one's hearing range, it is possible to isolate whatever conversation one chooses by tuning in certain voices and tuning out the rest.

In 1942 Licklider went to Cambridge, Massachusetts, to work as a research associate in Harvard University's Psycho-Acoustic Laboratory. During the war years, he studied the effects of high altitude on speech communication and the effects of static and other noise on reception by radio receivers. Licklider conducted experiments in B-17 and B-24 bombers at 35,000 feet. The aircraft weren't pressurized, and the temperatures on board were often well below freezing. During one field test, Licklider's colleague and best friend, Karl Kryter, saw Licklider turn white. Kryter panicked. He turned up the oxygen and yelled to his friend, "Lick! Speak to me!" Just as Kryter was about to ask the pilot to descend, the color returned to Licklider's face. He had been in tremendous pain, he said, but it had passed. After that, he stopped partaking of his favorite breakfast— Coca-Cola—before going on high-altitude missions.

By this time, Licklider had joined the Harvard faculty and was gaining recognition as one of the world's leading theorists on the nature of the auditory nervous system, which he once described as "the product of a superb architect and a sloppy workman."

Psychology at Harvard in those years was strongly influenced by the behaviorist B. F. Skinner and others who held that all behavior is learned, that animals are born as blank slates to be enscribed by chance, experience, and conditioning. When Skinner went so far as to put his own child in a so-called Skinner box to test behaviorist theories and other faculty members began doing similar experiments (albeit less radical ones), Louise Licklider put her foot down. No child of hers was going into a box, and her husband agreed.

Louise was usually the first person to hear her husband's ideas. Nearly every evening after dinner, he returned to work for a few hours, but when he got home at around 11:00 P.M. he usually spent an hour or so telling Louise his latest thoughts. "I grew up on his ideas," she said, "from when the seeds were first planted, until somehow or other he saw them bear fruit."

Everybody adored Licklider and, at his insistence, just about everybody called him "Lick." His restless, versatile genius gave rise through the years to an eclectic cult of admirers.

Lick stood just over six feet tall. He had sandy brown hair and large blue eyes. His most pronounced characteristic was his soft, down-home Missouri accent, which belied his acute mind. When he gave talks or led colloquia, he never prepared a speech. Instead, he would get up and make extensive remarks off the cuff about a certain problem he happened to be working on. Lick's father had been a Baptist minister, and Louise occasionally chided him by noticing the preacher in him. "Lick at play with a problem at a briefing or a colloquium, speaking in that soft hillbilly accent, was a *tour de force*," recalled Bill McGill, a former colleague. "He'd speak in this Missouri Ozark twang, and if you walked in off the street, you'd wonder, Who the hell is this hayseed? But if you were working on the same problem, and listened to his formulation, listening to him would be like seeing the glow of dawn."

Many of Lick's colleagues were in awe of his problem-solving ability. He was once described as having the world's most refined intuition. "He could see the resolution of a technical problem before the rest of us could calculate it," said McGill. "This made him rather extraordinary." Lick was not a formalist in any respect and seldom struggled with arcane theorems. "He was like a wide-eyed child going from problem to problem, consumed with curiosity. Almost every day he had some new fillip on a problem we were thinking about."

But living with Lick had its frustrations, too. He was humble, many believed, to a fault. He often sat in meetings tossing ideas out for anyone to claim. "If someone stole an idea from him," Louise recalled, "I'd pound the table and say it's not fair, and he'd say, 'It doesn't matter who gets the credit; it matters that it gets done.'" Throughout the many years he taught, he inspired all his students, even his undergraduates, to feel like junior colleagues. His house was open to them, and students often showed up at the front door with a chapter of a thesis or just a question for him. "I'd put my thumb up and they'd pound up to his third-floor office," said Louise.

In the postwar years, psychology was still a young discipline, inviting derision from those in the harder sciences with little patience for a new field that dealt with such enigmatic entities as the mind, or "the human factor." But Licklider was a psychologist in the most rigorous sense. As one colleague put it, he belonged with those "whose self-conscious preoccupation with the legitimacy of their scientific activity has made them more tough-minded than a good many of their colleagues in the better established fields."

By 1950, Lick had moved to MIT to work in the Institute's Acoustics Laboratory. The following year, when MIT created Lincoln Laboratory as a research lab devoted to air defense, Lick signed on to start the laboratory's human-engineering group. The cold war had come to dominate virtually the entire intellectual life of the institution. Lincoln Lab was one of the most visible manifestations of MIT's cold war alliance with Washington.

In the early 1950s many military theoreticians feared a surprise attack by Soviet bombers carrying nuclear weapons over the North Pole. And just as scientists had coalesced during the 1940s to deal with the possibility of German nuclear armament, a similar team gathered in 1951 at MIT to deal with the perceived Soviet threat. Their study was called Project Charles. Its outcome was a proposal to the Air Force for a research facility devoted to the task of creating technology for defense against aerial attack. Thus Lincoln Laboratory was quickly formed, staffed, and set to work under its first director, the physicist Albert Hill. In 1952, the lab moved off-campus to Lexington, about ten miles west of Cambridge. Its main projects centered around the concept of Distant Early Warning—the DEW line: arrays of radars stretching, ideally, from Hawaii to Alaska, across the Canadian archipelago to Greenland, and finally to Iceland and the British Isles. Problems of communication, control, and analysis for such an extended, complex structure could be handled only by a computer. To satisfy that requirement, Lincoln first took on Whirlwind, a computer project at MIT, and then developed a successor project called the Semi-Automatic Ground Environment, or SAGE.

Based on a large IBM computer, SAGE was so mammoth that its operators and technicians literally walked inside the machine. The system served three major functions: receiving data from various detection and tracking radars, interpreting data relating to unidentified aircraft, and pointing defensive weapons at incoming hostile aircraft. SAGE was only "semiautomatic," since the human operator remained an important part of the system. In fact, SAGE was one of the first fully operational, real-time interactive computer systems. Operators communicated with the computer through displays, keyboards, switches, and light guns. Users could request information from the computer and receive an answer within a few seconds. New information continuously flowed directly into the computer's memory through telephone lines to the users, making it immediately available to the operators.

The SAGE system inspired a few thinkers, including Licklider, to see computing in an entirely new light. SAGE was an early example of what Licklider would later call the "symbiosis" between humans and machines, where the machine functions as a problem-solving partner. Implied in this symbiotic relationship was the interdependency of humans and computers working in unison as a single system. For instance, in a battle scenario, human operators without computers would be unable to calculate and analyze threats quickly enough to counter an attack. Conversely, computers working alone would be unable to make crucial decisions.

In 1953 MIT decided to start a human factors group in the psychology section of the economics department, and Lick was put in charge. He recruited a handful of his brightest students and colleagues. Lick hired people based not on their doctoral work or class standing but on a simple test he applied: the Miller Analogies Test. (The test covers every field from geology to history and the arts. It requires both good general knowledge and an ability to apply that knowledge to relationships.) "I had a kind of a rule," he said. "Anybody who could do 85 or better on the Miller Analogies Test, hire him, because he's going to be very good at something."

In 1954 Lick's group moved in with the social psychologists and labor-management experts in the Sloan School of Management. But the group's ideas were far removed from management problems. As McGill, an early Licklider recruit, described it, he and his peers were far more interested in computers and computer memory devices as models for the versatility of human cognition. The first dissertation produced by the department under Lick's guidance came from Ph.D. candidate Tom Marill, who had examined the subject of ideal auditory detection. (Like others who came into Licklider's sphere, Marill would make his mark on the development of computer networking in years to come.) "Nothing like this had ever been seen before, at least not in a psychology department," said McGill. The department was the first cognitive science department in history. "The work was experimentally based cognitive psychology, as it would be defined today, but at the time we had no proper language or nomenclature."

But eventually MIT administrators wanted something more traditional, and Lick failed in his efforts to expand his new department with permanent appointments. As a result, all his protégés, young and marketable, drifted off. "We did not have the sophistication to promote what we did, and we were unaware that there was anything unique about it. So MIT let it all slip away," McGill said. Lick was a maverick, after all, and a little far-out, perhaps too much so for MIT.

Yet Lick did not lament the demise of the group, for he had a self-professed short attention span. His interests changed often and dramatically over the years. He once advised a young friend never to sign on for a project that lasted more than five to seven years, so he could always move on to other things. And anything Lick got interested in, he plunged into in great depth.

Perhaps the incident that most piqued Lick's interest in computers and their potential as interactive instruments was an encounter he had in the 1950s with a smart, opinionated young engineer at Lincoln Labs named Wesley Clark. Clark was a young researcher working on the TX-2 machine, the state of the art in digital computation and the successor to a computer called the TX-0. Clark had built the TX-0 with Ken Olsen before Olsen left to start Digital Equipment Corporation.

Clark's office was in the Lincoln basement. One day, on his way back from the stockroom at the other end of the corridor, Clark decided to venture into a room that had always seemed vaguely off-limits. Most lab doors stood open, but not this one. It was always closed. Clark tried the door, which he was surprised to find unlocked, and entered the room. "I wandered in and back through a little labyrinth of baffles and barriers," Clark recalled. "Off to one side was this very dark laboratory and I went in, and after probing around in the dark for a while I found this man sitting in front of some displays. He was doing some kind of psychometrics, and he was clearly an interesting fellow. I got interested in what he was doing and in his apparatus, and as I recall I suggested to him that he could achieve the same results by using a computer." The man was Licklider. Clark invited Lick to come down the hall to see the TX-2 and learn some fundamentals.

Teaching Lick actually to program the machine would have been too difficult. Programming a computer like the TX-2 was something of a black art. The TX-2, which contained 64,000 bytes of memory (as much as a simple handheld calculator today), took up a couple of rooms. What many years later became tiny microchips for the computer's central processing unit were, in those days, huge racks of many separate plug-in units, each consisting of dozens of transistors and associated electronic parts. Still more space was taken up with large consoles covered with switches and indicator lights to help the operator or troubleshooter understand what the system was doing. All of this equipment required rack upon rack of gear, only a tiny fraction of which—the video display screen and keyboard—might be recognizable today as ordinary computer parts. "To sit at the TX-2 with Lick was to be embedded in a welter of seemingly irrelevant stuff," Clark said. To become a TX-2 "user" would have been a daunting exercise even for someone as quick as Licklider. For one thing, there were no teaching tools per se, no instructional aids or help menus. For another, the operating system, which would standardize programming for the machine, had yet to be written.

One thing the TX-2 did do very well was display information on video screens. That made it one of the earliest machines for interactive graphics work. It was this feature that helped Clark demonstrate for Lick the main ideas of interactive use.

The sessions with Clark made an indelible impression on Lick. He drifted further from psychology and toward computer science. As his interests changed, Lick's belief in the potential for computers to transform society became something of an obsession. Succumbing to the lure of computing, he began spending hours at a time at the interactive display console. Louise believed that if he weren't being paid for this work, he'd have paid to do it.

The idea on which Lick's worldview pivoted was that technological progress would save humanity. The political process was a favorite example of his. In a McLuhanesque view of the power of electronic media, Lick saw a future in which, thanks in large part to the reach of computers, most citizens would be "informed about, and interested in, and involved in, the process of government." He imagined what he called "home computer consoles" and television sets linked together in a massive network. "The political process," he wrote, "would essentially be a giant teleconference, and a campaign would be a months-long series of communications among candidates, propagandists, commentators, political action groups, and voters. The key is the self-motivating exhilaration that accompanies truly effective interaction with information through a good console and a good network to a good computer."

Lick's thoughts about the role computers could play in people's lives hit a crescendo in 1960 with the publication of his seminal paper "Man-Computer Symbiosis." In it he distilled many of his ideas into a central thesis: A close coupling between humans and "the electronic members of the partnership" would eventually result in cooperative decision making. Moreover, decisions would be made by humans, using computers, without what Lick called "inflexible dependence on predetermined programs." He held to the view that computers would naturally continue to be used for what they do best: all of the rote work. And this would free humans to devote energy to making better decisions and developing clearer insights than they would be capable of without computers. Together, Lick suggested, man and machine would perform far more competently than either could alone. Moreover, attacking problems in partnership with computers could save the most valuable of postmodern resources: time. "The hope," Licklider wrote, "is that in not too many years, human brains and computing machines will be coupled . . . tightly, and that the resulting partnership will think as no human brain has ever thought and process data in a way not approached by the information-handling machines we know today."

Licklider's ideas, which had their beginnings just a few years earlier in a chance encounter in the basement of Lincoln Lab, represented some of the most daring and imaginative thinking of the day. One former MIT student, Robert Rosin, who had taken an experimental psychology course from Lick in 1956 and later went into computer science, read "Man-Computer Symbiosis" and was awestruck by the elder's intellectual versatility. "For the life of me, I could not imagine how a psychologist who, in 1956, had no apparent knowledge of computers, could have written such a profound and insightful paper about 'my field' in 1960," Rosin said. "Lick's paper made a deep impression on me and refined my own realization that a new age of computing was upon us."

In the moment that Licklider published the paper, his reputation as a computer scientist was fixed forever. He shed the mantle of psychology and took on computing. There was no turning him back. A couple of years before the paper was published, Licklider had left MIT to work at a small consulting and research firm in Cambridge called Bolt Beranek and Newman. The company had agreed to buy him two computers for his research, and he was having the time of his life.

One day in 1962, ARPA director Jack Ruina called Licklider with a new job possibility. What would Lick say to taking on not just

ARPA's command and control division, but a new behavioral sciences division as well? And there'd be a huge computer, the Q-32, thrown into the deal.

Ruina also called on Fred Frick, a friend and colleague of Lick's at Lincoln Lab. Frick and Licklider met with Ruina together. Licklider went in prepared just to listen but was soon waxing eloquent on the topic. The problems of command and control, he told Ruina, were essentially problems of human-computer interaction. "I thought it was just ridiculous to be having command and control systems based on batch processing," he recalled years later. "Who can direct a battle when he's got to write the program in the middle of the battle?" Licklider and Frick agreed that the job seemed interesting, but neither wanted to leave what he was doing.

Ruina's sales pitch was so intense, however, and he made the mission seem so critical, that Frick and Licklider decided one of them should do it. They tossed a coin, and Lick accepted the position on the condition that he be given the freedom to lead the program in any direction he saw fit. Partly because Ruina was very busy, and partly because he didn't understand computers himself, he agreed to the proviso without hesitation.

Lick belonged to a small group of computer scientists who believed that people could be much more effective if they had at their fingertips a computer system with good displays and good databases. Before moving to Washington in the fall of 1962, Lick gave a series of computer seminars at the Pentagon, well attended by Defense Department and military officials. His message, already something of a mantra up in Cambridge but still largely unfamiliar to a military audience, was that a computer should be something anyone could interact with directly, eliminating computer operators as the middlemen in solving their problems.

To this end, Lick saw great promise in time-sharing and was one of its most ardent evangelists. Time-sharing didn't exactly put a computer on everyone's desk, but it created the illusion of just that. It brought the power of the computer right to everyone's fingertips. It gave people a strong feel for the machine.

The promotion of time-sharing was by no means Lick's sole mission when he arrived at ARPA. He was just as keen on exploring the ideas that had been percolating around human-machine interaction for several years.

When Lick arrived for his first day at work, on October 1, 1962, his secretary said, "Well, Dr. Licklider, you have just one appointment today. There are some gentlemen coming from the Bureau of the Budget to review your program." When the budget officers arrived, they were amused to discover it was Licklider's first day. There wasn't much of substance to discuss yet. The command and control program consisted of one $9 million contract—with System Development Corporation—and the remaining $5 million or so in the budget was still unassigned. Instead of a budget review, the meeting was transformed into a private colloquium, in which Lick expounded on such topics as time-sharing, interactive computing, and artificial intelligence. Like many others before them, the accountants were infected by Licklider's enthusiasm. "I told them what I was excited about, and that turned out to work greatly to my favor, because they got interested in it," he said later. "And when we did have a meeting on it, they did not take any of my money away."

The principal charter he'd been given was to come up with uses for computers other than as tools for numerical scientific calculations. Lick developed new programs partly as a reaction against some of the applications the Defense Department had in mind for large computers. Air Force intelligence, for instance, wanted to harness huge mainframes to detect patterns of behavior among high-level Soviet officials. The computer would be fed intelligence information from a variety of human sources, such as hearsay from cocktail parties or observations at a May Day parade, and try to develop a best-guess scenario on what the Soviets might be up to. "The idea was that you take this powerful computer and feed it all this qualitative information, such as 'The air force chief drank two martinis,' or 'Khrushchev isn't reading *Pravda* on Mondays.'" recalled Ruina. "And the computer would play Sherlock Holmes and conclude that the Russians must be building an MX-72 missile or something like that."

First Ruina, then Licklider, tried putting a stop to such "asinine kinds of things," as Lick described the ill-conceived projects. Then Lick worked to find the country's foremost computer centers and set up research contracts with them. In short order, he had reached out to the best computer scientists of the day, from Stanford, MIT, UCLA, Berkeley, and a handful of companies, bringing them into ARPA's sphere. All told, there were about a dozen in Lick's inner circle, which Ruina called "Lick's priesthood." In typical fashion, where his most passionate beliefs masqueraded as a bit of a joke, Licklider nicknamed it the Intergalactic Computer Network.

Six months after his arrival at ARPA, Lick wrote a lengthy memo to the members of the Intergalactic Network in which he expressed his frustration over the proliferation of disparate programming languages, debugging systems, time-sharing system control languages, and documentation schemes. In making the case for an attempt at standardization, Lick discussed the hypothetical problem of a network of computers. "Consider the situation in which several different centers are netted together, each center being highly individualistic and having its own special language and its own special way of doing things," he posited. "Is it not desirable or even necessary for all the centers to agree upon some language or, at least, upon some conventions for asking such questions as 'What language do you speak?' At this extreme, the problem is essentially the one discussed by science-fiction writers: How do you get communications started among totally uncorrelated sapient beings?"

That said, Lick hedged his bets. "It will possibly turn out," he continued, "that only on rare occasions do most or all of the computers in the overall system operate together in an integrated network. It seems to me to be important, nevertheless, to develop a capability for integrated network operation." And therein lay the seed of Licklider's grandest vision yet. He would extend the concept of the Intergalactic Network to mean not just a group of people to whom he was sending memos but a universe of interconnected computers over which all might send their memos.

Licklider was no exception to the rule that people didn't spend a long time at ARPA. But by the time he left in 1964, he had succeeded in shifting the agency's emphasis in computing R&D from a command systems laboratory playing out war-game scenarios to advanced research in time-sharing systems, computer graphics, and improved computer languages. The name of the office, Command and Control Research, had changed to reflect that shift, becoming the Information Processing Techniques Office. Licklider chose his successor, a colleague named Ivan Sutherland, the world's leading expert in computer graphics. In 1965 Sutherland hired a young hotshot named Bob Taylor, who would soon sit down in ARPA's terminal room and wonder why, with so many computers, they were unable to communicate with one another.

❏ Taylor's Idea

Bob Taylor had started college in Dallas at the age of sixteen thinking he would follow his father's footsteps and become a minister. His family never lived in one place very long, moving from one Methodist church to another around Texas, in towns with names like Uvalde, Victoria, and Ozona. But instead of the service of the Lord, Taylor entered the service of the U.S. Navy when his reserve unit was called to active duty for the Korean War.

Taylor spent the war at the Dallas Naval Air Station—"the USS *Neverfloat*," he called it. At the end of the war, he entered the University of Texas on the GI Bill with no particular course of study in mind. He finally graduated in 1957 with a major in psychology and a minor in mathematics.

Taylor pursued his love for science into graduate school at UT and wrote his dissertation on psychoacoustics, a field from which some people were making a leap into computing. Taylor jumped, too. "When I was in graduate school, there was no computer science," Taylor recollected, "so I didn't really have much of an introduction to computing. But I began to feel that computing research was going to be much more rewarding."

Fresh from school, Taylor held a few jobs in the aerospace industry before landing a job at NASA in 1961, where he worked as a program officer in Washington, D.C., in the Office of Advanced Research and Technology. One day in 1963 Taylor was invited to join an unofficial committee of government program managers, all of whom were involved in funding computer research. It was an informal group that simply exchanged information about their projects, looked for ways of collaborating, and tried to avoid duplication or overlap. The invitation had come, as it turned out, from someone who had been Taylor's intellectual role model in psychoacoustics—J. C. R. Licklider. He was head of the committee. Licklider's early work in psychoacoustics had deeply influenced Taylor's own and he welcomed the chance to meet the illustrious Licklider.

Taylor was struck by how unassuming he was. "He flattered me right off by saying he knew my thesis work," Taylor said. Here was a man with a giant reputation who was probably one of the nicest, most easygoing people Taylor had ever met.

When Taylor first joined the committee, Licklider was in the process of pulling together the computer science community under ARPA, the new generation of researchers drawn to interactive computing. They were busily framing their bold new perspective, radically different from the mainstream in computer research and development during the previous two decades. Mountains of money and years of work had been invested in improving the technical parameters of speed, reliability, and memory size of computers. But this small avant-garde of researchers concentrated at MIT and around Boston had begun working on making the computer an amplifier of human potential, an extension of the mind and body.

Taylor was known for having a good bit of intuition himself. He was considered a farsighted program officer who had a knack for picking innovative winners—both projects and researchers. He joined ARPA in early 1965, following Licklider's departure, to work as deputy to Ivan Sutherland, IPTO's second director. Months later, in 1966, at the age of thirty-four, Taylor became the third director of IPTO, inheriting responsibility for the community and much of the vision—indeed the very office—established by Licklider. The only difference, which turned out to be crucial, was that ARPA—now headed by Charles Herzfeld, an Austrian physicist who had fled Europe during the war—was even faster and looser with its money than it had been during Ruina's tenure. A joke now circulated among its program directors: Come up with a good idea for a research program and it will take you about thirty minutes to get the funding.

The "terminal problem," as Taylor called it, was a source of frustration not just for him but for Sutherland before him and for Licklider before that. One day, shortly after becoming IPTO director, Taylor found himself rolling around an idea Lick had discussed with him several times but never actually acted on. Now that it was his watch, Taylor decided to act.

Taylor headed straight to Herzfeld's office. No memos. No meetings. Other program directors were slightly intimidated by Herzfeld, a large man with a thick rumbling Viennese accent. But Taylor saw nothing to fear about the man. In fact, Taylor behaved like such a good old boy around his boss that someone once asked him, "Taylor, what have you got with Herzfeld? You must be related to Lyndon Johnson. You're both from Texas, aren't you?"

Taylor told the ARPA director he needed to discuss funding for a networking experiment he had in mind. Herzfeld had talked about networking with Taylor a bit already, so the idea wasn't new to him. He had also visited Taylor's office, where he witnessed the annoying exercise of logging on to three different computers. And a few years earlier he had even fallen under the spell of Licklider himself when he attended Lick's lectures on interactive computing.

Taylor gave his boss a quick briefing: IPTO contractors, most of whom were at research universities, were beginning to request more and more computer resources. Every principal investigator, it seemed, wanted his own computer. Not only was there an obvious duplication of effort across the research community, but it was getting damned expensive. Computers weren't small and they weren't cheap. Why not try tying them all together? By building a system of electronic links between machines, researchers doing similar work in different parts of the country could share resources and results more easily. Instead of spreading a half dozen expensive mainframes across the country devoted to supporting advanced graphics research, ARPA could concentrate resources in one or two places and build a way for everyone to get at them. One university might concentrate on one thing, another research center could be funded to concentrate on something else, but regardless of where you were physically located, you would have access to it all. He suggested that ARPA fund a small test network, starting with, say, four nodes and building up to a dozen or so.

The Defense Department was the largest buyer of computers in the world. Investing in a particular make of computer was no trivial decision, and it often put the different services in a bind, particularly when faced with a federal rule dictating that all manufacturers be given equal opportunity. There seemed to be no hope of curtailing the purchase of a whole variety of machines. And the chances seemed slim to nonexistent that the computing world would gravitate anytime soon to a set of uniform operating standards. Research sponsors like ARPA would just have to find some other way of overcoming the industry's incompatibility problems. If the network idea worked, Taylor told Herzfeld, it would be possible for computers from different manufacturers to connect, and the problem of choosing computers would be greatly diminished. Herzfeld was so taken with that possibility that those arguments alone might have been enough to convince him. But there was another advantage, centering on the question of reliability. It might be possible to connect computers in a network redundantly, so that if one line went down, a message could take another path.

"Is it going to be hard to do?" Herzfeld asked.

"Oh no. We already know how to do it," Taylor responded with characteristic boldness.

"Great idea," Herzfeld said. "Get it going. You've got a million dollars more in your budget right now. Go."

Taylor left Herzfeld's office on the E-ring and headed back to the corridor that connected to the D-ring and his own office. He glanced at his watch. "Jesus Christ," he said to himself softly. "That only took twenty minutes."

A Block Here,
Some Stones There

By the time Taylor assumed the directorship of IPTO in 1966, man-ifestations of Licklider's philosophy were evident throughout the computer research establishment. The ranks of researchers hoping to extend the computer beyond the status of a calculating instru-ment continued to grow throughout the decade. Some of the earli-est and most important work in interactive graphics and virtual reality was taking place at the University of Utah using ARPA money. MIT in particular, seemed to breed one groundbreaking de-velopment after another. There Marvin Minsky and Seymour Papert were engaged in important early work in artificial intelligence. Pro-grams at other institutions focused on advanced programming techniques, time-sharing, and computer languages.

Building a network as an end in itself wasn't Taylor's principal objective. He was trying to solve a problem he had seen grow worse with each round of funding. Researchers were duplicating, and iso-lating, costly computing resources. Not only were the scientists at each site engaging in more, and more diverse, computer research, but their demands for computer resources were growing faster than

Taylor's budget. Every new project required setting up a new and costly computing operation. Depending on the computer being used and the number of graduate students being supported, IPTO's individual grants ranged from $500,000 to $3 million.

And none of the resources or results was easily shared. If the scientists doing graphics in Salt Lake City wanted to use the programs developed by the people at Lincoln Lab, they had to fly to Boston. Still more frustrating, if after a trip to Boston people in Utah wanted to start a similar project on their own machine, they would need to spend considerable time and money duplicating what they had just seen. In those days, software programs were one-of-a-kind, like original works of art, and not easily transferred from one machine to another. Taylor was convinced of the technical feasibility of sharing such resources over a computer network, though it had never been done.

Beyond cost-cutting, Taylor's idea revealed something very profound. A machine's ability to amplify human intellectual power was precisely what Licklider had had in mind while writing his paper on human-machine symbiosis six years earlier. Of course, Licklider's ideas about time-sharing were already bearing fruit at universities all over the country. But the networking idea marked a significant departure from time-sharing. In a resource-sharing network, many machines would serve many different users, and a researcher interested in using, say, a particular graphics program on a machine two thousand miles away would simply log on to that machine. The idea of one computer reaching out to tap resources inside another, as peers in a collaborative organization, represented the most advanced conception yet to emerge from Licklider's vision.

Taylor had the money, and he had Herzfeld's support, but needed a program manager who could oversee the design and construction of such a network, someone who not only knew Licklider's ideas but believed in them. This person had to be a first-rate computer scientist, comfortable with a wide range of technical issues.

How it was to be achieved didn't concern Taylor greatly, as long as the network was reliable and fast. Those were his priorities. Interactive computing meant you'd get a quick response from a computer, so in the modern computing environment it made sense that a network also should be highly responsive. And to be useful, it had to be working anytime you needed it. Whoever designed such a network needed to be an expert in telecommunications systems as well. It wasn't an easy combination to find. But Taylor already had someone in mind: a shy, deep-thinking young computer scientist from the Lincoln Labs breeding ground named Larry Roberts.

In early 1966, Roberts was at Lincoln working on graphics. But he had also done quite a lot of work in communications. He had just completed one of the most relevant proof-of-principle experiments in networking to date, hooking together two computers a continent apart. Taylor had funded Roberts's experiment. It had been successful enough to build Taylor's confidence and convince both himself and Herzfeld that a slightly more intricate network was feasible. And Roberts's knowledge of computers went deep. The son of Yale chemists, Roberts had attended MIT and received his introduction to computers on the TX-0. Although it was the first transistorized digital computer, the TX-0 was limited (subtraction was not in its repertoire; it could subtract only by adding a negative number). Using the TX-0, Roberts taught himself the basics of computer design and operation. Roberts, in fact, had written the entire operating system for its successor, the TX-2 computer at Lincoln, which Wes Clark (who built the TX-0 with Ken Olsen) had fatefully shown off to Licklider. When Clark left Lincoln in 1964, the job of overseeing the TX-2 had fallen to Roberts.

Taylor didn't know Roberts very well. No one, it seemed, knew Roberts very well. He was as reserved in his manner as Taylor was open in his. The people with whom Roberts worked most closely knew almost nothing about his personal life. What was known about him was that in addition to computing and telecommunications expertise, he had a knack for management. Roberts's style was simple, direct, unambiguous, and terribly effective.

Roberts had a reputation for being something of a genius. At twenty-eight, he had done more in the field of computing than many scientists were to achieve in a lifetime. Blessed with incredible stamina, he worked inordinately late hours. He was also a quick study: More than a few people had had the experience of explaining to Roberts something they had been working on intensively for years, and finding that within a few minutes he had grasped it, turned it around in his head a couple of times, and offered trenchant comments of his own. Roberts reminded Taylor of Licklider a little—but without Lick's sense of humor.

Roberts was also known for his nearly obsessive ability to immerse himself in a challenge, pouring intense powers of concentration into a problem. A colleague once recalled the time Roberts took a speed-reading course. He quickly doubled his already rapid reading rate, but he didn't stop there. He delved into the professional literature of speed-reading and kept pushing himself until he was reading at the phenomenal rate of about thirty thousand words a minute with 10 percent "selective comprehension," as Roberts described it. After a few months, Roberts's limiting factor had nothing to do with his eyes or his brain but with the speed at which he could turn the pages. "He'd pick up a paperback and be through with it in ten minutes," the friend observed. "It was typical Larry."

Taylor called Roberts and told him he'd like to come to Boston to see him. A few days later Taylor was sitting in Roberts's office at Lincoln Lab, telling him about the experiment he had in mind. As Taylor talked, Roberts murmured a nasal "hmm-hmm" as if to say, "please go on." Taylor outlined not just the project but a job offer. Roberts would be hired as program director for the experimental network, with the understanding that he would be next in line for the IPTO directorship. Taylor made it clear that this project had the full support of ARPA's director and that Roberts would be given ample latitude to design and build the network however he saw fit. Taylor waited for an answer. "I'll think about it," Roberts said flatly.

Taylor read this as Roberts's polite way of saying no, and he left Boston discouraged. Under any other circumstances, he'd have simply crossed Roberts off the list and called his second choice. But he didn't have a second choice. Not only did Roberts have the necessary technical understanding, but Taylor knew he would listen to Licklider and Wes Clark, both of whom were supporting Taylor's idea.

A few weeks later Taylor made a second trip to Lincoln. This time Roberts was more forthcoming. He told Taylor politely but unequivocally that he was enjoying his work at Lincoln and had no desire to become a Washington bureaucrat.

Disconsolate, Taylor went to Cambridge to visit Lick, who was now back at MIT ensconced in a research effort on time-sharing called Project MAC. They discussed who else might be well suited to the job. Lick suggested a few people, but Taylor rejected them. He wanted Roberts. From then on, every two months or so, during visits to ARPA's other Boston-area contractors, Taylor called on Roberts to try to persuade him to change his mind.

It had been nearly a year since Taylor's twenty-minute conversation with Herzfeld, and the networking idea was floundering for lack of a program manager. One day in late 1966, Taylor returned to the ARPA director's office.

"Isn't it true that ARPA is giving Lincoln at least fifty-one percent of its funding?" Taylor asked his boss.

"Yes, it is," Herzfeld responded, slightly puzzled.

Taylor then explained the difficulty he was having getting the engineer he wanted to run the networking program.

"Who is it?" Herzfeld asked.

Taylor told him. Then he asked his boss another question. Would Herzfeld call the director of Lincoln Lab and ask him to call Roberts in and tell him that it would be in his own best interest—and in Lincoln's best interest—to agree to take the Washington job?

Herzfeld picked up his telephone and dialed Lincoln Lab. He got the director on the line and said just what Taylor had asked him to say. It was a short conversation but, from what Taylor could tell, Herzfeld encountered no resistance. Herzfeld hung up, smiled at Taylor, and said, "Well, okay. We'll see what happens." Two weeks later, Roberts accepted the job.

Larry Roberts was twenty-nine years old when he walked into the Pentagon as ARPA's newest draftee. He fit in quickly, and his dislike of idle time soon became legendary. Within a few weeks, he had the place—one of the world's largest, most labyrinthine buildings—memorized. Getting around the building was complicated by the fact that certain hallways were blocked off as classified areas. Roberts obtained a stopwatch and began timing various routes to his frequent destinations. "Larry's Route" soon became commonly known as the fastest distance between any two Pentagon points.

Even before his first day at ARPA, Roberts had a rudimentary outline of the computer network figured out. Then, and for years afterward as the project grew, Roberts drew meticulous network diagrams, sketching out where the data lines should go, and the number of hops between nodes. On tracing paper and quadrille pad, he created hundreds of conceptual and logical sketches like these:

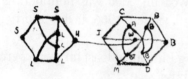

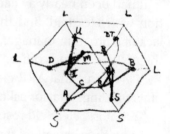

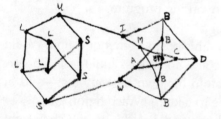

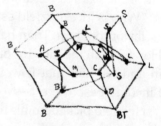

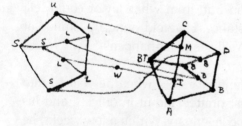

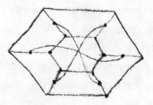

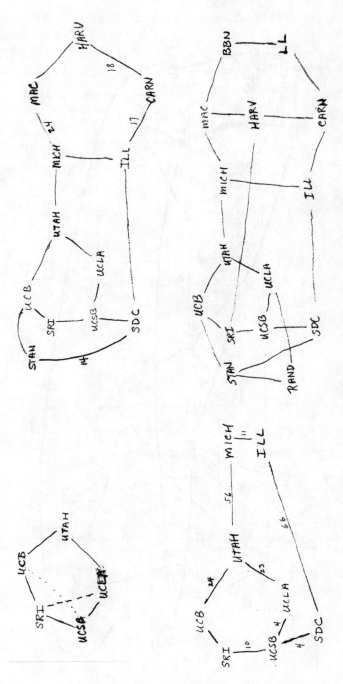

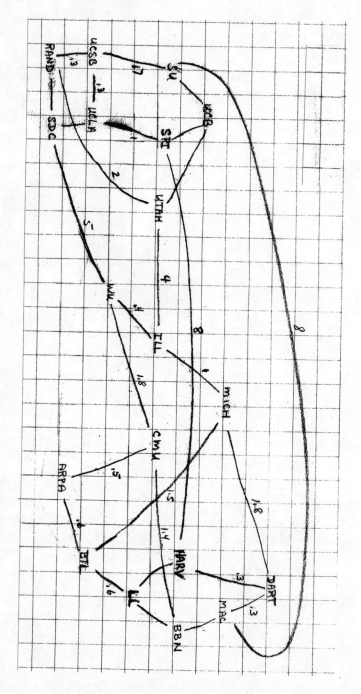

(Later, after the project was under way, Roberts would arrange with Howard Frank, an expert in the field of network topology, to carry out computer-based analyses on how to lay out the network most cost-effectively. Still, for years Roberts had the network's layout, and the technical particulars that defined it, sharply pictured inside his head.)

A lot was already known about how to build complicated communications networks to carry voice, sound, and other more elemental signals. AT&T, of course, had absolute hegemony when it came to the telephone network. But the systematic conveyance of information predated Ma Bell by at least a few thousand years. Messenger systems date at least as far back as the reign of Egyptian King Sesostris I, almost four thousand years ago. The first relay system, where a message was passed from one guard station to the next, came about in 650 B.C. For hundreds of years thereafter, invention was driven by the necessity for greater speed as the transmission of messages from one place to another progressed through pigeons, shouters, coded flags, mirrors, lanterns, torches, and beacons. Then, in 1793, the first tidings were exchanged using semaphores—pivoting vanes on a tower that resembled a person holding signal flags in outstretched arms.

By the mid-1800s telegraph networks were relying on electricity, and Western Union Telegraph Company had begun blanketing the United States with a network of wires for transmitting messages in the form of electric pulses. The telegraph was a classic early example of what is called a "store-and-forward network." Because of electrical losses, the signals had to be switched forward through a sequence of relay stations. At first, messages arriving at switching centers were transcribed by hand and forwarded via Morse code to the next station. Later, arriving messages were stored automatically on typed paper ribbons until an operator could retype the message for the next leg. By 1903, arriving messages were encoded on a snippet of paper tape as a series of small holes, and the torn tape was hung on a hook. Tapes were taken in turn from the hooks by clerks and fed through a tape reader that automatically forwarded them by Morse code.

By the middle of the twentieth century, after the telephone had supplanted the telegraph as the primary means of communication, the American Telephone and Telegraph Company held a complete—albeit strictly regulated—monopoly on long-distance communications within the United States. The company was tenacious about its stronghold on both telephone service and the equipment that made such service possible. Attachment of foreign (non-Bell) equipment to Bell lines was forbidden on the grounds that foreign devices could damage the entire telephone system. Everything added to the system had to work with existing equipment. In the early 1950s a company began manufacturing a device called a Hush-A-Phone, a plastic mouthpiece cover designed to permit a caller to speak into a telephone without being overheard. AT&T succeeded in having the Federal Communications Commission ban the device after presenting expert witnesses who described how the Hush-A-Phone damaged the telephone system by reducing telephone quality. In another example of AT&T's zeal, the company sued an undertaker in the Midwest who was giving out free plastic phone-book covers. AT&T argued that a plastic phone-book cover obscured the advertisement on the cover of the Yellow Pages and reduced the value of the paid advertising, revenues that helped reduce the cost of telephone service.

There was almost no way to bring radical new technology into the Bell System to coexist with the old. It wasn't until 1968, when the FCC permitted the use of the Carterfone—a device for connecting private two-way radios with the telephone system—that AT&T's unrelenting grip on the nation's telecommunications system loosened. Not surprisingly, then, in the early 1960s, when ARPA began exploring an entirely new way of transmitting information, AT&T wanted no part of it.

❑ Coincidental Inventions

Just as living creatures evolve through a process of mutation and natural selection, ideas in science and their applications in technology do the same. Evolution in science, as in nature—normally a gradual sequence of changes—occasionally makes a revolutionary leap breaking with the course of development. New ideas emerge simultaneously but independently. And so they did when the time was ripe for inventing a new way of transmitting information.

In the early 1960s, before Larry Roberts had even set to work creating a new computer network, two other researchers, Paul Baran and Donald Davies—completely unknown to each other and working continents apart toward different goals—arrived at virtually the same revolutionary idea for a new kind of communications network. The realization of their concepts came to be known as packet-switching.

Paul Baran was a good-humored immigrant from Eastern Europe. He was born in 1926, in what was then Poland. His parents sought refuge in the United States two years later, following a lengthy wait for immigration papers. The family arrived in Boston, where Paul's father went to work in a shoe factory, and later settled in Philadelphia, where he opened a small grocery store. As a boy, Paul delivered groceries for his dad using a small red wagon. Once when he was five, he asked his mother if they were rich or poor. "We're poor," she responded. Later he asked his father the same question. "We're rich," the older Baran replied, providing his son with the first of many such existential conundrums in his life.

Paul eventually attended school two streetcar hops from home at Drexel Institute of Technology, which later became Drexel University. He was put off by the school's heavy-handed emphasis in those days on rapid numerical problem solving: Two trivial arithmetic errors on a test (racing against a clock), and you failed, regardless of whether or not you fundamentally understood the problems. At the time, Drexel was trying to create a reputation for itself as a tough, no-nonsense place and took pride in its high dropout rate. Drexel instructors told their budding engineers that employers wanted only those who could calculate quickly and correctly. To his dismay, Baran saw many bright, imaginative friends forced out by the school's "macho attitude" toward math. But he stuck it out, and in 1949 earned a degree in electrical engineering.

Jobs were scarce, so he took the first offer that came, from the Eckert-Mauchly Computer Corporation. In the relatively mundane capacity of technician, he tested parts for radio tubes and germanium diodes on the first commercial computer—the UNIVAC. Baran soon married, and he and his wife moved to Los Angeles, where he took a job at Hughes Aircraft working on radar data processing systems. He took night classes at UCLA on computers and transistors, and in 1959 he received a master's degree in engineering.

Baran left Hughes in late 1959 to join the computer science department in the mathematics division at the RAND Corporation while continuing to take classes at UCLA. Baran was ambivalent, but his advisor at UCLA, Jerry Estrin, urged him to continue his studies toward a doctorate. Soon a heavy travel schedule was forcing him to miss classes. But it was finally divine intervention, he said, that sparked his decision to abandon the doctoral work. "I was driving one day to UCLA from RAND and couldn't find a single parking spot in all of UCLA nor the entire adjacent town of Westwood," Baran recalled. "At that instant I concluded that it was God's will that I should discontinue school. Why else would He have found it necessary to fill up all the parking lots at that exact instant?"

Soon after Baran had arrived at RAND, he developed an interest in the survivability of communications systems under nuclear attack. He was motivated primarily by the hovering tensions of the cold war, not the engineering challenges involved. Both the United States and the Soviet Union were in the process of building hair-trigger nuclear ballistic missile arsenals. By 1960, the escalating arms race between the United States and the Soviet Union heightened the threat of Doomsday—nuclear annihilation—over daily life in both countries.

Baran knew, as did all who understood nuclear weapons and communications technology, that the early command and control systems for missile launch were dangerously fragile. For military leaders, the "command" part of the equation meant having all the weapons, people, and machines of the modern military at their disposal and being able "to get them to do what you want them to do," as one analyst explained. "Control" meant just the opposite—"getting them *not* to do what you don't want them to." The threat of one country or the other having its command systems destroyed in an attack and being left unable to launch a defensive or retaliatory strike gave rise to what Baran described as "a dangerous temptation for either party to misunderstand the actions of the other and fire first."

As the strategists at RAND saw it, it was a necessary condition that the communications systems for strategic weapons be able to survive an attack, so the country's retaliatory capability could still function. At the time, the nation's long-distance communications networks were indeed extremely vulnerable and unable to withstand a nuclear attack. Yet the president's ability to call for, or call off, the launch of American missiles (called "minimal essential communication"), relied heavily on the nation's vulnerable communications systems. So Baran felt that working on the problem of building a more stable communications infrastructure—namely a tougher, more robust network—was the most important work he could be doing.

Baran wasn't the first at RAND to think about this problem. In fact, it was RAND's stock in trade to study such things. RAND had been set up in 1946 to preserve the nation's operations research capability developed during World War II. Most of its contracts came from the Air Force. The problem of the communications system's survivability was something that RAND's communications division was working on, but with limited success. Baran was one of the first to determine, at least on a theoretical level, that the problem was indeed solvable. And he was unquestionably the first to see that the way to solve it was by applying digital computer technology.

Few of the electronics experts in other departments at RAND knew much about the emerging field of digital computer technology, and even fewer seemed interested. Baran recalled his sense of how different his own thinking was from theirs: "Many of the things I thought possible would tend to sound like utter nonsense, or impractical, depending on the generosity of spirit in those brought up in an earlier world." And it wasn't just his colleagues at

RAND who cast a skeptical eye on Baran's thinking. The traditional communications community at large quickly dismissed his ideas as not merely racy, but untenable.

Instead of shying away, Baran just dove deeper into his work. RAND allowed investigators sufficient freedom to pursue their own ideas, and by late 1960 Baran's interest and knowledge of networks had grown into a small independent project. Convinced of the merit of his ideas, he embarked on writing a series of comprehensive technical papers to respond to objections previously raised and explain in increasing detail what he was proposing. The work, as he explained years later, was done not out of intellectual curiosity nor any desire to publish. "It was done in response to the most dangerous situation that ever existed," he said.

At the Pentagon, Baran found planners who were thinking in unemotional terms about postattack scenarios and making quantitative estimates of the destruction that would result from a Soviet nuclear ballistic missile attack. "The possibility of a war exists, but there is much that can be done to minimize the consequences," Baran wrote. "If war does not mean the end of the earth in a black-and-white manner, then it follows that we should do those things that make the shade of gray as light as possible: to plan now to minimize potential destruction and to do all those things necessary to permit the survivors of the holocaust to shuck their ashes and reconstruct the economy swiftly."

Baran's first paper revealed glimpses of his nascent, revolutionary ideas about the theory and structure of communications networks. He had arrived tentatively at the notion that a data network could be made more robust and reliable by introducing higher levels of redundancy. Computers were key. Independently of Licklider and others in computing's avant-garde, Baran saw well beyond mainstream computing, to the future of digital technologies and the symbiosis between humans and machines.

Baran was working on the problem of how to build communications structures whose surviving components could continue to function as a cohesive entity after other pieces were destroyed. He had long talks with Warren McCulloch, an eminent psychiatrist at

MIT's Research Laboratory of Electronics. They discussed the brain, its neural net structures, and what happens when some portion is diseased, particularly how brain functions can sometimes recover by sidestepping a dysfunctional region. "Well, gee, you know," Baran remembered thinking, "the brain seems to have some of the properties that one would need for real stability." It struck him as significant that brain functions didn't rely on a single, unique, dedicated set of cells. This is why damaged cells can be bypassed as neural nets re-create themselves over new pathways in the brain.

The notion of dividing a single large vulnerable structure into many parts, as a defense mechanism, can be seen in many other applications. The concept is not entirely dissimilar to the idea of segmented or compartmentalized structures used in modern ship hulls or gasoline tanker trucks. If only one or two areas of the skin are ruptured, only a section of the overall structure loses its utility, not the whole thing. Some terrorist groups and espionage operations employ a similar kind of compartmentalized organization to thwart authorities, who might eliminate one cell without jeopardizing the whole group.

Theoretically it might be possible to set up a network with numerous redundant connections, and you would "start getting structures sort of like neural nets," Baran said. But there was a technical limitation, since all signals on the telephone network were analog signals. The telephone-switching plan prohibited more than five links to be connected in tandem, because signal quality deteriorated rapidly with the increased number of tandem links. At each switched link, the signal would be slightly distorted and the quality incrementally degraded. This is similar to what happens when one makes copies of copies of audio tapes. With each new generation the quality deteriorates, eventually becoming hopelessly distorted.

Unlike analog systems, digital technologies essentially convert information of all kinds, including sound and image, to a set of 1s and 0s. Digitized information can be stored efficiently and replicated an unlimited number of times within the circuits of a digital device, reproducing the data with almost perfect accuracy. In a communications context, information that is digitally encoded can be passed from one switch to the next with much less degradation than in analog transmission.

As Baran wrote in his initial paper: "The timing for such thinking is particularly appropriate now, for we are just beginning to lay out designs for the digital data transmission system of the future." Technologists could realistically envision new systems where computers would speak to one another, allowing for a network with enough sequentially connected links to create adequate levels of redundancy. These linked structures resemble—in a very modest way—the astonishingly complicated billions of linkages among the neurons in the brain. And digital computers offered speed. Mechanical telephone switches of the time took twenty or thirty seconds just to establish a single long-distance connection over a typical phone line.

In speaking to various military commanders, Baran found that adequate communication in wartime requires the transmission of much more data than the conceptual "minimum essential communications." Exactly how much more was hard to know, so Baran changed the objective to a network able to support almost any imaginable traffic volume.

Baran's basic theoretical network configuration was as simple as it was dramatically different and new. Telephone networks have always been constructed using central switching points. The most vulnerable are those centralized networks with all paths leading into a single nerve center. The other common design is a decentralized network with several main nerve centers around which links are clustered, with a few long lines connecting between clusters; this is basically how the long-distance phone system still looks in schematic terms today.

Baran's idea constituted a third approach to network design. He called his a distributed network. Avoid having a central communications switch, he said, and build a network composed of many nodes, each redundantly connected to its neighbor. His original diagram showed a network of interconnected nodes resembling a distorted lattice, or fish net.

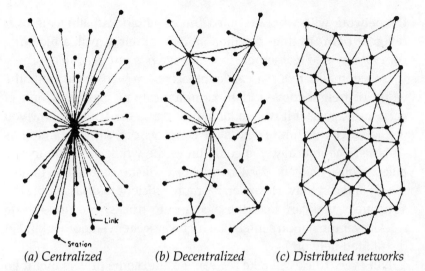

(a) Centralized   (b) Decentralized   (c) Distributed networks

The question remained: How much redundancy in the interconnections between neighboring nodes would be needed for survivability? "Redundancy level" was Baran's term for the degree of connectivity between nodes in the network. A distributed network with the absolute minimum number of links necessary to connect each node was said to have a redundancy level of 1, and was considered extremely vulnerable. Baran ran numerous simulations to determine the probability of distributed network survival under a variety of attack scenarios. He concluded that a redundancy level as low as 3 or 4—each node connecting to three or four other nodes—would provide an exceptionally high level of ruggedness and reliability. "Just a redundancy level of maybe three or four would permit almost as robust a network as the theoretical limit," he said. Even after a nuclear attack, it should be possible to find and use some pathway through the remaining network.

"That was a most fortunate finding because it meant that we would not need to buy a huge amount of redundancy to build survivable networks," Baran said. Even low-cost, unreliable links would suffice as long as there were at least three times the minimum number of them.

Baran's second big idea was still more revolutionary: Fracture the messages too. By dividing each message into parts, you could flood the network with what he called "message blocks," all racing over different paths to their destination. Upon their arrival, a receiving computer would reassemble the message bits into readable form.

Conceptually, this was an approach borrowed more from the world of freight movers than communications experts. Think of each message as if it were a large house and ask yourself how you would move that house across the country from, say, Boston to Los Angeles. Theoretically, you could move the whole structure in one piece. House movers do it over shorter distances all the time— slowly and carefully. However, it's more efficient to disassemble the structure if you can, load the pieces onto trucks, and drive those trucks over the nation's interstate highway system—another kind of distributed network.

Not every truck will take the same route; some drivers might go through Chicago and some through Nashville. If a driver learns that the road is bad around Kansas City, for example, he may take an alternate route. As long as each driver has clear instructions telling him where to deliver his load and he is told to take the fastest way he can find, chances are that all the pieces will arrive at their destination in L.A. and the house can be reassembled on a new site. In some cases the last truck to leave Boston might be the first to arrive in L.A., but if each piece of the house carries a label indicating its place in the overall structure, the order of arrival doesn't matter. The rebuilders can find the right parts and put them together in the right places.

In Baran's model, these pieces were what he called "message blocks," and they were to be of a certain size, just as (in the truck analogy) most tractor-trailer vehicles share the same configuration. The advantage of the packet messaging technique was realized primarily in a distributed network that offered many different routes.

Baran's innovation also provided a much needed solution to the "bursty" nature of data communications. At the time, all communications networks were circuit-switched, which meant that a communications line was reserved for one call at a time and held open for the duration of that session. A phone call between teenagers will tie up a line for as long as they commiserate over their boyfriends and tell stories about their rivals. Even during pauses in their conversation, the line remains dedicated to that conversation until it ends. And technically this makes a lot of sense, since people tend to keep up a fairly steady flow of talk during a phone call.

But a stream of data is different. It usually pours out in short bursts followed by empty pauses that leave the line idle much of the time, wasting its "bandwidth," or capacity. One well-known computer scientist liked to use the example of a bakery with one counter clerk, where customers usually arrive in random bursts. The clerk has to stay at the counter throughout the day, sometimes busy, sometimes idle. In the context of data communications network, it's a highly inefficient way to utilize a long-distance connection.

It would be dramatically more cost-effective, then, to send data in "blocks" and allocate bandwidth in such a way that different messages could share the line. A message would be divided into specific blocks, which would then be sent out individually over the network through multiple locations, and reassembled at their destination. Because there were multiple paths over which the different blocks could be transmitted, they could arrive out of sequence, which meant that once a complete message had arrived, however helter-skelter, it needed to be reassembled in the proper order. Each block would therefore need to contain information identifying the part of the message to which it belonged.

What Baran envisioned was a network of unmanned switches, or nodes—stand-alone computers, essentially—that routed messages by employing what he called a "self-learning policy at each node, without need for a central, and possibly vulnerable, control point." He came up with a scheme for sending information back and forth that he called "hot potato routing," which was essentially a rapid store-and-forward system working almost instantaneously, in contrast with the old post-it-and-forward teletype procedure.

In Baran's model, each switching node contained a routing table that behaved as a sort of transport coordinator or dispatcher. The routing table at each node reflected how many hops, or links, were required to reach every other node in the network. The table indicated the best routes to take and was constantly updated with information about neighboring nodes, distances, and delays—much like dispatchers or truck drivers who use their CB radios to keep one another informed of accidents, construction work, detours, and speed traps. The continuous updating of the tables is also known as "adaptive" or "dynamic" routing.

As the term "hot potato" suggests, no sooner did a message block enter a node than it was tossed out the door again as quickly as possible. If the best outgoing path was busy—or blown to bits— the message block was automatically sent out over the next best route. If that link was busy or gone, it followed the next best route, and so forth. And if the choices ran out, the data could even be sent back to the node from which it originated.

Baran, the inventor of the scheme, also became its chief lobbyist. He hoped to persuade AT&T of its advantages. But it wasn't easy. He found that convincing some of the communications people within RAND of the feasibility of his ideas was difficult enough. The concepts were entirely unheard of in traditional telecommunications circles. Eventually he won his colleagues' support. But winning over AT&T management, who would be called upon if such a network were to be built, proved nearly impossible.

Baran's first task was to show that the nation's long-distance communications system (consisting of almost nothing but AT&T lines) would fail in a Soviet first strike. Not only did AT&T officials refuse to believe this but they also refused to let RAND use their long-distance circuit maps. RAND resorted to using a purloined set of AT&T Long Lines maps to analyze the telephone system's vulnerability.

Vulnerability notwithstanding, the idea of slicing data into message blocks and sending each block out to find its own way through a matrix of phone lines struck AT&T staff members as totally preposterous. Their world was a place where communications were sent as a stream of signals down a pipe. Sending data in small parcels seemed just about as logical as sending oil down a pipeline one cupful at a time.

AT&T's officials concluded that Baran didn't have the first notion of how the telephone system worked. "Their attitude was that they knew everything and nobody outside the Bell System knew anything," Baran said. "And somebody from the outside couldn't possibly understand or appreciate the complexity of the system. So here some idiot comes along and talks about something being very simple, who obviously does not understand how the system works."

AT&T's answer was to educate. The company began a seminar series on telephony, held for a small group of outsiders, including Baran. The classes lasted for several weeks. "It took ninety-four separate speakers to describe the entire system, since no single individual seemed to know more than a part of the system," Baran said. "Probably their greatest disappointment was that after all this, they said, 'Now do you see why it can't work?' And I said, 'No.'"

With the exception of a few supporters at Bell Laboratories who understood digital technology, AT&T continued to resist the idea. The most outspoken skeptics were some of AT&T's most senior technical people. "After I heard the melodic refrain of 'bullshit' often enough," Baran recalled, "I was motivated to go away and write a series of detailed memoranda papers, to show, for example, that algorithms were possible that allowed a short message to contain all the information it needed to find its own way through the network." With each objection answered, another was raised and another piece of a report had to be written. By the time Baran had answered all of the concerns raised by the defense, communications, and computer science communities, nearly four years had passed and his volumes numbered eleven.

In spite of AT&T's intransigence, Baran believed he was engaged in what he called an "honest disagreement" with phone company officials. "The folks at AT&T headquarters always chose to believe their actions were in the best interest of the 'network,' which was by their definition the same as what was best for the country," he said.

By 1965, five years after embarking on the project, Baran had the full support of RAND, and that August RAND sent a formal recommendation to the Air Force that a distributed switching network be built, first as a research and development program and later as a fully operational system: "The need for a survivable . . . flexible, user-to-user communications system is of overriding importance. We do not know of any comparable alternative system proposals to attain this capability, and we believe that the Air Force should move swiftly to implement the research and development program proposed herein."

The Air Force agreed to it. Now the only people holding out were the AT&T officials. The Air Force told AT&T it would pay the phone company to build and maintain the network. But the phone company was not to be swayed.

The Air Force, determined not to let the plan die on the drawing boards, decided that it should proceed without AT&T's cooperation. But the Pentagon decided to put the newly formed Defense Communications Agency (DCA), not the Air Force, in charge of building the network. Baran pictured nothing but trouble. The agency was run by a group of old-fashioned communications officers from each of the various services, with no experience in digital technology. To make matters worse, DCA's enthusiasm for the project was on a par with the response from AT&T. "So I told my friends in the Pentagon to abort this entire program—because they wouldn't get it right," Baran recalled. "It would have been a damn waste of government money and set things back. The DCA would screw it up and then no one else would be allowed to try, given the failed attempt on the books."

Baran felt that it was better to wait until "a competent organization came along." And with that, after five years of struggle, Paul Baran shifted his attention to other things. It was, in no small way, a visit back to the "Are we rich or are we poor?" question he had posed decades earlier to his parents, whose starkly contrasting answers helped him understand that most things in life are a matter of perspective.

In London in the autumn of 1965, just after Baran halted work on his project, Donald Watts Davies, a forty-one-year-old physicist at the British National Physical Laboratory (NPL), wrote the first of several personal notes expounding on some ideas he was playing with for a new computer network much like Baran's. He sent his set of notes to a few interested people, but—certain he would encounter stiff resistance from the authorities in charge of the British Post Office's telephone service monopoly—mostly he kept his ideas to himself. Davies wanted time to validate his concepts. By the following spring, confident that his ideas were sound, he gave a public lecture in London describing the notion of sending short blocks of data—which he called "packets"—through a digital store-and-forward network. As the meeting was breaking up, a man from the audience approached Davies and said that he was from the Ministry of Defence. He told Davies about some remarkably similar work that had been circulated in the American defense community by a man named Paul Baran. Davies had never heard of Baran or his RAND studies.

Donald Davies was the son of working-class parents. His father, a clerk at a coal mine in Wales, died the year after Donald and his twin sister were born. Their mother moved her young family to Portsmouth, a British naval port, where she went to work as a counter clerk in the post office. Donald experimented with radio at a young age and took an early interest in physics. He was not yet fourteen the day his mother brought home a book, something an engineer had left behind at the post office, all about telephony. The technical volume described the logic and design of telephone-switching systems and "made hours of fascinating reading," Davies recalled years later.

An exceptional student, Davies was offered scholarships to several universities. To celebrate its star student, his school declared a half-day holiday. "For a short time I was the most popular boy in the school," he recalled. Davies chose the University of London's Imperial College, and by the time he was twenty-three had earned degrees in physics and mathematics. In 1947 he joined a team of scientists led by the mathematician Alan Turing at the National Physical Laboratory and Davies played a leading part in building the fastest digital computer in England at the time, the Pilot ACE. In 1954 Davies won a fellowship to spend a year in the United States; part of that year, he was at MIT. He then returned to England, rose swiftly at the NPL, and in 1966, after describing his pioneering work on packet-switching, he was appointed head of the computer science division.

The technical similarity between Davies' and Baran's work was striking. Not only were their ideas roughly parallel in concept, but by coincidence they had even chosen the same packet size and data-transmission rate. Independently, Davies also came up with a routing scheme that was adaptive, like Baran's, but different in detail.

There was just one major difference in their approaches. The motivation that led Davies to conceive of a packet-switching network had nothing to do with the military concerns that had driven Baran. Davies simply wanted to create a new public communications network. He wanted to exploit the technical strengths he saw in digital computers and switches, to bring about highly responsive, highly interactive computing over long distances. Such a network would have greater speed and efficiency than existing systems. Davies was concerned that circuit-switched networks were poorly matched to the requirements of interacting computers. The irregular, bursty characteristics of computer-generated data traffic did not fit well with the uniform channel capacity of the telephone system. Matching the network design to the new types of data traffic became his main motivation.

Rather than conduct the kind of redundancy and reliability studies to which Baran had devoted so much time, Davies focused on working out the details of configuring the data blocks. He also foresaw the need to overcome differences in computer languages and machine-operating procedures—differences in hardware and software—that would exist in a large public network. He envisioned the day when someone would sit down at one kind of computer and interact with a machine of a different kind somewhere else. To bridge the gap between the widely divergent computer systems of the era, he began outlining the features of an intermediary device—a new computer—that would serve as a translator, assembling and disassembling digital messages for the other machines.

The idea of splitting messages into uniform data "packets"—

each the length of one typical line of text—was something Davies hit upon after studying advanced time-sharing systems and how they allocated processing time to multiple users. On a trip to the United States in 1965 he had observed MIT's Project MAC time-sharing system. A few months later, the NPL had played host in London to a group from MIT, including Larry Roberts, for further discussions about time-sharing. It was in those meetings that the packet idea first struck Davies. Unlike AT&T's chilly reaction to Baran, the British telecommunications establishment embraced Davies' ideas. He was encouraged to seek funding for an experimental network at NPL.

Time-sharing systems had already solved the nagging problem of slow turnaround time in batch processing by giving each user a slice of computer processing time. Several people could be running jobs at once without noticing any significant delay in their work. Analogously, in a digital communications network, a computer could slice messages into small pieces, or packets, pour those into the electronic pipeline, and allow users to share the network's total capacity. Davies, like Baran, saw in the digital age the feasibility for a new kind of communications network.

Davies' choice of the word "packet" was very deliberate. "I thought it was important to have a new word for one of the short pieces of data which traveled separately," he explained. "This would make it easier to talk about them." There were plenty of other possibilities—block, unit, section, segment, frame. "I hit on the word packet," he said, "in the sense of small package." Before settling on the word, he asked two linguists from a research team in his lab to confirm that there were cognates in other languages. When they reported back that it was a good choice, he fixed on it. Packet-switching. It was precise, economic, and very British. And it was far easier on the ear than Baran's "distributed adaptive message block switching." Davies met Baran for the first time several years later. He told Baran that he had been thoroughly embarrassed to hear of Baran's work after he had finished his own, and then added, "Well, you may have got there first, but I got the name."

❑ Mapping It Out

In December 1966, when Larry Roberts arrived at the Pentagon, he knew Donald Davies from his trip to London the previous year, but didn't know about Davies' subsequent work in packet switching. And he had never heard the name Paul Baran.

A few years earlier, Roberts had decided that computing was getting old and everything worth doing *inside* a computer had already been done. This had come to him as a revelation at a 1964 conference held in Homestead, Virginia, where Roberts, Licklider, and others stayed up until the small hours of the morning talking about the potential of computer networks. Roberts left the meeting resolved to begin work on communications *between* computers.

His first opportunity came a year later when he oversaw one of the first real experiments in uniting disparate machines over long distances. In 1965 psychologist Tom Marill, who had studied under Licklider and who was similarly entranced by computers, started a small time-sharing company, Computer Corporation of America (CCA). When Marill's largest investor backed out at the last minute, Marill cast about for some R&D work. He proposed to ARPA that he conduct a networking experiment tying Lincoln's TX-2 computer to the SDC Q-32 in Santa Monica. Marill's company was so small, however, that ARPA recommended carrying out his experiment under the aegis of Lincoln Laboratory. Officials at Lincoln liked the idea and put Larry Roberts in charge of overseeing the project.

The objective was clear. As Marill argued in a letter to Roberts in 1965, computing had reached an unfortunate state of affairs; time-sharing projects were proliferating, but there was no "common ground for exchange of programs, personnel, experience, or ideas." His impression of the computer science community was "of a number of essentially similar projects, each going off in its own direction with complete disregard for the others." Why waste resources?

As far as it went, the TX-2 experiment was ambitious. The link between the two computers was made using a special Western Union four-wire full-duplex service (full duplex provides simultaneous transmission in both directions between two points). To this

Marill attached a crude form of modem, operating at 2,000 bits per second, which he called an automatic dialer. By directly linking the machines, Marill got around the problem of incompatibilities between them. The idea was to connect the computers like a pair of Siamese twins, running programs *in situ*. Though not transferring files back and forth, the experiment did allow the machines to send messages to each other. Marill set up a procedure for grouping characters into messages, sending them across the link, and checking to see if the messages arrived. If no acknowledgment followed, the message was retransmitted. Marill referred to the set of procedures for sending information back and forth as a message "protocol," prompting a colleague to inquire, "Why do you use that term? I thought it referred to diplomacy."

In a 1966 report summarizing the initial results of the experiment, Marill wrote that he could "foresee no obstacle that a reasonable amount of diligence cannot be expected to overcome." Diligence notwithstanding, when Marill and Roberts actually connected the two machines, the results were mixed. The connection itself worked as planned. But the reliability of the connection and the response time were, as Roberts would describe them several years later, just plain lousy.

Bringing together two different computers was one thing, but the project for which Roberts had been pulled away from Lincoln to work at ARPA was another, much greater challenge. Interconnecting a matrix of machines, each with distinct characteristics, would be exceedingly complicated. To pull it off was probably going to require calling on every expert Roberts knew in every area of computing and communications.

Fortunately, Roberts's circle of colleagues was wide. One of his best friends from Lincoln Laboratory, with whom he had worked on the TX-2, was Leonard Kleinrock, a smart and ambitious engineer who had attended MIT on a full scholarship. If anyone influenced Roberts in his earliest thinking about computer networks, it was Kleinrock.

Kleinrock's dissertation, proposed as early as 1959, was an important theoretical work that described a series of analytical models of communication networks. And in 1961, while working with Roberts, Kleinrock had published a report at MIT that analyzed the problem of data flow in networks. Kleinrock had also worked on random routing procedures, and had some early thoughts on dividing messages into blocks for efficient use of communication channels. Now Kleinrock was at UCLA, and Roberts gave him an ARPA contract to set up the official Network Measurement Center there, a lab devoted to network performance testing.

The friendship between Roberts and Kleinrock went well beyond the professional interests they shared. Brain teasers were one common interest. Money-making schemes were another. Each reinforced the other's openness to fiscal adventure. Those who thought Roberts was all work and no play had never seen him in action with his friends.

Roberts and Kleinrock were inveterate casino gamblers. Roberts developed a "high-low" counting scheme for blackjack and taught it to Kleinrock. They never made it into the official rogues' gallery of blacklisted card counters, but more than once, they were spotted by casino detectives and asked to leave.

And in another daring episode, Roberts and Kleinrock cooked up a plan to cash in on the physics of roulette. The idea was to predict, employing rudimentary laws of motion, just when the ball would fall off its trajectory. To do this, they needed to know the speed of the ball, which traveled in one direction, and the speed of the wheel, which traveled in the other. They decided to build a small machine that would make the predictions, but they needed a little data. So Roberts got a tape recorder, put a microphone in his hand, and made a cast that made it appear he had a broken wrist. The two sat down at the table and Roberts placed his hand next to the wheel to record the sound of the passing ball, from which they could later extrapolate its speed. Kleinrock's job was to distract the pit boss by playing several rounds of roulette. "Everything was working fine except for one thing," Kleinrock said. "I started winning. It drew attention to me. The pit boss looks over and sees this guy with a broken arm with his hand near the roulette wheel, and he grabs Larry's arm and says, 'Let me see your arm!' Larry and I made fast tracks out of there."

. . .

Roberts agreed with Taylor that fast response time for the network was critical, because a low message delay time was crucial to inter-activity. Anyone who had used time-sharing systems that passed data over standard communications lines knew how sluggish they could be. Data traveled to and from the main computer at excruci-atingly slow rates of a few hundred bits per second. Retrieving or sending even a small amount of information was a process that left plenty of time to pour yourself a cup of coffee, or even brew an en-tire pot, while the modem churned away. No one wanted a sluggish network.

During an early meeting of the loose group of advisors Roberts had assembled, someone banged his fist on the table and said, "If this network can't give me a one-second response, it's no good." Optimistically, a half-second response time was written into the re-quirements. The second priority, of course, was reliability. If a net-work was to be effective, users needed complete confidence in its ability to send data back and forth without snafus.

Another source of consternation was the question of how the network would be mapped out. Several people had proposed that the resource sharing be done on a single centralized computer, sit-ting in, say Omaha, a popular place for long-distance telephone switches because it lay at the nation's geographic center. If central-ization made sense for a telephone network, why not for a com-puter network? Perhaps the network should use dedicated phone lines—a question that was still unresolved—which would help keep costs uniform. Baran had avoided a centralized system be-cause that increased its vulnerability. Roberts, too, was opposed to a centralized approach, but decided to delay his final decision until he could bring up the topic with a large group. His chance came soon, at a meeting for ARPA's principal investigators in Ann Arbor, Michi-gan, in early 1967.

Taylor had called the meeting, and the principal item on the agenda was the networking experiment. Roberts laid out his initial plan. The idea, as he described it, was to connect all of the time-sharing computers to one another directly, over dial-up telephone lines. The networking functions would be handled by the "host" computers at each site. So, in other words, the hosts would do double duty, as both research computers and as communications routers. The idea was greeted with little enthusiasm. People from the proposed host sites foresaw no end of trouble. No one wanted to relinquish an unknown portion of valuable computing resources to administer a network about which they were hardly excited. Then there were dozens of idiosyncratic variations to cope with, not the least of which was the fact that each machine spoke a language substantially different from the others. It seemed nearly impossible to standardize around one set of protocols.

The Ann Arbor meeting revealed the lack of enthusiasm, if not downright hostility, to Taylor and Roberts's proposal. Few ARPA principal investigators wanted to participate in the experiment. This attitude was especially pronounced among researchers from the East Coast universities, who saw no reason to link up with campuses in the West. They were like the upper-crust woman on Beacon Hill who, when told that long-distance telephone service to Texas was available, echoed Thoreau's famous line: "But what would I possibly have to say to anyone in Texas?"

Douglas Engelbart, a computer scientist at Stanford Research Institute (SRI) in 1967, remembered the meeting clearly. "One of the first reactions was, 'Oh hell, here I've got this time-sharing computer, and my resources are scarce as it is.' Another reaction was, 'Why would I let my graduate students get sucked off into something like this?'" Nonetheless, it quickly became clear just how serious Roberts was. First he tried to allay the skepticism about resource-sharing by pointing out that everyone had something of interest on his computer that others might want. "I remember one guy turning to the other and saying, 'What have you got on your computer that I could use?'" Engelbart recalled, "And the other guy replied, 'Well, don't you read my reports?'" No one was taken with the idea. "People were thinking, 'Why would I need anyone else's computer when I've got everything right here?" recalled Jon Postel, then a graduate student at UCLA. "What would they have that I want, and what would I have that I want anyone else to look at?"

An even more difficult problem lay in overcoming the communications barriers between disparate computers. How could anyone program the TX-2, for instance, to talk to the Sigma-7 at UCLA or the computer at SRI? The machines, their operating systems, their programming languages were all different, and heaven only knew what other incongruities divided them.

Just before the meeting ended, Wes Clark passed a note up to Roberts. It read, "You've got the network inside out." Roberts was intrigued, and he wanted to hear more; however, the meeting was breaking up, and people were already leaving. Roberts, Taylor and a few others huddled around Clark afterward, and a small group decided to continue the discussion during the ride back to the airport. In the car, Clark sketched out his idea: Leave the host computers out of it as much as possible and instead insert a small computer between each host computer and the network of transmission lines. (This was, by coincidence, precisely what Davies had concluded separately in England.)

The way Clark explained it, the solution was obvious: a subnetwork with small, identical nodes, all interconnected. The idea solved several problems. It placed far fewer demands on all the host computers and correspondingly fewer demands on the people in charge of them. The smaller computers composing this inner network would all speak the same language, of course, and they, not the host computers, would be in charge of all the routing. Furthermore, the host computers would have to adjust their language just once—to speak to the subnet. Not only did Clark's idea make good sense technically, it was an administrative solution as well. ARPA could have the entire network under its direct control and not worry much about the characteristics of each host. Moreover, providing each site with its own identical computer would lend uniformity to the experiment.

The most curious thing about the idea was that Clark thought it up. He hadn't been paying much attention to the proceedings in Ann Arbor. In fact, he was a bit bored by it all. He had already told Roberts in no uncertain terms that he had no desire to put his computer at Washington University in St. Louis on the network. Clark was not friendly toward time-sharing, or even resource-sharing. He had been working on computers designed for individual use and saw no particular reason to share his facility with people on a network. But when he heard the discord over how the ARPA experiment should be deployed, he couldn't help but hazard a suggestion. Perhaps it was Clark's antipathy toward time-sharing that enabled him to think of this. By assigning the task of routing to the host computers, Roberts and others were essentially adding another time-sharing function. Clark's idea was to spare the hosts that extra burden and build a network of identical, nonshared computers dedicated to routing.

During the ride to the airport, the discussion turned lively. Wouldn't an entire subnetwork composed of individual computers be prohibitively expensive and defeat the original goal of saving money? And who, Roberts wanted to know, did Wes Clark think could build such a thing? "There's only one person in the country who can do that," Clark responded. "Frank Heart."

Larry Roberts knew Frank Heart. The two had worked together at Lincoln Lab, and Roberts had shared an office with Heart's wife, Jane, a programmer at Lincoln. Roberts and Heart had never worked together directly, but Roberts knew Heart to be an exacting systems engineer. He was an expert in real-time systems built for when the physical world demands a response within fractions of seconds—or at least before the next set of data arrives. Anything dealing with incoming information in a time-critical fashion, such as radar tracking data sent to the SAGE system, and seismic information generated during an earthquake, was considered a real-time system, and in the 1960s few people understood real-time systems as well as Heart did.

Roberts also knew that Heart and Clark were good friends from Lincoln, where Heart had shown Clark the ropes of programming more than a decade earlier. Now, as far as Roberts knew, Heart was at Bolt Beranek and Newman in Cambridge, where he had moved in 1966 to work on the use of computers in medicine.

The ARPA network wasn't intended as a real-time system, not in the same sense of the word that true real-timers understand it.

(Anything that takes more than 10 to 20 milliseconds, the point at which delays become humanly perceptible, is not considered real-time.) Strictly speaking, the ARPA network was to be a store-and-forward system. But data would zip in and out of the nodes so quickly, and the response time from a human perspective would be so rapid, that it qualified as a real-time problem. The system would have to cope with dozens of problems involving closely sequenced events and extremely tight timing. The status of the network would change constantly, and whoever programmed the computers that composed Clark's proposed subnet would need to know how to make the system handle incoming and outgoing data reliably at very fast rates.

Despite the logic of Clark's recommendation, however, Roberts couldn't simply turn the job over to Heart. ARPA had to play by the government's contracting rules. Over the years, most proposals requesting funding arrived at ARPA unsolicited. Seldom had the agency actually requested proposals. But this one was different. The agency had come up with the network idea internally, and in that respect it was unusual. Also, because the network would be government property controlled centrally by ARPA and wouldn't reside on one campus, say, or at one research firm, Roberts and others decided they had to send this project out for competitive bids.

When he returned to Washington, Roberts wrote a memorandum describing Clark's idea and distributed it to Kleinrock and others. He called the intermediate computers that would control the network "interface message processors," or IMPs, which he pronounced "imps." They were to perform the functions of interconnecting the network, sending and receiving data, checking for errors, retransmitting in the event of errors, routing data, and verifying that messages arrived at their intended destinations. A protocol would be established for defining just how the IMPs should communicate with host computers. After word of Clark's idea spread, the initial hostility toward the network diminished a bit. For one thing, a separate computer to carry out the switching functions removed the burdensome kludge (a kludge is an inelegant solution to a technical problem) that could result from adding those functions to the host computer. People also saw it as a way of getting another computer to play with.

At the end of 1967 another computer conference, this one in Gatlinburg, Tennessee, helped advance the network plan. This symposium was sponsored by the Association for Computing Machinery, the oldest and most prestigious of professional organizations for the growing computer industry. Though small in number, the attendees represented the highest levels of the computer science establishment.

Gatlinburg was a perfect venue for Roberts to present his first paper on what he called the "ARPA net." In his presentation, Roberts focused on the reasons for the network and described the subnet of IMPs, but said little else about how the network would actually work. One big puzzle still to solve was the question of how the data would actually be transmitted—over what kind of channel. Ever mindful of cost, Roberts closed his presentation with a brief discussion of what he called "communication needs." He was thinking of using the same type of telephone lines that he and Marill had used for their small TX-2 experiment: full-duplex, four-wire lines. Talk of the matter ended on a note of frustration. Ordinary dial-up phone lines (as opposed to dedicated, leased lines) were slow, and holding a line open was wasteful. Roberts still hadn't found a highly efficient means of carrying the data.

Whereas the Ann Arbor meeting months earlier had been the intellectual equivalent of a barroom brawl, Gatlinburg was high tea. People were politely coming around to the idea of a network. Roberts's presentation was generally well received, even greeted enthusiastically by some.

Another paper was presented by Roger Scantlebury. It came from Donald Davies' team at the National Physical Laboratory and discussed the work going on in England. His paper presented a detailed design study for a packet-switched network. It was the first Roberts had heard of it. Afterward, Roberts and a few others approached Scantlebury, and they began to discuss the NPL work. The discussion continued at the hotel bar and went late into the night. Scantlebury raised the issue of line speed with Roberts. He said that he and Davies were planning to use lines that operated much faster than the 2,000 bits per second speed Roberts was proposing. He suggested Roberts build the ARPA network with fewer lines carrying data at speeds more than twenty times higher to improve the response time.

Roberts also learned from Scantlebury, for the first time, of the work that had been done by Paul Baran at RAND a few years earlier. When Roberts returned to Washington, he found the RAND reports, which had actually been collecting dust in the Information Processing Techniques Office for months, and studied them. Roberts was designing this experimental network not with survivable communications as his main—or even secondary—concern. Nuclear war scenarios, and command and control issues, weren't high on Roberts's agenda. But Baran's insights into data communications intrigued him nonetheless, and in early 1968 he met with Baran. After that, Baran became something of an informal consultant to the group Roberts assembled to design the network. The Gatlinburg paper presented by Scantlebury on behalf of the British effort was clearly an influence, too. When he visited Roberts during the design of the ARPA network, Davies said, "I saw that our paper had been used so much that its pages were falling apart."

Roberts thought the network should start out with four sites— UCLA, SRI, the University of Utah, and the University of California at Santa Barbara—and eventually grow to around nineteen. UCLA was chosen as the first site because Len Kleinrock's Network Measurement Center was there. At each of the other sites, ARPA-sponsored research that would provide valuable resources to the network was already under way. Researchers at UCSB were working on interactive graphics. Utah researchers were also doing a lot of graphics work as well as investigating night vision for the military. Dave Evans, who, with Ivan Sutherland, later started Evans and Sutherland, a pioneering graphics company, was at Utah putting together a system that would take images and manipulate them with a computer. Evans and his group were also interested in whether the network could be used for more than just textual exchanges.

Stanford Research Institute (later it severed its ties to Stanford and became just SRI) had been chosen as one of the first sites because Doug Engelbart, a scientist of extraordinary vision, worked there. Several years earlier, when Bob Taylor was at NASA he had funded Engelbart's invention of the first computer mouse (Engelbart received a patent for the device as an "X-Y position indicator for a display system"), and for years afterward Taylor pointed with pride to his support of Engelbart's mouse.

Engelbart had been in attendance at the 1967 Ann Arbor meeting of ARPA's principal investigators when Taylor and Larry Roberts announced that a dozen or so of them would be expected to tie their computers together over an experimental network and that each site would be expected to make its computer resources available on the network. While others had responded skeptically to the plan, Engelbart had been delighted with it. At the time, he was directing an SRI computer research lab. Not unlike Licklider, Engelbart was interested in using computers to augment human intellect. Under a contract from ARPA, he was developing a system (called NLS, for oNLine System) that depended on computer-literate communities. He saw the ARPA experimental network as an excellent vehicle for extending NLS to a wide area of distributed collaboration. "I realized there was a ready-made computer community," Engelbart recalled. "It was just the thing I was looking for."

Part of the strength of NLS was its usefulness in creating digital libraries and in storing and retrieving electronic documents. Engelbart also saw NLS as a natural way to support an information clearinghouse for the ARPA network. After all, if people were going to share resources, it was important to let everyone know what was available. At the Michigan meeting, Engelbart volunteered to put together the Network Information Center, which came to be known as the NIC (pronounced "nick"). Engelbart also knew that his research group back home in Menlo Park would be equally enthusiastic about the network. His colleagues were talented programmers who would recognize an interesting project when they saw it.

The conversation with Scantlebury had clarified several points for Roberts. The Briton's comments about packet-switching in particular helped steer Roberts closer to a detailed design. In specifying the network requirements, Roberts was guided by a few basic principles. First, the IMP subnet was to function as a communications system whose essential task was to transfer bits reliably from a source location to a specified destination. Next, the average transit time through the subnet should be less than half a second. Third, the subnet must be able to operate autonomously. Computers of that era typically required several hours per week of maintenance downtime. IMPs could not afford to be dependent on a local host computer or host-site personnel; they should be able to continue operating and routing network traffic whether or not a host was running. The subnetwork also had to continue functioning when individual IMPs were down for service. This idea that maintaining reliability should be incumbent on the subnetwork, not the hosts, was a key principle. Roberts and others believed the IMPs should also attend to such tasks as route selection and acknowledgment of receipt.

By the end of July, 1968, Roberts had finished drafting the request for proposals. He sent it out to 140 companies interested in building the Interface Message Processor. The document was thick with details of what the network should look like and what the IMPs would be expected to do. It was a rich piece of technical prose, filled with an eclectic mix of ideas. Kleinrock had influenced Roberts's earliest thoughts about the theoretical possibilities. Baran had contributed to the intellectual foundation on which the technical concept was based, and Roberts's dynamic routing scheme gave an extra nod to Baran's work; Roberts had adopted Davies' term "packet" and incorporated his and Scantlebury's higher line speeds; Clark's subnet idea was a stroke of technical genius. "The process of technological development is like building a cathedral," remarked Baran years later. "Over the course of several hundred years new people come along and each lays down a block on top of the old foundations, each saying, 'I built a cathedral.' Next month another block is placed atop the previous one. Then comes along an historian who asks, 'Well, who built the cathedral?' Peter added some stones here, and Paul added a few more. If you are not careful, you can con yourself into believing that you did the most important part. But the reality is that each contribution has to follow onto previous work. Everything is tied to everything else."

But in 1968 the network's principal architect was Larry Roberts: He made the initial decisions, and he established the parameters and operational specifications. Although he would get input from others, Roberts would be the one to decide who built it.

The first responses to the request for proposals were from IBM and Control Data Corporation (CDC). IBM was then the world's largest computer manufacturer and dominated the market for large computer systems. CDC, though dwarfed by IBM, was another company that had invested heavily in developing large systems. Both declined to bid, and their reasons were identical: The network could never be built, they said flatly, because there existed no computers small enough to make it cost-effective. For the IMP, IBM had thought about proposing a 360 Model 50 computer, a large mainframe. But at a price many times that of a minicomputer, the Model 50 was too expensive to consider buying in large quantities.

Roberts, on the other hand, was thinking small. The first computer he had thought of was the PDP-8, a minicomputer made by Digital Equipment Corp. Digital had released the PDP-8 in 1965. Not only was it the company's first big hit but the PDP-9 also established minicomputers as the new vanguard of the computer industry. Roberts knew Ken Olsen from Lincoln, and he thought Digital might even offer a quantity discount on the machine.

When bids started coming in, the majority had chosen a Honeywell computer instead. It was a minicomputer called the DDP-516; Honeywell had just introduced it. Part of the new machine's cachet was that it could be built to heavy-duty specifications. In its "ruggedized" version, it cost about $80,000. Shortly after the machine's introduction, at a computer conference in Las Vegas, the hardened military version was hoisted off the showroom floor by a crane. As it swung from ropes attached to the crane, a Honeywell employee took a sledgehammer to it. The point of the exercise was to demonstrate that the machine was tough enough to operate on a battlefield. For bidders, the more likely appeal of the 516 was its impressive cost-performance ratio and the design of its input/output system.

More than a dozen bids were submitted, resulting in a six-foot stack of paper. Marill's company, CCA, bid jointly with Digital. Raytheon bid, and so did Bunker-Ramo. Roberts was pleasantly surprised that several of the respondents believed they could construct a network that performed faster than the goal listed in the specifications.

Raytheon was a frontrunner. A major defense contractor in the Boston area specializing in electronic systems components, Raytheon had already proposed to build a high-speed, short-distance computer network. In the middle of December, Roberts entered into final negotiations with Raytheon for the IMP contract. Raytheon officials answered ARPA's remaining technical questions and accepted the price.

So it surprised everyone when, just a few days before Christmas, ARPA announced that the contract to build the Interface Message Processors that would reside at the core of its experimental network was being awarded to Bolt Beranek and Newman, a small consulting firm in Cambridge, Massachusetts.

The Third University

When Richard Bolt and Leo Beranek started their consulting company in 1948, advanced computing was not on their minds. Beranek was an electrical engineer, Bolt an architect and physicist. Both were acousticians and members of the MIT faculty during the 1940s. Bolt had worked for the Navy in World War II on methods for using sound to detect submarines. Following the war, as head of MIT's acoustics laboratory, Bolt did consulting work, as did Beranek. MIT began receiving requests for aid in acoustical planning for new buildings around the country and passed them on to Bolt and Beranek. Independently of each other, the two had already done quite a bit of work in what is known as airborne acoustics—the sound carried in concert halls and movie theaters—as well as in noise control and noise reduction in buildings.

When the United Nations asked Bolt to design the acoustics for its new complex of buildings in an old slaughterhouse district on Manhattan's East River, Bolt called Beranek into his office and showed him the pile of papers spelling out the UN job. It was too much for one person to take on. At the time, Beranek was busy on a

project to improve the acoustics in a chain of Brooklyn movie theaters. But Bolt convinced Beranek to join him in starting a consulting firm to take on the UN project. A year later they took in Robert
Newman, an architect with a physics background who had been a
student of Bolt's, and Bolt Beranek and Newman was born.

In its earliest days, BBN was truly a consulting company. That is,
Bolt and Beranek hired people, provided them with office space—
and expected them to find the work. And find work they did. The
UN project was such a conspicuous success that the company didn't
need to advertise for the first ten years of its existence. The business
grew as BBN consulted on the design of acoustical systems for office
buildings, apartment complexes, and performing arts centers.
When a large wind tunnel was built for testing jet engines near
Cleveland, the noise disturbed people within a ten-mile radius,
and local residents threatened to have the facility shut down. BBN
engineers figured out a way to muffle the sound. The company
was developing expertise in analyzing audio tapes: It was called in
after the assassination of President John F. Kennedy in 1963 and
would be called on again after the shootings at Kent State University in 1970. Its most famous tape analysis would come during the
Watergate scandal in 1974, when BBN would be involved in the
analysis of the infamous 18.5-minute gap in the Nixon tapes. A
committee headed by Dick Bolt would conclude that the erasure
was deliberate.

In 1957 Beranek had recruited Licklider to BBN. He had worked
with Lick at Harvard during the war, and when he went to MIT, he
convinced Lick to go there too. When Beranek hired Lick at BBN, it
wasn't so much Lick's background in psychoacoustics but his interest in human-machine interaction that Beranek thought was interesting. Beranek sensed that consulting jobs would pick up in the
business of helping companies build machines that were more efficient amplifiers of human labor, which meant bringing about some
kind of compatibility between humans and machines. "I didn't
know how big a business it was," Beranek later recalled. "But I
thought it was a good supplement to what we were doing."

Lick, of course, had thought it through more fully. He believed the future of scientific research was going to be linked to high-speed computers, and he thought computing was a good field for BBN to enter. He had been at BBN for less than a year when he told Beranek he'd like to buy a computer. By way of persuasion, Lick stressed that the computer he had in mind was a very modern machine—its programs and data were punched on paper tape rather than the conventional stacks of IBM cards.

"What will it cost?" Beranek asked him.

"Around $25,000."

"That's a lot of money," Beranek replied. "What are you going to do with it?"

"I don't know."

Licklider was convinced the company would be able to get contracts from the government to do basic research using computers. The $25,000, he assured Beranek, wouldn't be wasted.

None of the company's three principals knew much about computers. Beranek knew that Lick, by contrast, was almost evangelistic in his belief that computers would change not only the way people thought about problems but the way problems were solved. Beranek's faith in Licklider won the day. "I decided it was worth the risk to spend $25,000 on an unknown machine for an unknown purpose," Beranek said. The computer he purchased for Lick was an LGP-30, manufactured in 1958 by Royal-McBee, a subsidiary of the Royal Typewriter Company. It had a drum memory and was slow even by the standards of its day. Yet Lick went straight to work tinkering with it, using it for lengthy statistical calculations and psychoacoustics experiments.

Not long after the computer arrived, Ken Olsen stopped by to see the Royal-McBee machine and to tell BBN about the computer he was building at his new company, Digital Equipment. Olsen wanted to lend Beranek a prototype of the machine, which he called the PDP-1, so BBN engineers could take a look at it. Beranek agreed. But the computer measured four feet by eight feet, and there were few doorways at BBN through which to squeeze it. So it was set up in the lobby. A month or so later, after everyone had a chance to play with it, BBN sent it back to Olsen with recommendations for fine-tuning. When the PDP-1 went on the market for slightly less than $150,000, BBN bought the first one.

The presence of the PDP-1 and the work Licklider was doing with it attracted a number of leading computer scientists to BBN. The firm had also become well known as a place whose hiring philosophy was to recruit MIT dropouts. The idea was that if they could get into MIT they were smart, and if they dropped out, you could get them cheaper. Beranek gave Lick a great deal of freedom to hire whomever he pleased, and Licklider did just that, occasionally forgetting to tell Beranek. "I was wandering around the building one day to see what was going on in the computer side, and I saw two strange guys sitting in one of the large rooms there," Beranek said. (Lick would have been happy to wear a suit to a picnic, but his hirees were decidedly less formal.) Beranek had no idea who the two men were. "I walked up to the first fellow and said, 'Who are you?' and he said, 'Who are you?'" The two young men, it turned out, were friends of Licklider's from MIT—Marvin Minsky and John McCarthy, two of the most prominent figures in the emerging field of artificial intelligence.

The PDP-1 had computing power roughly equivalent to today's pocket organizers and a little less memory. People at BBN kept the computer going day and night doing interactive programming. They even built a time-sharing system around it, dividing the screen for four simultaneous users. The time-sharing demonstration was a success, and BBN decided to start a time-sharing service in the Boston area by placing terminals throughout the city. Soon, however, General Electric mounted a similar effort and quickly stole the bulk of BBN's time-sharing business.

The presence of an accessible computer inspired a change in the company. Everyone began thinking up things that could be done with it. One BBN scientist, Jordan Baruch, decided hospitals could use computers to keep more accurate information on patients, so he set out to computerize the record handling at Massachusetts General Hospital. Lick and others began exploring ways in which computers could transform libraries. But computers in the early 1960s were still too underpowered to do much.

By this time, BBN had begun to concentrate seriously on computer technology. The richly academic atmosphere at BBN earned the consulting firm a reputation as "the third university" in Cambridge. "I had the policy that every person we hired had to be better than the previous people," said Beranek. Next to MIT and Harvard, BBN became one of the most attractive places to work in the Boston area. Some people even considered it better than the universities because there was no teaching obligation and no worry over earning tenure. It was a rarefied environment—the cognac of the research business.

The firm's architectural-acoustics division went through a crisis in the early 1960s, when Beranek was hired to design the acoustics for the new Philharmonic Hall (later renamed Avery Fisher Hall) at New York's Lincoln Center. Both Beranek and the chief architect were criticized for overlooking certain acoustical principles important in designing concert halls. After many attempts at minor adjustment, it became clear that the situation was hopeless. The problem had to be solved by brute force: The walls and balconies were torn out, along with the ceiling—ten thousand tons of building material in all—and carted to dumps. The repair took several years and millions of dollars to carry out, under the supervision of a new consultant. In its exhaustive coverage of the problems, the *New York Times* focused its attention on Leo Beranek.

If BBN hadn't already diversified into computer research, the Lincoln Center debacle could have spelled its end. By the mid-1960s, however, the company's offices had expanded into a row of low, fairly nondescript buildings, mostly old warehouses that stood along a quiet side street near Fresh Pond on Cambridge's western edge. The offices had a casual architectural uniformity best described as low-rent modernism—Mondrian without the colors. These were stripped-down, spare, boxlike buildings whose flat roofs, few windows, and thin walls exuded simplicity and economy in design. Four of the buildings had been built for other purposes, mainly as warehouse space, before BBN bought and converted them into offices, shops, and laboratories. Building Number 2 was designed by Bolt himself and had a couple of unusual features: Its foundation "floated" in the Cambridge mud, effectively isolating the entire structure from external vibrations; and it was designed for the kind of people BBN was hiring—academicians—whom Bolt expected to fill their offices with books. Therefore he designed the new building to withstand an unusual amount of weight. There were corridors and enclosed footbridges between all of the BBN buildings, making it possible to follow a kind of meandering path through the complete row without going outside during the winter. For a while, BBN depended on borrowed steam piped in from an adjacent laundry to heat some of the quarters.

Among the computer researchers were Wally Feurzeig and Seymour Papert, who were working on educational applications. Papert was a consultant to BBN for about four years in the late 1960s. While there, he conceived of and made the first rough design of a programming language that would be accessible to school-age children. The idea was adopted as a research theme by BBN's education group, which Feurzeig ran, and the language came to be called LOGO.

While the acousticians usually came to work in jackets and ties, the atmosphere on the computer side was decidedly more relaxed. "When we got into the computer business we had the strangest people working for us," said Beranek. He appreciated the brilliance of the people Lick hired but seldom felt comfortable around them. He recalled being invited to a New Years' Eve party at the home of a computer engineer around 1965. "It was like going to the Addams Family house," Beranek said. "They were all in bare feet. The women were wearing tight-fitting clothing. I showed up with a tie on and had to take it off."

Frank Heart was a notable exception. Conservative in his attire and prone to caution in general, Heart was at that time a computer systems engineer at MIT's Lincoln Lab. In 1966 BBN embarked on a campaign to hire him for its hospital computer project. Heart was an engineer with a reputation for making things happen. Tell him you wanted something built and, by god, you would have it. But Heart was also hardheaded and not easy to pry away from Lincoln.

A self-described "overprotected Jewish kid from Yonkers," Heart was bookish and, in high school, a bit of a nerd. Frank wanted desperately to attend MIT, which posed a problem for his parents, who were of modest means. (Through the Depression, Heart's father managed to keep his job as an engineer for Otis Elevator.) The thought of sending her only son to a school so far away was particularly difficult for Frank's mother, who did most of the overprotecting. MIT admitted him in 1947, but with a scholarship so small as to guarantee continued financial struggles for his parents.

Following the example set by his father, who built elevator control systems, Frank had decided to become an electrical engineer before entering MIT. To ease the financial strain on his family, he enrolled in a five-year master's degree program, in which work and school were combined in alternate semesters. He worked one summer at a General Electric factory testing large power transformers. "That was something you want to do just once," Heart recalled. In his second year, he chose to specialize in power engineering—the design of large-scale electrical systems, such as power plants, building transformers, generators, and motors.

Then he discovered computers. In 1951, Heart's senior year, MIT offered its first course ever in computer programming, taught by a visiting professor named Gordon Welchman. Heart signed up. "It was an unbelievable revelation to me that a thing like a computer could exist," Heart said. He dropped out of the work-study program, a decision that shocked many people because it was such a difficult program to get into. "I got all sorts of nasty letters from MIT and G.E." But he had caught the computer bug and never looked back.

Thanks to Welchman's introduction, Heart became so interested in computers that he earned his bachelor's degree one term early and finished his master's degree while working as a research assistant on the Whirlwind Project. Whirlwind controlled a radar defense system for tracking aircraft. A radar (RAdio Detection And Ranging) system measures electromagnetic pulses reflected from an object to provide information concerning its direction and distance. Jamming devices can destroy data from a single radar, but an array of radars can compensate if they are working in concert with a computer. Whirlwind gave Heart his first taste of programming in a real-time environment. When Whirlwind was transferred to Lincoln Lab, Heart was transferred with it. "It was the most painless kind of job change one could imagine," Heart said.

Many programs in the 1950s were written in "machine language," the actual instructions in the "natural language" of the computer. Commands had to be specified in exhaustive detail; there was a one-to-one correspondence between each line of the program and each instruction to the machine. Working in machine language could be tedious, and mistakes were difficult to find and correct. But it gave programmers a strong sense of identification with the machine. Computer programming was still so new that few people understood its intricacies. Many who worked in the more traditional sciences ignored (or dismissed) those who were exploring computers as a science.

Lincoln Laboratory was proving to be a perfect incubator for the kind of genius that ARPA would need to push computing into the interactive, and interconnected, age. It had already turned into a breeding ground for some of the most important early work in computing and networking. Many of its alumni—among them, Licklider, Roberts, Heart, and others still to come—would play crucial roles in the design and development of the ARPA network. In the early days, computer programmers at Lincoln were poorly regarded. Only full-fledged physicists and mathematicians were allowed on the research staff, and many programmers left Lincoln as a result. But Heart broke through the prejudice. He started out as a graduate student programmer, became a staff member, and before long he was running a group.

Heart also disregarded the rules. He had little tolerance for professional delineations and didn't take titles too seriously. When a young programmer named Dave Walden came to work at Lincoln, he was hired on with the title of technical assistant. The fact that this was not a staff-level post was clearly indicated on his security badge. Titles were important at Lincoln, and among other things, the badge kept him out of staff-member seminars. Ignoring all that, and flouting the protocol that assigned nonstaff to the least-desirable work space, Heart set Walden up in an office with one of

Walden's mentors, a young MIT graduate named Will Crowther. Crowther was a physicist turned computer scientist.

In the late 1950s and early 1960s, Heart, Crowther, and others close to them worked on one groundbreaking project after another. In time, Heart and his team at Lincoln became experts at connecting a variety of measuring devices to computers via phone lines for information gathering. This in turn made them experts in building real-time computing systems.

When a group of Heart's colleagues left to start MITRE Corporation in 1958, Heart remained firmly moored to Lincoln, partly because he had always disliked change and partly because he loved what he was doing. He couldn't imagine ever having a more interesting job or a more talented group with which to work.

In the summer of 1965, Heart met Danny Bobrow, who had been working on artificial intelligence at BBN. Bobrow suggested to Heart that he leave Lincoln for a job at BBN, overseeing a project to introduce computer technology into hospitals. When Heart declined, Dick Bolt stepped in.

One of the reasons the principals at BBN were anxious to woo Heart was that he had fruitful experience in putting together systems that worked efficiently in the field. The company needed someone like that. For all its innovation, BBN hadn't been very successful at turning its ideas into functioning, usable systems. "The culture at BBN at the time was to do interesting things and move on to the next interesting thing," said one former employee. There was more incentive to come up with interesting ideas and explore them than to try to capitalize on them once they had been developed.

Bolt invited Heart to his house. They had more meetings at BBN. They met at the local Howard Johnson's. Heart remained reluctant, but there were aspects of the BBN job that appealed to him. Like Licklider, Heart had always held what he described as a "do-gooder's" view: Heart believed computers and technology could help society. Wedded as it was to the military, Lincoln Lab had never gone very far afield of the Air Force's needs. In fact, the lab's narrow focus had precipitated the departure of people like Ken Olsen and Wes Clark, who left to build computers. Heart was also interested in the application of computers to the life sciences, and Bolt let him know he would have the opportunity to pursue that interest at BBN. Moreover, a friend of Heart's from Yonkers, Jerry Elkind, was at BBN, and Heart respected Elkind quite a bit. "It also occurred to me," Heart admitted, "that there was a chance I could make some money at a private corporation."

In the end, Bolt convinced him to take the job, but by the time Heart got to BBN, the company's computer research was being carried out by two separate divisions: information sciences and computer systems. As a general rule, those with Ph.D.'s worked in the information sciences, or research, division, while those without Ph.D.'s worked in the computer systems division. One member of the information sciences division described the computer systems division as consisting of a bunch of guys with soldering irons. In other words, they just got things built, while those in the research division considered themselves more concerned with inventing the future. There was not much cross-pollination between the two groups. They worked in separate buildings, divided by a narrow, glass-enclosed footbridge. It wasn't animosity, exactly, that separated them, nor was it rivalry. Each was aware of the other's limitations, resulting in a conspicuous lack of interest in what happened in the other camp. Frank Heart was a systems guy through and through.

❑ Bidding

When ARPA's request for proposals to build the IMP arrived at BBN in August 1968, the company had thirty days to respond. Jerry Elkind, who now was Heart's boss, was in charge of both computer divisions. He thought BBN should bid, and he thought Heart was the best person at the company to manage it. Since the demise of the hospital computer project shortly after he had arrived, Heart had been searching for a long-term project in which to immerse himself. Moreover, Heart probably had the most experience in building the kind of computer system that ARPA was seeking.

Nonetheless, when Elkind suggested he take it on, Heart was typically cautious.

Heart could be difficult to interpret at first. Alex McKenzie, who worked for Heart on and off for twenty-seven years, recalled the first time he encountered his new boss—from the other end of a hallway. Heart was speaking in a loud, high-pitched voice to someone else and seemed agitated. "He was really yelling, and I thought it must be trouble," McKenzie recalled. "Then later I found out it was simply enthusiasm." A few years later, while on an airplane with Heart, McKenzie finally told him about his initial impression. Heart raised his eyebrows. "YELLING?!" Heart yelled, his voice reaching for its trademark falsetto, loud enough to attract the attention of everyone around them. "I don't yell!" Not, that is, when angry. "When he's angry he gets very quiet," McKenzie said.

Meetings with Heart occasionally involved a lot of shouting. "And then the next day it turns out he's heard what you said through all the yelling and shouting," recalled another longtime employee. "If you were willing to put up with the yelling and shouting, he made things come out right, unlike most people who yell and shout." Heart had prodigious energy, which made it difficult for him to sit still for more than a few minutes at a time. He was most relaxed when he was at home, working in his basement woodworking shop, where he whistled long complex pieces of music flawlessly, seldom aware that he was doing so. When things were tense or uncertain, he bit his fingernails or drummed his fingers on tabletops.

Heart was intensely loyal to the people who worked for him and they in turn were loyal to him. He was also nurturing, not just toward his three children (he happily took on many child-care chores not expected of husbands in those days) but also toward his employees. At the same time, he took a lot of things personally, particularly when people left his group to go work somewhere else, even if it was only across the hall to another division.

One of Heart's greatest strengths was making certain that jobs he signed up for really got done, and in taking on the ARPA job he was concerned about the risk of committing the company to something

it might not be able to accomplish. The project was packed with uncertainties and unexplored technology. Heart found it difficult to
gauge exactly what was involved. There wasn't time to do the kind
of detailed planning he'd like to do on a systems software project,
such as estimating the number of lines of code that would be
needed.

Risk assessment is essential in any engineering enterprise. Because no significant technological project can be entirely risk-free,
the probabilities for success and failure of particular designs are factored and weighed. The potential for trouble falls into three cate-
gories: the foreseen, the unforeseen but foreseeable, and the
unforeseeable. In the last case engineers are forced to make decisions with their fingers crossed. The situation facing Heart fell
largely into this last category, since so much of the system had no
precedent on which to base risk estimates.

The software uncertainties were serious enough, but a plethora
of other unknowns existed. For example, how much traffic could
such a network handle without encountering logjams? What was
the chance that the failure of one node would propagate through
the network? In November 1965, for example, one overloaded relay
caused a ripple effect that brought down the electric power grid
serving the entire northeastern United States. Above all, what was
the probability that the network would even work? Signing on for a
project like the ARPA network required a certain amount of sheer
faith, and that disturbed Heart.

Elkind was motivated by his sense that ARPA was pushing the
state of the art of computing into a new era, and from a business
point of view, it made a lot of sense to launch BBN toward that future. Elkind recognized that Heart's concerns were rational. "But it
struck me that this was a contract we had to do and could do as well
as anybody," Elkind said. "We knew how to work with ARPA and
had computer skills as good as anyone around."

Elkind suggested to Heart that a small group from BBN get together to decide what to do with ARPA's request for proposals. They
agreed to meet informally and chose Danny Bobrow's house in Bel-
mont as the location. The first meeting went well into the night. By

the time it was over, Heart was converted and BBN's participation had been as much as guaranteed.

That was the easy part. They then had just one month to write a detailed proposal. One of the first people to get involved with the proposal was Bob Kahn, a professor of electrical engineering on leave from MIT and working in BBN's information sciences division. At MIT, Kahn had been an applied mathematician working on communications and information theory. Most of his colleagues possessed a combination of theoretical and applied engineering skills. One day Kahn had been talking with a senior colleague at MIT about the different technical problems in which he was interested, and he asked, "How can you tell when one problem is more interesting than another?" "It's just experience," Kahn's colleague responded. "How does one get that?" Kahn inquired. "Find someone who has a lot of experience and go work with him." One obvious place for Kahn to acquire that experience was BBN. So he went.

By coincidence, in 1967, at the time that Larry Roberts was in Washington formulating the network project and its requirements, Kahn was at BBN having his own thoughts about networking. Still more coincidentally, at Jerry Elkind's urging he had been sending unsolicited technical memos to Bob Taylor and Roberts. When Roberts told Kahn that ARPA was planning to fund a nationwide network, it was a pleasant revelation to Kahn. Then Elkind told him that a group in the BBN computer systems division was interested in putting together a proposal for the ARPA network and suggested that Kahn get involved in the process.

Not long afterward, Frank Heart wandered over to Kahn's office. "I understand from Jerry that you've been thinking about the networking area. Can we chat about it?"

"Yes, sure," Kahn responded. "Who are you?"

In 1968 BBN had more than six hundred employees. Frank Heart's group occupied a row of offices along a stretch of linoleum tiled corridor in Building Number 3. At one end of the hall was a conference room with plenty of chalkboards and seating for large gatherings. The offices themselves were small and unassuming, with desks fashioned from doors to which legs had been attached by BBN's construction shop. Stiff-backed wooden chairs and canvas-backed director's chairs were the preferred styles. Fluorescent lighting, a few personal effects, lots of shelves and little else completed the picture.

Heart liked working with small, tightly knit groups composed of very bright people. He believed that individual productivity and talent varied not by factors of two or three, but by factors of ten or a hundred. Because Heart had a knack for spotting engineers who could make things happen, the groups he had supervised at Lincoln tended to be unusually productive.

One of the first people Heart called upon to help with the IMP proposal was Dave Walden, who had followed Heart from Lincoln to BBN. Though young, with only four or five years of programming experience, Walden had a highly cultivated expertise in real-time systems—ideal for the ARPA network job. Next Heart drafted Bernie Cosell, a young programmer who had been working in BBN's computer systems division. Cosell was a debugger par excellence, someone who could go poking around in a computer program he had never seen before and in two days fix a problem that had gone unsolved for weeks. Heart also enlisted Hawley Rising, a soft-spoken electrical engineer who was an old friend from Heart's student days at MIT.

Heart's hardware ace was Severo Ornstein, a thirty-eight-year-old Lincoln alumnus who had worked for Heart on and off for years. Ornstein was an intense man of many and diverse interests. The son of a virtuoso pianist and prominent composer, Ornstein had attended Harvard and had flirted briefly with a major in music before his parents argued him out of it. He finally settled on geology. After leaving Harvard, Ornstein had become interested in computers and had gone to work at Lincoln. When his colleague Wes Clark left for Washington University in St. Louis to build a computer of his own design, Ornstein went with him. After three years in St. Louis, Ornstein itched to return to Cambridge, so he called Heart, who offered him a position at BBN.

When the request for proposals arrived from ARPA, Heart handed a copy to Ornstein and said, "Why don't you take this home and have a look at it, see what you think?" Ornstein returned to Heart's office the next day and said, "Well, sure, I suppose we could build that if you wanted to. But I can't see what one would want such a thing for." Nonetheless, Ornstein thought the IMP-building project looked like fun, which was always a primary consideration for him.

Heart had a predilection for judging people not by their looks or manners or political views, but almost purely by how smart he believed them to be. Or, as he liked to put it, by how many neurons per cubic centimeter their brains contained. If he decided the number was unusually high, Heart was likely to tolerate a lot more idiosyncrasy in one than in another whose gray matter he thought was less densely packed. When talking, Heart often used computer jargon in nontechnical circumstances. "It's a no-op," he might say to his wife Jane if they decided to leave a Sunday afternoon free. (No-op, or no operation, refers to a line of code that accomplishes nothing.) Or he might say, "It's binary," to one of their small children, meaning it is a black-and-white situation.

Heart's knack for putting together effective engineering teams had made him a highly regarded and valuable project manager. He looked for people who would be committed to a common mission rather than a personal agenda. He preferred to keep teams small so that everyone was always talking to everyone else. Heart chose the kind of people who took personal responsibility for what they did. And while Heart tolerated idiosyncrasy, he shied away from ego-centric "head cases," no matter how smart they were.

In assembling BBN's team for the ARPA proposal, Heart made certain he pulled in engineers with all the requisite skills for such an ambitious undertaking. Kahn, for instance, was the consummate theoretician. He, more than anyone at BBN, understood the problems associated with sending information over telephone lines, and he had clear ideas about the best error-control mechanisms. Ornstein was a perfectionist, and it showed in the hardware he built, while Walden brought with him both his knowledge of real-time systems and a resolute willingness to work long hours. Cosell had the ability to burrow into complex software programs and find bugs faster than anyone else at BBN. Because of this, Cosell was one of the company's human insurance policies: Projects would be worked on by teams, but every BBN manager knew that if his project got into trouble, he could throw Cosell into the job and superhuman things would happen in a hurry. Although there remained a great deal of detailed design work, among them the team members understood the most important technical issues.

As the team got started, Heart already knew what was in store: four weeks of working around the clock. Heart was expected home for dinner every evening at six-thirty, and he always made it. But after dinner he disappeared into his study and didn't emerge until long after his family had gone to bed.

An important initial decision was which hardware to use. Reliability was, by far, Heart's chief concern. His fifteen years at Lincoln Lab building antennae and radar systems for the military had taught him to worry about reliability above all else. Intuitively, Heart believed that the graduate students who would be knocking around the IMPs at the university sites wouldn't be able to keep their hands off the equipment. He had been a student, and he had probably even done the very kinds of things he feared—hell, he *knew*—they would try to do. They'd go poking around in the box to see how it worked.

Heart's choices were limited. The minicomputer industry was still relatively young. Its leaders were Digital Equipment and Honeywell. From the start, the reliability issue led Heart to favor the new Honeywell DDP-516, the machine housed in the heavy-duty steel cabinet. The Navy had a reputation for setting rigorous engineering standards. And some of BBN's people knew some of Honeywell's people, who made the machine at a plant not far from BBN's Cambridge location. The 516 also helped to settle Heart's fear that inquisitive graduate students might bring down the network with their tinkering. He could rest much easier knowing the IMPs would be housed in a box built to withstand a war.

The functionality of the Honeywell computer's sophisticated input/output (I/O) capability—the speed and efficiency with which it could communicate with external devices such as modems—also helped propel it to the top of the list. As the handling of I/O traffic was the main function of the IMP, a machine with a good I/O structure was absolutely essential.

Not long into writing the proposal, Dave Walden began feeling that he might be out of his depth. As the first programmer Heart brought to the project, Walden did a lot of the early thinking about general coding issues, and he did some of the original charts sketching out in block form the logical flow and timing of the program. Walden had outlined enough of the program to realize they were undertaking something difficult. He decided that the ARPA proposal would provide a good excuse to recruit Will Crowther, the ingenious programmer for whom Walden had worked at Lincoln, to lead the software effort. Walden wasn't in the least reluctant to bring in someone above him. He was confident enough in his own talents to shrug off pecking-order concerns that might worry a lot of other people. The two had worked closely at Lincoln, and Walden was happier to be on a team with Crowther than on one without him. And besides, Crowther was exceptional.

Having Crowther on the team wouldn't just boost the chances of making the software work. Having Crowther at BBN would make doing the work more pleasant. Crowther was quiet, easy to work with, and when it came to writing code, he was downright inspiring. He was also Ornstein's good friend and rock-climbing companion. Crowther seemed to concentrate best while hanging from door frames by his fingertips, doing chin-ups. And he was known for his mathematical doodling. While others passed the time at lengthy meetings by drawing squiggles and curlicues, Crowther filled his page with a thicket of differential equations.

Walden, Heart, and Ornstein were pretty sure that Crowther hadn't been entirely happy at Lincoln since Heart had left. Crowther liked working for Heart, and while reporting to Heart at Lincoln, he had grown accustomed to seeing things built. After Heart left, a lot of the people who had worked for him had gone back to less productive tinkering. Ornstein called Crowther and said, "Willy, you ought to come to BBN," to which Crowther readily agreed.

In Crowther, BBN gained an invaluable addition. He specialized in producing complex, tightly written pieces of code, which were exactly what was required in the IMP. In fact, writing small intricate bits of code was one of Crowther's greatest pleasures in life. His code was among the leanest anyone who worked with him had ever seen. Since the IMPs were to be hooked up to phone lines, with data constantly flowing in and out, the idea was to have a data packet arrive at an IMP, be processed, and immediately either be sent forward or placed in a queue to await its turn—all in less time than it took to snap your fingers. Every instruction took one or two millionths of a second (microseconds) to execute. Since every unnecessary instruction ate up one or two extra microseconds, each little task, or piece of software code, had to be written with intense frugality, using the fewest instructions possible.

Central to the design of the network was the idea that the subnet of IMPs should operate invisibly. So, for instance, if someone seated at a host computer at UCLA wanted to log on to a computer at the University of Utah, the connection should appear to be direct. The user should not have to be bothered with the fact that a subnet even existed. The effect was similar to direct dialing in the telephone system, which freed callers from the annoyance of having to wait for an operator to make their connections. Like the maze of automated switching equipment at a phone company, the IMPs were to be "transparent" to the user. As Roberts described it in the call for proposals, "Each transmitting host looks into the network through its adjacent IMP and sees itself connected to the receiving host."

To achieve that transparency, the network was going to have to be fast, free of congestion, and extremely reliable. These were relatively straightforward requirements that Roberts had written into the request for proposals, but no one expected that actually accomplishing them would be easy.

However, one of the first things BBN's software team discovered was that they could make the code process ten times the number of packets per second that Roberts was requiring. Before doing anything else, Crowther and Walden wrote the code for the inner loop— the heart of the program—and counted the number of instructions.

Roberts would have been content with an inner loop of 1,500 instructions; Crowther and Walden used 150. From that, the two programmers calculated just how quickly the IMP could process each packet. With that information, they were able to predict how many packets could be moved per second. "We actually sat down and wrote the hundred and fifty lines of code, counted them, and then we knew," Crowther said. They had figured out the kernel.

"We take the position that it will be difficult to make the system work," BBN wrote hedgingly in its proposal. In this cautious way the BBN team let Roberts know that it didn't take for granted a task that was unprecedented in its complexity, revolutionary in concept, and filled with technical details of uncertain feasibility. Yet the proposal then went on to demonstrate that BBN seemed to have the problem solved.

By the time the proposal was finished, it filled two hundred pages and cost BBN more than $100,000, the most the company had ever spent on such a risky project. The BBN team had covered so much of the design of the IMPs that a large fraction of the entire system was already clearly defined. BBN's finished proposal was more blueprint than outline. Its engineers had designed test programs and regular performance checks for IMPs and the network. They described how the network would handle congestion in the buffers (storage areas in the machines that served as waiting areas and staging areas for the flow of packets into and out of the network), and how it would recover from line and computer failures. They provided ARPA with flowcharts outlining how the IMP software would handle such difficult problems as timing and the continual updating of routing tables. They came up with detailed computations, equations, and tables that covered, among other things, transmission delays and the queueing of packets. It was all there for Roberts to see.

The BBN team submitted its proposal on September 6, 1968, relatively certain that no one else had prepared a bid as detailed as theirs. Years later, when people who worked on the BBN proposal were asked how long it took to put the document together, some of them said honestly they thought it had taken six months.

Heart's team had obviously done an impressive amount of extra spade work, resolving some problems Larry Roberts hadn't expected to see covered. BBN held another advantage: its relatively small size. Roberts didn't want to deal with a lot of bureaucracy, and the other proposals were fraught with it. The team Raytheon was putting forth, for example, spanned five layers of management. Roberts could see that just finding the right person with whom to talk over the slightest problem might require a dozen phone calls. The BBN team, on the other hand, had a very simple hierarchy. Everybody reported to Heart, who handed out the tasks and saw that they got done. Heart had a boss, but he appeared to be giving Heart ample latitude to do as he pleased with this project.

The first sign that BBN's bid was being taken seriously came when Roberts called a meeting to review parts of the proposal. Heart, Crowther, Kahn, and Ornstein, their spirits high, took the train to Washington. (Heart tried, unsuccessfully, to convince Crowther to wear something on his feet besides sneakers.) During the meeting, they defended and expanded on their proposal. Roberts tested, prodded, and poked the engineers to see if they had really thought deeply and thoroughly about the system. And his questions continued for some weeks afterward. "At some level I think that the continued questioning by Larry kept us thinking about the problems and continuing to fill out design details subliminally," recalled Ornstein. "But I think the more important thing was that we took it to heart more than the other contenders. We made the design our problem and did our best to find solutions we believed in without bowing too much to the specifications others had put down."

But for the most part, all they could do was wait. If Roberts had a favorite proposal, he wasn't letting anyone know it. It could take months before they heard anything definite. By midautumn they all returned to what they had been doing before the proposal marathon. Time slowed down again. Crowther went caving, which, next to rock climbing and writing code, was his passion. Heart got home at dinnertime and didn't go back to work. Kahn was about the only one who, by force of habit, routinely kept working late into the night. Everyone was anxious. "I personally swung from certainty that our proposal couldn't be beaten," said Ornstein, "to a belief that there was no way we could win, given the size of BBN compared to the other contenders."

Throughout the evaluation process, as the competition for the Interface Message Processor got whittled down, the BBN team heard rumors through the ARPA grapevine, though never from Roberts himself, who remained sphinxlike. Naturally, they did a lot of second-guessing. In their more pessimistic moments, the BBN engineers were inclined to believe that since Roberts knew many of them from Lincoln, it might be difficult or awkward or impossible for him to award the contract to BBN. Nonetheless, ARPA did just that.

When news reached Massachusetts Senator Edward Kennedy's office just before Christmas that a million-dollar ARPA contract had been awarded to some local boys, Kennedy sent a telegram thanking BBN for its ecumenical efforts and congratulating the company on its contract to build the "Interfaith Message Processor."

Head Down
in the Bits

New Year's Day, 1969, was the last time Frank Heart's group would be able to rest for quite a while. The following week, the contract to build the first Interface Message Processors officially began. For a little more than $1 million, BBN would build four IMPs; the first was due at UCLA by Labor Day, followed by one every month through December. In twelve months the network was supposed to be up and running, with four sites on-line. The BBN team had already done a great deal of work in generating the proposal. Now looking ahead, they saw at least eight more months of late nights and intensive systems engineering work. There were still many unknown challenges, a point emphatically underscored by BBN in its proposal. Furthermore, the members of Heart's team all had different ideas about how difficult building the IMPs would be.

Heart encountered any number of skeptics—phone company people and academicians mostly—who didn't believe a packet-switching network would work. Building the hardware wasn't really the hard part, they argued; rather, making it all work together—the systems part—was the trick. Even if you could integrate all the hardware and software and demonstrate the feasibility of a computer network, some pointed out, there still wasn't any profit in it for a company like AT&T or IBM, not as a business proposition. Who but a few government bureaucrats or computer scientists would ever use a computer network? It wasn't as if computing had a mass market like the television networks or the phone company.

During the weeks before winning the bid, BBN's biggest doubt had been whether ARPA would entrust the job to such a small company. The members of BBN's team knew there was a lot riding on them now. If the IMPs didn't work, networking and packet-switching would fall into the oblivion of failed experiments. Some people—other bidders mostly—expressed astonishment that little BBN had won the contract. "This kind of large systems job just didn't seem to be up BBN's alley," said one competitor.

By and large, Heart ignored the detractors, although he too worried occasionally about the technical challenges that lay ahead. To be effective, a data network would have to send packets reliably, despite errors unavoidably introduced during transmission over ordinary phone lines. Human ears tolerate telephone line noise, which is often barely audible, but computers receiving data are nit-pickers about noise, and the smallest hiss or pop can destroy small bits of data or instruction. The IMPs would have to be able to compensate.

Then there were circuit outages to anticipate, especially if the four-node experiment expanded coast to coast as ARPA envisioned. A spot of bad weather somewhere, a thunderstorm in the Midwest or a New England blizzard, would knock out service on a long-distance phone line carrying network data traffic. Brief interruptions in service couldn't be prevented and would have to be dealt with by the IMPs. On top of that, in the best of conditions, there was a vastly complicated matrix of routing problems to be resolved. Heart's team had to prevent messages from circulating endlessly in the network, bouncing from node to node without ever reaching their final destination. Finally, the team had to consider the possibility of jam-ups in the memory buffers. Messages could be a maximum of 8,000 bits; IMPs were to break such messages into a sequence of packets with a maximum size of 1,000 bits each. One packet would contain the equivalent of about two lines of text on this page.

The system had to deliver packets and messages within the time specifications Roberts had set—half a second for a message to go from any source host to any destination host via the IMP subnet. It would mean processing data at speeds on the order of one hundred messages per second, which was certainly possible although synchronizing everything would be difficult.

As if the technical challenges weren't enough, the ARPA network project schedule was on a fast track; the schedule set by Roberts was tied to the budget cycle and political realities facing him in Washington. Eight months weren't enough for anyone to build the perfect network. Everyone knew it. But BBN's job was more limited than that; it was to demonstrate that the network concept could work. Heart was seasoned enough to know that compromises were necessary to get anything this ambitious done on time. Still, the tension between Heart's perfectionism and his drive to meet deadlines was always with him, and sometimes was apparent to others as an open, unresolved contradiction.

BBN faced countless other issues that had pushed other bidders and potential bidders out of the running. Now all these problems belonged to Frank Heart.

❑ Getting Started

"It's one thing when you plug into a socket in the wall and electrons flow," said Bob Kahn. "It's another thing when you have to figure out, for every electron, which direction it takes." To Kahn's way of thinking, this summed up the difficulty of building a network that switched packets of bits, and did so dynamically. Kahn knew very little about hardware design. He was a scientist who mainly did conceptual work on system designs and architecture. Because he pondered the larger conceptual aspects of the problem perhaps a little more deeply than his colleagues, he worried more about the complexity of building the network. To Kahn the network was more of an abstraction, perfectible and whole, than it was to the other team members, involved as they were in the actual programming and wiring of its many parts.

The packet-switching concept opened a rich universe in which a theoretically oriented and trained engineer like Kahn could investigate a wide range of hypothetical scenarios. Kahn's analyses had already helped shape the ARPA network project. Kahn had contributed ideas freely to Larry Roberts, urging him to launch the ARPA networking experiment on a large scale using long-distance telephone lines. Other people had said a small-scale experiment would be fine to begin with, but Kahn had worried that nothing meaningful could be learned from a small experiment. Roberts agreed and decided on a transcontinental network of at least nineteen nodes.

You could certainly build a network experiment in a single laboratory—if you wanted to. By this time Donald Davies had finally been given the go-ahead and some funding to do just that at the National Physical Laboratory in London, using short lines, each hundreds of yards at most. Kahn was sure that a small-network experiment wouldn't "scale up," at least not in practical terms. He reasoned that short links in a laboratory wouldn't have the same real-world error rates and problems as the long lines used in the telephone system. The real goal was to link computer scientists, and eventually other computer users, cross-country. So a real network would have to cover thousands of miles, and would have to be designed to handle packets—and correct phone-line errors—at a much higher rate than any small network.

Roberts seemed to trust Kahn's judgment. Before the request for proposals hit the streets and BBN became a bidder, the two men spoke occasionally. Once Kahn had been enlisted to contribute to BBN's proposal effort, he worked into the early-morning hours, night after night, occasionally in Severo Ornstein's living room, helping to design the system for BBN's bid. The work paid off, BBN won the contract, and Kahn had already decided to return to his own research work after Christmas.

But as the new year rolled around, Kahn began to have second thoughts. The technical issues were complicated. Perhaps he should stick around for the implementation. It couldn't hurt. Besides, Kahn was eager to learn more about the hardware side of things from Ornstein. And moving over to Heart's shop was the only way for Kahn to continue his own network research, or so the folks who ran BBN led him to believe.

Jerry Elkind, the man to whom both Heart and Kahn reported, urged Kahn to join the IMP group because Heart now had the one contract at BBN specifically devoted to networking. Although he continued to report to Elkind, Kahn moved into Heart's systems group. Soon he found himself picking up his office and crossing over the BBN footbridge from Bolt's scholarly haven into the re-designed warehouse where the group of young men who had started calling themselves the "IMP Guys" were already hard at it. (And guys they were. In keeping with the norms of the time, with the exception of Heart's secretary, the people who designed and built the ARPA network were all men. Few women held positions in computer science. Heart's wife, Jane, had quit her programming job at Lincoln to raise their three children.)

The team Heart had assembled knew how to make things that worked, if not perfectly, then well enough. They were engineers and pragmatists. All of their lives they had built things, connected wires, and made concepts real. Their ethos was utilitarian. At its core, all engineering comes down to making tradeoffs between the perfect and the workable.

Functionality mattered now, not elegance or beauty. Unlike, say, fine Swiss watchmakers, whose engineering and art are inseparable in a $40,000 watch, Heart's team naturally separated artistry from the craft of building a reliable computer. Looking down into the bits, lesser engineers with larger egos might attempt to show off, to infuse the mechanism with art, to create some wonder of engineer-ing, a gold inlaid, filigreed marvel of complexity. The inner strength of Heart's team was its restraint, its maturity. This was no place for signature craftsmanship. "There was an infinity of ways we could go wrong, and a substantial number of ways to go right," said Walden, the first programmer Heart had signed on. "Good engineers find one of the ways of going right."

The real-time radar systems, the systems for seismic detection of A-bomb tests and earthquakes, and the other systems that Heart, Ornstein, Crowther, and Walden had all worked on at Lincoln Lab had been more complicated than the IMP. Years later, some people would say that the IMP was nothing but a big I/O device and actually very simple. To the user, the IMP was to be as simple as an electrical outlet or a wall switch that does its job without calling attention to itself. Then again, building the IMP to perform as well and as unobtrusively as a household socket or switch was precisely the challenge.

The software team had been working together closely since the proposal. Each member had a specific role. Crowther worked on IMP-to-IMP communications, Walden concentrated on the IMP-to-host issues, while Cosell worked on development and debugging tools.

Willy Crowther, thirty-two years old, quiet but opinionated, was the soul of the team. In the first few weeks of 1969, Crowther did a lot of hanging from office-door frames. Everyone around him just accepted the behavior as Willy's way of warming up. It helped strengthen his hands for rock climbing and seemed to help his thinking even more. Crowther's style, recognized by the rest of the team, was to appear as if he were doing nothing for days, or doing just a lot of door-frame chin-ups, before finally releasing in a torrent whatever had been forming in his mind.

If Crowther and his colleagues were confident about their programming and software design, Ornstein was equally confident about directing the hardware effort. He was responsible for designing high-speed I/O devices that BBN planned to add to the Honeywell 516. The considerable effort that he'd already invested in drafting the proposal was time well spent. After making only a few further refinements and finishing touches, the team would be ready to move into the hardware construction and programming phases of the project. Ornstein's first task was to bring the hardware design to a point where he could go to Honeywell with a set of detailed modifications to the 516. After that, Honeywell would start to build the specialized I/O devices the IMP needed to communicate with the hosts and other IMPs.

The IMP team had to decide which network operations would be handled by the IMP software and which would be hardwired, or built into, the IMP hardware. Simple tasks that had to happen quickly were best handled by hardware. But once designed and built, a piece of equipment was harder to modify than any piece of software. So as a rule, the IMP Guys favored software solutions. If something could be done fast enough in software they did it there, designing the system to give themselves more leeway for revisions later on.

By February, BBN had firmed up its contract with Honeywell for the purchase of the DDP-516s. Within days, Honeywell delivered and installed the first 516 computer in a room at the front of BBN's Moulton Street complex. This machine wasn't the modified, military-grade version on order but a plain vanilla, off-the-shelf 516. It was a tester, the "development" machine, with which the programmers would experiment as they set to work. Programmers are usually not willing (or able) to go far in writing code for a specific computer until the actual hardware it will run on is at hand. Ornstein had just begun the process of working out all the final details of the specialized I/O interfaces; it might be weeks before Honeywell could make those interfaces available to conduct experiments.

Like virtually all computers of its era, the Honeywell machine had no disk—no hard drive, no floppy (floppies hadn't been invented yet). It had a core memory—a dense matrix of hair-thin copper wires and magnetized ferrite rings, or cores, each about the size of a mustard seed. The total size of the memory ordered (12k) was miniscule by today's standards. The amount of memory in a desktop computer circa mid-1990s, if it consisted of ferrite cores, would take up an area roughly the size of a football field.

One interesting advantage of core memory is its nonvolatile nature. If you turned the machine off in the middle of working on something, it wouldn't lose its place; it would pick right back up again where it had left off. Heart's team had also designed an automatic restart feature: If the power failed, the machine was supposed to come to a clean stop and then restart automatically when power returned. With the core memory, the machine would restart at the beginning of the program as soon as power was restored. The only time a program had to be reloaded was when a new release was issued or when some hardware or software glitch caused the memory to be over-written. In these cases, the IMP program would be reloaded from a paper tape reader, a kludgy electro-mechanical device which shone light from an incandescent bulb through a paper tape that was pulled across a line of photocells. The IMP had other self-sufficiency measures, one of which was called a "watchdog" timer. "If the program went wild," Heart explained, a small timer in the machine would run down to zero (but a healthy program would continually reset it). If the timer reached zero and went off, the IMP was assumed to have a trashed program. It would then throw a relay to turn on the paper tape reader, give it a while to warm up, and then reload the program. BBN would ship each machine with a copy of a tape that had three copies of the entire IMP operating program in sequence, giving each IMP the chance to do three auto-reloads before someone had to go and rewind the tape. Later, an even more ingenious scheme would be invented by BBN to reload crashed IMPs from the nearest neighbor IMPs, and start fresh. These were all unusual features at the time.

The IMP Guys set to work on writing the code, and by the time they finished, it would turn out to be about six thousand words. "A tiny program," said Heart. They did all their programming in Honeywell 516 "assembly" language.

Computers are instruction-following mechanisms. Assembly-language programming requires thinking through a vast number of minute steps, then writing the instructions to carry them out. For instance, let's say you want to find the elevator. An equivalent set of instructions in a high-level language might go something like this: "Go out the door, turn right, go past the water fountain, and it's on your left."

The equivalent in assembly language would begin more like this: "Find your left foot; find your right foot. Place your left foot in front of your right foot. Now place your right foot in front of your left foot. Repeat this ten times. Stop. Turn ninety degrees to the right." Et cetera.

To program in assembly language was to dwell maniacally on the mechanism. It was easy for programmers to lose sight of the larger goal and difficult to write short, economical programs. Unskilled programmers often ended up writing assembly-language programs that wandered aimlessly, like some hapless Arctic expedition in a blizzard.

Crowther managed to keep the detailed steps of assembly-language programming straight in his head without getting lost. But he was forever drawing big flowcharts so he could picture everything at once. One colleague likened the process to designing a whole city while keeping track of the wiring to each lamp and the plumbing to every toilet. Sometimes, though, Crowther eschewed the flow diagrams and did them in his head. Where others struggled to apply the rudimentary programming tools of the time, Crowther was out there operating on a higher plane.

Writing the IMP software began in the offices of the programming team members, where each would type code on a Model 33 Teletype into a PDP-1 "editor." After the code was created on the PDP-1, it was transferred on paper tape to the Honeywell computer, where it was converted into the Honeywell's machine language, a chore handled by a program known as an assembler, which converted the code into the 1s and 0s the 516 could understand. The assembled code was then punched onto paper tape. For a while the programmers tried using the assembler that came with the Honeywell 516, but it was so inefficient they soon abandoned it: Walden and Cosell spent fourteen hours one weekend on an assembly of the IMP system code, using almost an entire box, nearly half a mile, of tape.

Not long after that, Cosell wrote some code to modify the much better assembler on BBN's time-shared PDP-1 computer down the hall. This made it possible for the PDP-1 to produce machine-language tapes for the Honeywell 516. From then on the team wrote pieces of IMP code, edited them, and assembled them under the PDP-1 time-sharing system. Once he was satisfied with an assembly process, the programmer would instruct the PDP-1 to punch out the assembled code on a paper tape, then carry the tape back to the lab where the 516 sat. He would load the tape into the 516, run it, and wait to see what happened. Usually there would be some bugs, and so the process would be repeated. Naturally, when one of the programmers saw something interesting or quirky happening as a new piece of code ran on the 516, the team members would gravitate to the event and stand around the Honeywell talking it over.

Most of the IMP Guys lived close to Cambridge, and it was easy for them to check in and out of the lab at any hour. Chef Joyce Chen's original Chinese restaurant was next door to BBN, and that helped when they worked late, as they often did. Cosell and Walden drank a lot of Coke to keep themselves going; Crowther never touched the stuff. He was a notoriously finicky eater (anything beyond the culinary level of a plain bologna sandwich was a risk), making him an impossible dinner guest or dining companion.

Early in the project, BBN was asked to brief a group of high-level ARPA and military personnel at the Pentagon. Crowther was among those planning to make the trip on behalf of the IMP Guys. Heart grew nervous just thinking about what Crowther might wear to the briefing. People were sure to notice his feet, thought Heart. The only time that anyone could remember Crowther wearing shoes you could shine was the day he got married. Heart went to Ornstein and asked him to tell Crowther not to wear sneakers to the Pentagon. Ornstein did.

"Willy, Frank says you shouldn't wear your sneakers to this meeting."

There was a long silence at the other end of the line. And then Crowther's calm voice. "Tell Frank they've seen my sneakers in JSAC [Joint Services Advisory Committee] meetings before and it'll be okay." It was.

Crowther and Ornstein were among Heart's most devoted

staffers. But they loved to kid the boss when the chance arose. "Frank took things very, very seriously," Ornstein observed.

Ornstein was an outspoken opponent of the Vietnam War. By 1969 a lot of people who had never questioned their own involvement in Pentagon-sponsored research projects began having second thoughts. Ornstein had taken to wearing a lapel pin that said RESIST. The pin also bore the Ω sign, for electrical resistance, a popular antiwar symbol for electrical engineers. One day, before a Pentagon briefing, Ornstein conceived a new use for his pin. In meetings at the Pentagon, it wasn't unusual for the men around the table to remove their jackets and roll up their shirt sleeves. Ornstein told Heart that he was going to pin his RESIST button onto a general's jacket when no one was looking. "I think Frank actually worried that I would," said Ornstein. (Ornstein didn't, but he did wear his pin to the meeting.)

As the IMP Guys laid out their plans in Washington, it became apparent that the ARPA network would be a hybrid of the original ideas of Baran and Davies. The ARPA network would use an adaptive routing scheme that the IMP Guys had developed on their own, but which was similar to the basic idea that Baran had sketched. However, unlike Baran's theoretical network, the ARPA network would not have nearly the same redundancy level or number of links to each node. Nodes in the BBN scheme were normally linked to two neighboring nodes, occasionally to one or three. As it was now conceived, just two failed links could divide, or partition, the network into isolated segments. Paul Baran had said that a network with a multitude of redundant links could be built of inexpensive parts; if a part malfunctioned, there would be others to back it up. The low level of redundancy in the ARPA network was closer to Davies' plan. Heart's approach was to make every part of the network as robust and reliable as possible.

During the proposal period, Crowther and Walden had already done some very crucial work, with amazing results. First, they had found a way to make adaptive routing work efficiently. They had also discovered that they could make the system run much faster than anyone imagined. Observers said their code wouldn't work; Crowther and Walden knew it would. In writing the "kernel" of their program ("the very small part that is the only thing that matters," as Crowther put it), they had discovered how few commands would actually be needed in a software program to pull packets into the IMP, figure out where to send them, and push them out on the next line.

Crowther and Walden quickly worked out the critical algorithms—the basic rules for solving the packet-processing and routing problems. That had lead them to the determination that it would take only one hundred fifty lines of code to process a packet through one of the IMPs. But without a real machine to test it on, running the code would have to wait. Nonetheless, they had a good feeling the IMP would work.

A key task that Heart worried about, but didn't have to handle, was the subcontract with AT&T. It was Larry Roberts's responsibility to arrange for the 50-kilobit lines (able to transmit about two pages of text per second) into each host site by the date the IMPs were ready. Roberts turned the job over to another Pentagon agency, now working with AT&T on the terms for the installation and leasing of the proper lines, modems, and other communications gear necessary to form links in the network. The physical connection from the IMPs to the local telephone office was to be made by normal telephone wire—two twisted pairs of copper wires wrapped in a cable containing about a thousand other twisted pairs—with special terminating equipment at each end to support the high data rates. The dedicated lines and other equipment were to be in place at the California sites by the time the first IMPs arrived in the fall. Heart knew the telephone company was going to have to scramble to meet its obligations, and he was glad that securing AT&T's cooperation wasn't his problem.

Roberts was a distant but persistent force, vital to the project. His style was to stay out of the way of principal investigators most of the time. Whenever he did inject himself into a project, he never wasted anyone's time. He always made his point and moved on. People in the growing computer community came to regard Roberts highly.

These were great days to be running the Information Processing Techniques Office at ARPA. With Taylor and Roberts there, the budget for computing research kept growing even as the rest of ARPA's funds were being slashed because of the escalating cost of the Vietnam War. IPTO's managers could spend money on priorities of their own choosing. And they could just as easily rescind funding if they didn't receive the kind of cooperation they wanted from contractors.

Giving ample authority to people like Roberts was typical of ARPA's management style, which stretched back to its earliest days. It was rooted in a deep trust of frontline scientists and engineers. On his deathbed in 1969, Dwight Eisenhower asked a friend about "my scientists" and said they were "one of the few groups that I encountered in Washington who seemed to be there to help the country and not help themselves." Indeed, many of the best scientists in the country, Roberts among them, came to view working for the agency as an important responsibility, a way of serving.

But ARPA administrators were not well paid. Ornstein once hooked up with Roberts at an out-of-town meeting and saw Roberts driving a banged-up little rental car. Ornstein asked him why on earth he would rent such a heap. Roberts muttered something about how Ornstein didn't understand government rules and expenses. "I always thought of him as passing out these millions of dollars," said Ornstein. "It hadn't occurred to me that he was in fact living, personally, on quite a limited budget. People like Larry sacrificed themselves for a while in order to get their hands on a big throttle."

Roberts was treated in most respects as if he were a member of the BBN team, even though he was in Washington. He didn't travel to Cambridge often, yet his presence was constantly felt. Since only a few people were working on the project at BBN, Roberts sat down with everyone together when he visited. These were informal talks about their progress, lengthy high-level rump sessions. As principal investigator and group manager, Frank Heart was Roberts's main point of contact at BBN—but Roberts also stayed in close touch with Kahn.

Each site was responsible for building a custom interface between host and IMP. Since computers of various makes were involved, no single interface would do for all the sites. This entailed a separate hardware- and software-development project at each site and was not something the host teams could throw together overnight.

The IMP Guys had to write the host-to-IMP specification before the hosts could start building anything. Heart's most urgent order of business was to complete BBN's design of the host-to-IMP specification, so people at UCLA could begin working in time to meet Roberts's schedule. Heart was already predicting difficulty in getting the host sites to complete their work on time. He knew how heavily the principal investigators relied on graduate students, and Heart worried that the project could be derailed because of a graduate student's failure to treat the schedule seriously enough.

Days spent discussing the host-to-IMP specification turned into weeks. It became obvious that unless someone on Heart's team seized the task of just writing the specification, there would be more talk and little writing. Kahn took it upon himself to draft the specification, and his colleagues were happy to let him. Heart thought Kahn was the best writer the group had, so he stood back and let Kahn produce the specification that became known as BBN Report 1822.

Some people thought Heart worried excessively about potential engineering failures. He was a most defensive driver when it came to engineering. Heart had learned cautious engineering early on from his mentor at Lincoln Lab, Jay Forrester, the inventor of core memory. Forrester had drummed reliability into the heads of a whole generation of MIT engineers. Above cost, performance, or anything else, reliability was their top priority—design for it, build for it, prepare for the worst, and above all, don't put your machine in a position to fail. Heart's mantra built reliability into the IMP in a thousand ways right from the start.

Computer manufacturers were known to cut corners in order to compete on price and build new machines on time. They almost always paid some price in terms of higher failure rates—bugs and computer crashes—but usually it didn't ruin reputations. From Roberts to Heart, on down the line, all of the IMP Guys expected a higher standard in this project. A network running twenty-four hours a day would demand solid performance from the BBN-built IMPs. The accepted imperative was that the IMPs would do their best to deliver each and every message accurately. A line might fail, even a host machine might fail, but the IMPs should not. Reliability was, in a sense, the founding principle of the network. The ARPA network would always reflect Frank Heart's own steady character.

Ornstein had a reputation as a hard taskmaster, and he was very effective as a technical examiner. His trademark line was, "I'm just a dumb hardware guy, convince me!" He wouldn't let go until the explanation made sense to him. Often he uncovered some hidden soft spot.

Many of the planning sessions at BBN took place in the Weiner Room, a high-ceilinged conference room with a big square table and plenty of chalkboards. It was conveniently located at an intersection of corridors in the middle of BBN's systems division, a crossroads between the 516 computer room, the lunchroom, and Heart's office. The Weiner Room served as a regular gathering place for the IMP Guys. The IMP team was small enough, their offices close enough, and contact among team members frequent enough that formal design reviews were unnecessary. They talked in the hallways, sat in one another's offices, debated, and shared ideas constantly. In the Weiner Room, chalk was applied liberally and often to explain, diagram, outline, argue, and teach. Ornstein used the room to hold an informal lecture series, in which software and hardware were explained in detail, and occasionally visitors would come in to talk about technical subjects. The whole team shared information. "Everybody knew everything," as Crowther put it.

The team members also wrote a numbered series of informal technical notes that they circulated among themselves. The notes didn't have a strict format but always began "The IMP Guys' Notes." They wrote down their ideas, exchanged them, and then usually got together to discuss them. The notes also gave Heart a way of monitoring their progress.

Heart's reviews of the work as it matured were nothing like traditional design reviews. A design review is usually a major event in the course of an engineering project. An engineering team may work for weeks preparing a design for review, then come together to submit, elaborate on, and debate it under the scrutiny of colleagues and senior engineers. Heart's reviews tended to be ad hoc and ongoing, which isn't to say that they were easy. "It was like your worst nightmare for an oral exam by someone with psychic abilities," recalled Bernie Cosell, the team's ace software troubleshooter. "He could intuit the parts of the design you were least sure of, the places you understood least well, the areas where you were just song-and-dancing, trying to get by, and cast an uncomfortable spotlight on parts you least wanted to work on, meanwhile virtually ignoring the parts you were so proud of for having gotten really nailed down and done right."

Like the less-frequent meetings with Roberts, Heart's design reviews were meant "to help thrash through the hard parts," Cosell said. Heart had implicit respect for the things his engineers did that worked well. But he was sparing with his praise. His attitude seemed to be, Why waste time with that? Younger and less experienced engineers might have been devastated by the lack of positive feedback from Heart, but the IMP Guys were a seasoned, closely knit, self-assured bunch well accustomed to Heart's ways.

Because of Heart's insistence on reliability, and Kahn's early analysis of this area, a large number of error-control mechanisms were designed into the system. Every communications system is prone to errors in transmission caused by noise in the communication circuits. Voices passing through telephones, an analog transmission, can be garbled or ambiguous—as when the sounds of "s" and "f" are confused. Digital transmissions can also be distorted: a "1" can come through as a "0" and vice versa. Errors occur in bursts. If a given bit is in error, the probability of surrounding bits being in error is much higher than normal. Despite these problems, there are good techniques for detecting and even correcting digital errors, and the IMPs would have to rely on them.

Digital error correction rests upon the basic idea of the "checksum," a relatively small number that is calculated from the data at its source, then transmitted along with the data, and recalculated at the destination. If the original and recalculated numbers do not agree, there has been an error in the transmission, unless perhaps the checking hardware itself failed, a very unlikely proposition.

Checksums appear in data transmissions of all kinds. For instance, every beep you hear at the supermarket checkout counter signifies that a tiny laser has scanned a bar code and transmitted its digits to a computer where the checksum has been calculated and found to be correct. The machine at the checkout counter has done some sophisticated decimal arithmetic along the way by shuffling, multiplying, and adding the scanned digits—all in the blink of an eye. In most supermarket systems the result must end in 0, the single-digit checksum used for all products.

If a product is scanned and the computer fails to beep, it means the arithmetic didn't check. If the computer had a way of correcting the error, it would beep on every pass and save time. But error-correcting techniques add cost to the system, so the checkout person must pass the item through the scanner again, perhaps two or three times until the code is transmitted without error.

The IMP Guys faced a similar problem: If a checksum detected a packet error on the network, how should it be handled? Should the transmitting IMP send the packet again, or should the receiving IMP be augmented with hardware to correct the error? In a network, error correction eats up space on the communications circuits and increases hardware expense in the switching equipment. Consequently, the BBN team decided that if an IMP detected an error in a packet, it would discard the packet without acknowledging receipt. The source IMP, still possessing a duplicate packet and still awaiting acknowledgment but not getting it, would then retransmit the duplicate.

Before issuing the request for proposals, Roberts had had to decide on the type of checksum for the IMPs. How many bits should be assigned to it and how sophisticated should it be? The precise requirement, based on an average number of errors in the phone lines, was difficult to determine because there was no hard information available about error rates on the high-speed lines over which the data was to be sent. Still, it was obvious that a 1-bit checksum would never do. Nor would a 2-bit, or even an 8-bit. Even a 16-bit checksum might not be good enough.

Kahn had earlier documented that a 16-bit checksum might not be sufficiently powerful to reach the desired level of reliability in the network, especially given the uncertainty in error performance of the high-speed lines. Kahn shared with Roberts some rough calculations that strongly suggested a 24-bit checksum would be a much better choice, pointing out that the extra 8 bits added very little expense to the hardware. The checksum was one of many technical issues on which Roberts listened to Kahn's advice, and a 24-bit checksum got written into the RFP. Later, Kahn argued the same case convincingly to Crowther and the others, and the IMP Guys settled on the 24-bit checksum as one vital piece of the error-control system.

The BBN engineers had good intuition for which problems to solve in hardware and which ones to solve in software. It made sense to let the IMP's hardware calculate the checksum, because a software calculation would be too slow. The final IMP-to-IMP error-detection scheme was a clever mix of known engineering techniques and others of the BBN team's own invention. As Crowther put it, "We'd steal ideas from anywhere, but most of the time we had to roll our own."

On Valentine's Day 1969, Cambridge was socked in by a snowstorm. About two dozen people were in attendance at an all-day meeting at BBN. This was the first meeting between Heart's team and the researchers and graduate students from the host sites.

Through Heart's cautious eyes, this crowd of mostly graduate students looked hungry to get their hands on the IMPs. He suspected that when ARPA decided to put the IMPs out at the sites, the researchers expected to have another computer to play with. He imagined they'd want to use the IMPs for all sorts of other things—to play chess or calculate their income taxes. "I took an extraordinarily rigid position," Heart recalled. "They were not to touch, they weren't to go near it, they were to barely look at it. It was a closed box with no switches available."

Kahn was still hard at work on the host-to-IMP interface specification, so it remained unclear to host team members exactly what they'd be required to build. Some people from the host sites asked to see what BBN had in mind, but the IMP Guys hadn't settled on a plan among themselves. On that issue nothing much was resolved at the meeting.

The graduate students decided to share with BBN a plan they had devised for the hosts to compute an end-to-end checksum. This would provide an extra layer of protection against errors in host-to-host communications. It was designed to catch various imagined errors, including the possible misassembly of message packets by the IMPs.

Heart was distressed to hear this, because it would slow down the hosts and make the entire system appear slow. Nor did the very idea that the IMPs might pass damaged packets up to the hosts sit well with him. The students argued that BBN's 24-bit checksum didn't cover the paths from the IMPs to the host computers, and that bits traveled "naked" between the two machines. Heart assured everyone, in no uncertain terms, that the IMP checksum would be reliable. It remained to be seen, and in time the students would be more right than wrong, but with Heart's confidence on display, the host sites dropped their plans to include a checksum in the host protocols.

More problematic was the idea of connecting multiple host computers to the IMP at each site. When Roberts first designed the network, his idea was to connect one—and only one—host computer to each IMP. However, by the Valentine's Day meeting, representatives from the sites were making it clear that they wanted to connect more than one host computer to each IMP. Every research center had multiple computers, and it made sense to try to connect more than one machine per site, if possible. Roberts sent word to Cambridge that BBN was to redesign the IMP to handle up to four hosts apiece. Walden, Crowther, and Cosell invented a clever way to do it.

After Valentine's Day, the IMP Guys really went to work. Their working hours stretched long into the night. Heart, who lived in the rural town of Lincoln, tried to get home in time to have dinner, but often he didn't make it. It was easier for the others to go home for dinner and return to work, or not go home at all. When he was deep into the project, Crowther would sit at his terminal until he fell asleep.

Now the real pressure was on Kahn. He spent much of the next two months on the phone with people at the host sites, grinding away at the interface specification. Kahn became BBN's main point of contact with the host research community. Researchers called him regularly to check what was happening, and what the schedule was, or simply to pass along new ideas.

By mid-April, Kahn finished the specification, a thick document describing how a host computer should communicate with a packet switch, or IMP. "It had been written partly keeping in mind what we'd been told the hosts wanted, and quite a lot keeping in mind what was going to be possible to implement, and what made sense to us," said Walden. A committee of representatives of the host sites reviewed it and told BBN where they didn't think it would work. The specification was revised until an acceptable design was reached. The host sites had something to build now. The UCLA team, which would be first, had less than five months to get ready for the arrival of its IMP.

Heart had drawn a clear line between what the IMPs would handle and what the hosts would do. "Early on, Frank made a decision, a very wise decision, to make a clean boundary between the host responsibilities and the network responsibilities," said Crowther. Heart and his team decided to put "maximum logical separation" between the IMP and the host. It made conceptual and design sense for them to draw the line there to avoid cluttering or crowding the IMP's functions. This also made building the IMPs more manageable. All IMPs could be designed the same, rather than being customized for each site. It also kept BBN from being caught in the middle, having to mediate among the host sites over the network protocols.

BBN had agreed with Roberts that the IMPs wouldn't perform any host-to-host functions. That was a large technical problem. There were neither language standards nor word-length standards, and so far nothing that would facilitate easy communication between hosts. Even individual manufacturers, such as Digital, built a number of wholly incompatible computers.

The last thing BBN wanted was the additional headache of solving the host-to-host problems. Furthermore, Roberts didn't want to give BBN or any other contractor that much control over the network design. Roberts was determined to distribute responsibilities evenly. Between Roberts and BBN it was settled: The IMP would be built as a messenger, a sophisticated store-and-forward device, nothing more. Its job would be to carry bits, packets, and messages: To disassemble messages, store packets, check for errors, route the packets, and send acknowledgments for packets arriving error-free; and then to reassemble incoming packets into messages and send them up to the host machines—all in a common language.

The IMPs were designed to read only the first 32 bits of each message. This part of the message, originally called a "leader" (and later changed to "header"), specified either the source or destination, and included some additional control information. The leader contained the minimal data needed to send and process a message. These messages were then broken into packets within the source IMP. The burden of reading the content of the messages would be on the hosts themselves.

The host computers spoke many different languages, and the hardest part of making the network useful was going to be getting the hosts to communicate with each other. The host sites would have to get their disparate computers to talk to each other by means of protocols they agreed on in advance. Spurred by ARPA, the host community was making an organized effort to begin resolving those protocol issues, knowing it would be quite a while before anything was settled definitively.

❏ IMP Number 0

One spring day, a delivery truck from Honeywell turned down Moulton Street. Inside was the first 516 machine built to BBN's specifications. The refrigerator-sized computer was brought off the truck and onto a loading dock at the back of the systems division building and then was rolled into a large room, soon to be known as the IMP room, adjacent to the dock. The team had converted a storeroom into space for testing the IMPs by adding a raised computer floor, bright fluorescent lighting, and air-conditioning. The windowless room was where the youngest man on the team, twenty-two-year-old Ben Barker, would soon spend a lot of time.

Barker was an undergraduate student whose brilliance had caught Ornstein's attention in one of the classes he taught at Harvard. When BBN was awarded the ARPA contract, Heart had offered Barker a job, and Barker had taken a leave of absence to accept it. Barker, like Ornstein, was a hardware engineer and he showed signs of becoming an ace debugger—someone who could rescue a project when the time came. He was placed in charge of setting up each IMP Honeywell delivered and debugging the hardware before it left BBN's shop.

This first machine was the prototype (IMP Number 0), a non-ruggedized 516 containing Honeywell's initial implementation of BBN's interfaces. With the machine in the middle of the room, Barker ran power to the computer, plugged everything in, and turned it on.

Barker had built a tester and had written some debugging code. He was looking forward to working out whatever bugs the machine had. Undoubtedly there would be something that would need fixing, because there always was; bugs were part of the natural process of computer design. Heart and the whole team looked forward to finding out which parts of the IMP design worked and which needed more attention.

Barker tried loading the first IMP diagnostic program into the untested machine. He couldn't get it to work. So he loaded some other code, and that didn't work either. Barker tried a few other things and discovered that nothing worked. "The machine didn't come close to doing anything useful," he said. So far, the first IMP was a fizzling dud.

Prior to the IMP project, people at BBN and Honeywell had interacted casually and relations were friendly. In the days leading up to the IMP project a sense of teamwork grew. Honeywell had devoted a special systems crew to work on the BBN contract from day one. At BBN's request, Honeywell had assigned one of its technicians exclusively to the task of shepherding Honeywell's part of the job to completion.

This was unusual. In general, minicomputer manufacturers like Honeywell didn't cater much to the special demands of their customers. "Most computer companies won't build specials at all," said Heart. "Or if they do, it's under great duress." Minicomputer salespeople went after a broad market, while mainframe computer makers were known to treat customers like royalty. Nobody in the minicomputer business did much hand-holding.

In the wake of IMP Number 0's gross failure, BBN's hardware chief Ornstein began to go over the design with the Honeywell team. He discovered that no one at Honeywell seemed to understand in much detail how the BBN-designed interfaces were supposed to work. He was surprised to learn that the technicians building the first interface didn't really understand the drawings. Honeywell hadn't attempted to develop any diagnostics to test the design; it had simply tried to produce a faithful implementation of the block diagrams that Ornstein had drawn and that BBN had included in its proposal to ARPA. The trouble was that in furnishing Honeywell with a set of fairly generic block diagrams, BBN assumed that Honeywell's familiarity and expertise with its own machines would enable the computer manufacturer to anticipate any peculiar problems with BBN's requested modifications to the model 516. Honeywell had its own logic modules, its own design system. But instead of working out the essential details in the blueprints, Honeywell had built BBN's machine without verifying that the BBN-designed interfaces, as drawn, would work with the 516 base model.

Of course, neither BBN in drawing the block diagrams nor Honeywell in implementing the design actually had all of the necessary tools to create a perfectly working prototype IMP on the first pass. In building new computers, said Barker, the operative assumption is that you design something you think will work, get the prototype ready, start testing, then gradually fix the design errors until the machine passes the test. It would have been an engineering fluke if the machine ran perfectly straight away. But even as a first pass, the condition of this prototype machine was unacceptable.

If Ornstein was concerned about Honeywell's performance, Barker was downright nervous. As the chief debugger, he was the one responsible for getting the machine to actually work. At this stage in the IMP project, the interfaces on the 516, he said, "wouldn't have come close to working even if Honeywell had implemented them properly."

Barker was staring at weeks of concentrated work ahead. He felt the weight of the schedule suddenly grow heavier. If the BBN hardware team intended to hand off to the BBN programming team a working version of the modified Honeywell 516 any time soon, so that Crowther, Walden, and Cosell would have time for final debugging of their operating code, then the hardware specialists would have to hustle. With Ornstein's help, Barker would have to "take the stuff Honeywell had built," he said, "and figure out how to make it actually do what it was intended to do."

The arrival of the prototype IMP in its initial state marked a real setback; correcting the course would take time, and soon there would be precious little of that.

Armed with an oscilloscope, a wire-wrap gun, and an unwrap tool, Barker worked alone on the machine sixteen hours a day. The circuitry of the computer relied on pin blocks, or wire-wrapped boards, that served as the central connection points to which wires, hundreds upon hundreds of wires, were routed. There were numerous blocks of thirty-four pins into which logic boards were plugged and which carried components to form the correct circuits. After figuring out where the wires should actually go, Barker had to unwrap each tightly wound misconnected wire from its pin. The pins in each block were about an inch long, and were closely spaced (1/20th of an inch apart) in a square matrix; each block looked like a miniature bed of nails with wires streaming Medusa-like into and out of it. Once he determined where the correct wires should be re-connected, Barker used the wire-wrap gun to wrap each wire care-fully on its correct pin. It was a long, laborious, and delicate process.

To complicate matters, Barker had a slight palsy in his hands. Working with a wire-wrap gun called for a steady hand and good concentration. The close spacing of the pins, the weight of the wire-wrap gun, and the size of the nozzle on the gun that had to be slipped down over a single pin amid a small forest of pins all con-spired against him. The risk was in getting the wire on the wrong pin or bending or breaking a pin. You could destroy a lot of fine work if you weren't careful. So the shake in Barker's hands caused quite a stir among the other IMP Guys when Barker took his wire-wrap gun to the pin blocks inside the IMP.

Most of the rewiring was done with the power off. When some-thing had to be done with the power on, it was done with little clip-leads that slipped onto the pins. Here, though, there was a very real danger of shorting things out and blowing circuits.

Barker spent months debugging the machine. Ornstein was overseeing the design corrections in the prototype and making sure they got relayed back to Honeywell's engineers. The next machine Honeywell was scheduled to deliver would be the first ruggedized 516 with all the design bugs worked out: IMP Number One des-tined for UCLA. "The sweat was to get working designs in time to ship," said Barker. The summer was upon them.

Heart's wariness about the hordes of curious graduate students drove BBN to conceptualize even greater measures of protection for the IMPs. In time, among the most creative things Heart's team did was invent ways of obtaining critical operating data from the net-work IMPs—reading the machines' vital signs—unobtrusively from a distance. Heart wanted to be able to sit at a terminal in Cambridge and see what an IMP in Los Angeles, Salt Lake City or any place else was doing. BBN's full implementation of remote diagnostic tools and debugging capabilities would later become a huge asset. When the network matured, remote control would enable BBN to monitor and maintain the whole system from one operations center, collecting data and diagnosing problems as things changed. Periodically, each IMP would send back to Cambridge a "snapshot of its status," a set of data about its operating conditions. Changes in the network, minor and major, could be detected. Heart's group envisioned someday being able to look across the network to know whether any machine was malfunctioning or any line was failing, or perhaps if anyone was meddling with the machines.

Nonetheless, BBN still hadn't even gotten the prototype IMP to a state in which it could run operational code. And the programming team—Crowther, Walden, and Cosell—was now moving into difficult territory: the design of a flexible, or "dynamic" routing system, allowing alternative routing, so that packets would automatically flow around troubled nodes and links. A fixed-routing scheme would have been straightforward: You would send a packet with clear instructions to travel via x, y, and z points on the map. But if point y was knocked out, all traffic would be held up. And that would thwart one of the advantages of a network with multiple links and nodes.

The original request from ARPA had specified dynamic routing, without offering a clue as to how to make it work. Crowther had found a way to do it. He was building a system of dynamic-routing tables that would be updated every split second or so. These tables would tell the IMPs in which direction to forward each packet that hadn't yet reached its destination. The routing tables would reflect such network conditions as line failures and congestion, and they would route packets the shortest way possible. Making this design actually work seemed a mind-bending problem—until Crowther came up with a simple, perfect set of code. Crowther "always had his head right down in the bits," as Ornstein described Crowther's uncanny, intuitive talent.

Crowther's dynamic-routing algorithm was a piece of programming poetry. "It was incredibly minimalistic and worked astoundingly well," Walden observed. Crowther was regarded by his colleagues as being within the top fraction of 1 percent of programmers in the world. On occasion the graceful minimalism of Crowther's code wasn't enough to handle the complexity of real-world systems. Other programmers would have to fine-tune what Crowther had created. But his core ideas were more often than not brilliant. "Most of the rest of us made our livings handling the details resulting from Will's use of his brain," Walden observed.

Flow control was another programming challenge. But when Kahn looked at Crowther's code and saw how he had implemented control of the flow of packets from one side of the network to the other, he was worried. Messages between hosts were to be transmitted by the subnet over logical "links." The subnet would accept one message at a time on a given link. Messages waiting to enter the subnet were stored in a memory buffer (a waiting area inside the machine), in a queue. The next message wasn't sent until the sending IMP received an acknowledgment (similar to a return receipt) saying that the previous message had arrived error-free at the destination host. When one link was cleared and a new message could be sent, the subnet would notify the sending IMP by means of a special control signal that the BBN engineers called Ready for Next Message, or RFNM (pronounced RUFF-num). Messages in the sending host's buffers, waiting for links to clear, were like patrons in a restaurant waiting for tables; RFNMs were the equivalent of the maître d's announcing "Your table is ready."

This meant it was impossible to send a continuous stream of messages over any single link through the system from one host to another. RFNM was a congestion-control strategy designed to protect the IMPs from overload, but at the expense of reducing service to the host. Kahn had studied the problem of congestion control even before the ARPA network project began. His reaction to Crowther's solution was that the links and RFNMs would still allow fatal congestion of the network's arteries. The IMP's buffers would fill up, he said. You'd have incomplete messages sitting in the receiving IMPs waiting for their final packets to arrive so the entire message could be reassembled, and there would be no room for the packets to arrive.

Kahn's reassembly lockup scenario has an analog in the shipping business. Say that a Toyota dealership in Sacramento orders sets of replacement engine blocks and pistons from a warehouse in Yokohama. Both items together are essential for the jobs the dealer has at hand. In the Yokohama harbor, freighters are loading large containers, all the same size, filled with products of many kinds. The engine blocks and pistons wind up in separate ships. When the container of engine blocks arrives in San Francisco, it is unloaded to a warehouse of containers whose contents are also partial shipments awaiting the arrival of other parts before being sent onward: components for television sets, pin blocks for pianos, and so on. When the freighter with the pistons arrives, it finds the warehouse full. Every later ship has the same problem: Nobody can unload; nothing can leave the warehouse. Deadlock. Solution? The Yokohama shipper agrees to call ahead next time to reserve space for all containers that go together. If space is unavailable, he waits until it becomes available before shipping.

Kahn also predicted another type of deadlock that might lead to loss of packets. He said that it would occur in heavy traffic within the subnet when the buffers of one IMP were filled with packets routed to another, and vice versa. A kind of standoff would result, in which neither one would be able to accept the other's packets. The way the routing software had been written the IMPs would discard the packets.

Kahn and Crowther debated the gridlock question at length. Over points such as these Kahn's conceptual views came into open conflict with the pragmatic bent of the rest of the IMP Guys and cracked open a wide disagreement between them. The rest of the team just wanted to get the network up and running on schedule. As the network grew they'd have time to improve its performance, work out problems, and perfect the algorithms.

But Kahn persisted. "I could see things that to me were obvious flaws," he said. "The most obvious one was that the network could deadlock." Kahn was certain the network would lock up, and he told Heart and the others so immediately. They argued with him. "Bob was interested in the theory of things and the math, but he wasn't really interested in the implementation," said Crowther. Crowther and Kahn began to talk it through, and the two had what Crowther described as "grand little fights." The flow-control scheme wasn't designed for a huge network, and with a small number of nodes Crowther thought they could get by with it.

Heart thought that Kahn was worrying too much about hypothetical, unlikely network conditions. His approach was to wait and see. Some of the others thought Kahn didn't understand many of the problems with which they were grappling. "Some of the things he was suggesting were off-the-wall, just wrong," said Ornstein. Kahn wanted to watch simulations of network traffic on a screen. He wanted to have a program that would show packets moving through the network. In fact, the packets would never move at a humanly observable speed; they'd be going "zip-zip" in microseconds and milliseconds. "We said, 'Bob, you'll never understand the problems looking at it that way.'" The other IMP Guys respected Kahn, but some believed he was going in the wrong direction. Gradually, they paid less attention to him. "Most of us in the group were trying to get Kahn out of our hair," Ornstein said.

Heart scotched Kahn's suggestion that they use a simulation. Heart hated to see his programming team spend time on simulations or on writing anything but operational code. They were already becoming distracted by something else he disliked—building software tools. Heart feared delay. Over the years he had seen too many programmers captivated by tool building, and he had spent a career holding young engineers back from doing things that might waste money or time. The people in Heart's division knew that if they asked him for the okay to clock hours writing editors, assemblers, and debuggers, they would meet with stiff resistance, perhaps even a shouting match. So no one ever asked; they just did it, building tools when they thought it was the right thing to do, regardless of what Heart thought. This was software they would eventually need when the time came to test the system. All were customized pieces of programming, specifically designed for the ARPA project.

As summer peaked, a troubling problem loomed: BBN was still awaiting Honeywell's delivery of the first production IMP, with all the debugged interfaces built to BBN's specifications. The programming team had given up waiting and gone ahead with its work by loading a lower-grade development machine with a simulation program the team had designed to mimic the operations of the production model IMP and its I/O interfaces. Still, testing the software on the real machine was the preferred approach. And whenever the machine came in, Barker would first need time to debug it. The time left was dwindling. By late summer, the machine still hadn't crossed BBN's loading dock. Scheduled delivery of the IMP to California was now only a few weeks away, and BBN's own reputation was on the line.

❑ The Bug

Finally, about two weeks before Labor Day, Honeywell rushed the first ruggedized 516 IMP out its shop door and over to Cambridge. As soon as the machine touched the floor at BBN, Barker was ready to work on it. He powered up IMP Number One in the backroom.

Barker loaded the IMP diagnostic code. When he tried running it, nothing happened. The machine didn't respond. On closer inspection, it was apparent that the machine BBN received was not what it had ordered. This 516 had few of the modifications that Barker and Ornstein had worked out painstakingly in debugging the prototype; in fact, it was wired just like the original dysfunctional prototype had been wired. With the deadline closing in, Barker had only one recourse: fix it at BBN. This time at least he already knew where every wire should go. With the machine sitting in the middle of the large room, Barker went to work implementing all of the design modifications necessary to make it a functioning IMP.

Within a few days, Barker had coaxed the machine to life. He managed to activate the IMP's interfaces—whereupon the computer began crashing at random intervals. The randomness of the crashes was unusually bad. Intermittent problems of this sort were the devil. The IMP would run for anywhere from twelve hours to forty hours at a stretch, then die and be somewhere "off in the boonies." What to do? Recalled Ornstein, "We couldn't figure out what the hell was going on."

As Labor Day approached, they pressured the IMP, putting it through as many hard tests as possible. It might run fine for twenty-four hours, then inexplicably die. Barker would look for a clue, chase what appeared to be a problem, fix it, and still the machine would crash again. With only a few days left before the delivery deadline, it looked like they were not going to make it.

Barker, who had been nursing the computer, suspected the problem was in the machine's timing chain. It was just a hunch.

The IMP had a clock used by the operating system to keep time in the machine, not as humans would by marking seconds, minutes or hours, but counting time in 1-microsecond (one million ticks per second) increments—fast for its day but a hundred times slower than today's personal computers. This clock provided a framework in which the IMP operated, and it regulated the computer's many functions synchronously. In a communications system, messages arrive unannounced; signals interrupt the machine asynchronously. Like a telephone call in the middle of dinner, an incoming packet shows up on its own schedule at the IMP's door and says, "Take me now."

The computer had a sophisticated system for handling the incoming interruptions in a methodical manner, so as not to upset the synchronous operation of all its functions. If not properly designed, such synchronizers can be thrown off by an incoming signal occurring at just the wrong moment. Synchronizer bugs are rare. But when they occur and the synchronizer fails to respond properly to an interrupt, the consequences are profoundly disturbing to the machine's total operation. One might call it a nervous breakdown; computer scientists have another term for it: The synchronizer goes into a "metastable" condition. "Under such circumstances," Ornstein said, "the machine invariably dies in a hopelessly confused state—different each time."

Ornstein knew all too well about synchronizer bugs. He had dealt with the problem in the computer he and Wes Clark had built a few years earlier in St. Louis. Ornstein was the author of some of the first published papers on the subject, and was one of the few people in the world who actually had any experience with this particular gremlin.

Their unpredictability made synchronizer bugs among the most frustrating of bugs because of the absence of any recognizable pattern to the resulting crashes. Unlike most other problems that could cause computers to crash, a synchronizer bug left behind virtually no useful forensic evidence that might point a diagnostician to the problem. In fact, the absence of clues was one of the most useful clues. Furthermore, the failures caused by this bug were so infrequent (only once every day or so even in full-bore tests), that it was impossible to detect any evidence on an oscilloscope. Only the most astute debuggers had any idea what they were dealing with.

This seemed to be the problem Ornstein and Barker had on their hands. But who knew, because you couldn't actually trace it. What to do now? The Honeywell 516 had never been used in an application as demanding as the packet-switching network. It was a fast machine; the IMP Guys had chosen it precisely for its I/O capabilities. No one else was likely ever to see the problem in a typical application of the 516 computer. "If their machine died once a year," Ornstein said, "they'd never notice. They would just restart." But the IMP Guys were driving the machine hard. The flow of packets into and out of the IMP happened faster than the Honeywell designers had anticipated. The 516 machine didn't seem capable of handling such traffic. Maybe BBN had been overly optimistic. Ornstein and Barker went to Honeywell and insisted that the manufacturer "dig out of the woodwork, way in the backroom" the designer of the 516 computer. He was a very smart guy, Ornstein had to admit, but at first the Honeywell man refused to admit that a metastable state was possible in the machine. He had never read Ornstein's papers, and had never seen the problem. "Though filled with disbelief," said Ornstein, he "at least understood what we were saying."

Under normal conditions, the 516 would run for years without experiencing the synchronizer problem. However, under ARPA's packet-switching network conditions, the machine was failing once every day or so. Try telling Frank Heart, Mr. Reliability, that he'd just have to live with that.

Ornstein and Barker huddled. It was only a guess that the IMP had a synchronizer problem. To test the hypothesis, Ornstein designed and wired an "aggravator" that deliberately produced data requests at what Barker called a "fierce rate." It increased the probability of getting interruptions at the exact nanosecond that would reveal the problem. The aggravator had a knob that worked like a tuner. Using the knob, Ornstein and Barker could "tune" the timing of requests to bring in a signal perfectly out of kilter with the clock, the worst case. Then, using an oscilloscope, they observed the machine's "heartbeat" and other internal functions.

The debugging crew went to work. The patterns they were looking for on the oscilloscope would be so faint as to be visible only in a darkened room. So with all the lights out in the IMP room and with all their diagnostic equipment and the Honeywell turned on, they watched, while fooling with the aggravator. The traces they saw on the scope were bright, regularly positioned, and steadily paced—the vital signs of a healthy machine.

Even with the aggravator, it took the debugging team quite a while to find what it was looking for. Still, every few minutes a very faint ghost trace flitted across the oscilloscope. Was that it? The fleeting trace was perhaps the only telltale sign that the crashes were caused by a timing problem: a synchronizer stalled in a metastable condition for a few nanoseconds too long. It was the computer equivalent of the one split second of confusion or indecision by a race car driver that ends suddenly in a fatal crash. The evidence seemed fairly incontrovertible, and Honeywell finally acknowledged it.

In the meantime, Barker designed a possible fix, and rewired the

IMP's central timing chain. When Barker brought the machine back up, loaded in his diagnostic code, and looked in the scope, the ghost traces were gone.

While Barker and Ornstein were reasonably certain that the problem was fixed, they had no way of knowing for sure unless the machine ran for a few consecutive days without crashing. And they didn't have a few days. Heart had already approved shipping the first Interface Message Processor to California the next day. IMP Number One was almost out the door.

Do It To It Truett

Steve Crocker and Vint Cerf had been best friends since attending Van Nuys High School in L.A.'s San Fernando Valley. They shared a love for science, and the two spent more than a few Saturday nights building three-dimensional chess games or trying to re-create Edwin Land's experiments with color perception.

Vint was a wiry, intense, effusive kid. He joined his high school ROTC unit to avoid gym class. On the days he didn't show up at school in his ROTC uniform, Vint wore a jacket and tie. And he always toted a large brown briefcase. By local standards, it was an unusual mode of dress, even in the late 1950s. "I used the coat and tie to distinguish myself from the crowd—maybe a nerd's way of being different," he recalled. Nonetheless, much to the consternation of his friends, Vint never had trouble attracting the attention of the opposite sex. He was, everyone agreed, one of a kind.

From an early age, Vint aspired to match the accomplished track record of his father, who had risen through the ranks to become a senior executive at North American Aviation (now Rockwell International). Both of Vint's younger brothers played football and took turns as president of the student body. Vint was the bookworm. His literary tastes tilted toward fantasy. Well into his adult life, he regularly set aside several days to reread *The Lord of the Rings* trilogy. Vint did particularly well in chemistry, but his passion was math. When Steve Crocker started the math club at Van Nuys High, Vint was one of the first to join.

As a result of premature birth, Vint was hearing-impaired. Although hearing aids in both ears later corrected much of the deficit, he grew up devising clever strategies for communicating in the hearing world. Years later, after they became friends, Bob Kahn brought some of Cerf's aural tricks to his friends' attention and Cerf eventually wrote a paper called "Confessions of a Hearing-Impaired Engineer," in which he shared some of his secrets.

> In particularly noisy environments (cafeterias, restaurants, and homes with dogs and small children), the deaf person's reliance on conversational context often suffers badly. A typical strategy here is to dominate the conversation, not by doing all the talking, but by asking a lot of questions. In this way, the deaf listener will at least know what question the speaker is addressing, even if he cannot hear all of the response. In a group conversation, this can backfire embarrassingly if the question you ask is one which was just asked by someone else. A variation (equally embarrassing) is to enthusiastically suggest something just suggested, for example:
>
> Friend A: I wonder what the origin of this term is?
> Friend B: Why don't we look it up in *The Oxford English Dictionary*?
> Friend A: Yeah, but too bad we don't have an *O.E.D.*
> Cerf: I know. Why don't we look it up in *The Oxford English Dictionary*?

Steve Crocker drifted in and out of Vint's life. Steve's parents were divorced, and he spent his high school years shuttling between suburban Chicago and the San Fernando Valley. Always precocious, Steve grew up knowing he was probably the smartest kid in any given room. At age thirteen, while home one day with a cold, he taught himself the elements of calculus. And at the end of tenth grade, he learned the rudiments of computer programming. "I remember being thrilled when I finally understood the concept of a loop," Crocker recalled, "which enabled the computer to proceed with a very lengthy sequence of operations with only a relatively few instructions. I was a bit callow, but I remember thinking this was the kind of revelation that must have led Archimedes to run down the street naked yelling, 'Eureka!'"

Around 1960, when Steve had returned to L.A., Vint followed him into the computer lab at UCLA. Although still in high school, Steve had gotten permission to use the UCLA computer, but the only free time he and Vint had was on the weekends. One Saturday they arrived to find the computer lab building locked. "I couldn't see any choice but to give up and go home," said Crocker. But they looked up and saw an open second-story window. They looked at each other. "Next thing I know, Vint is on my shoulders," Crocker recalled. Cerf went through the window and, once inside, opened the door and taped the latch so they could get in and out of the building. "When the Watergate burglars did the same thing a dozen years later and got caught, I shuddered," said Crocker.

After high school, Cerf attended Stanford on a four-year scholarship from his father's company. He majored in math but soon got hooked on serious computing. "There was something amazingly enticing about programming," he said. "You created your own universe and you were the master of it. The computer would do anything you programmed it to do. It was this unbelievable sandbox in which every grain of sand was under your control."

After graduating in 1965, Cerf decided he wanted to work for a while before going on to graduate school. IBM was recruiting on the Stanford campus, and Cerf took a job at IBM in Los Angeles. He went to work as the systems engineer for an IBM time-sharing system. Realizing he needed better grounding in computer science, he soon joined his friend Crocker, now a graduate student in UCLA's computer science department. Computer science was still a young discipline, and UCLA's Ph.D. program—one of the first in the country—was one of only a dozen in existence at the time. Cerf arrived just as Crocker was leaving for MIT. Crocker's thesis advisor at UCLA was Jerry Estrin, the same professor Paul Baran had worked with a few years earlier. Estrin had an ARPA contract for the "Snuper Computer," which used one computer to observe the execution of programs running on a second machine. Estrin took on Cerf as a research student for the project; it became the basis for Cerf's doctoral thesis. In the summer of 1968 Crocker returned to UCLA and joined Cerf in Estrin's group.

For both Cerf and Crocker, 1968 marked the beginning of a lifelong fascination with the networking of computers. For Cerf, computer networking would become the centerpiece of his professional career. Although Crocker would move on to other things for long stretches at a time, he too would eventually return to the field of networking.

In the fall of 1968, ARPA transferred its contract from Estrin to Len Kleinrock at UCLA. Kleinrock was setting up his Network Measurement Center, with a $200,000 annual contract from ARPA. By coincidence, when Kleinrock got the contract, the person in the office next door conveniently moved out, so Kleinrock expanded his domain; he tore down the wall between the two offices and installed a large conference table for meetings with students and staff. The meetings were frequent as Kleinrock busily built a small empire.

In planning the ARPA network, Larry Roberts had conceived of the Network Measurement Center as the organization that would be responsible for most of the performance testing and analysis. The measurement center was intended to be roughly analogous to a test track where drivers push the outer limits of high-performance cars. Kleinrock and his group were in charge of gathering data—total network response time, traffic density, delays, and capacity—the measures needed to evaluate how the network is performing. Like Bob Kahn, Kleinrock had a theoretician's bent; his business was simulation, modeling, and analysis. Through simulations, he had come as close as he could to monitoring the ways in which networks perform without actually having a network to run. He welcomed the chance to test his theories on the real thing.

The engineers at BBN didn't pay too much attention to Kleinrock. They thought he was a trifle heavy on theory and fairly light on engineering. The skepticism was mutual, for Kleinrock believed that the BBN team was largely uninterested in performance. BBN's programmers were outstanding, but, said Kleinrock, "By and large, a programmer simply wants to get a piece of software that works. That's hard enough. Whether it works efficiently or well is not usually the issue." He was unaware, perhaps, of Walden and Crowther's obsession with software efficiency, but in any case, perfecting *network* performance, Kleinrock decided, was his job.

Before long Kleinrock was managing forty students who helped run the center. Crocker and Cerf were among the senior members of Kleinrock's group. Another important member was Jon Postel. He had a long bushy beard, wore sandals year-round and had never put on a tie in his life. Always dapper and generally more conservative, Cerf presented a striking contrast to Postel's steadfastly casual appearance. Crocker, the unofficial leader, was somewhere in the middle. He had grown a beard at MIT ("Cops looked at me a little harder, but girls were a lot friendlier, and that was a trade-off I could live with," Crocker said), but was willing to put on a pair of dress shoes every now and then.

While Cerf and Crocker were academic stars, Postel, who was twenty-five, had had a more checkered academic career. He had grown up in nearby Glendale and Sherman Oaks, and he too had attended Van Nuys High School, where his grades were mediocre. Postel's interest in computers developed at a local community college. By the time he got to UCLA to finish an undergraduate degree in engineering (the closest thing to computer science at the time) computing was his life. UCLA eventually decided to establish computer science as a formal department, at just about the time Postel was entering the university's graduate school. Postel was quiet, but he had strong opinions. The people running the computer science department occasionally interpreted the firmness of Postel's opinions as a bad attitude.

In 1966 Cerf had married a young illustrator named Sigrid. She was profoundly deaf. Their first meeting had been contrived by their hearing-aid dealer, who scheduled adjacent appointments for them one Saturday morning in hopes that they would cross paths and hit it off. They went to lunch and Sigrid was awestruck by her companion's eclectic curiosity. Vint seemed to dance in his chair with excitement as he described his work with computers. They extended their *tête-à-tête* with a visit to the Los Angeles County Museum of Art to see some of Sigrid's favorite paintings. Unschooled in art but eager to learn, Cerf stared for a long time at a huge Kandinsky. "This thing reminds me of a green hamburger," he finally remarked. A year later they were married, with Steve Crocker as Vint's best man (roles that would be reversed a few years later). Crocker's electronics expertise came in handy when, minutes before the ceremony was to begin, he discovered the tape recorder for the wedding music was malfunctioning. Best man and frantic groom retreated to a tiny room near the altar and fixed it just in time.

Kleinrock, although only ten years older than the rest of his group, had a great reputation in queueing theory (the study of how long people and things spend waiting in lines, how long the lines get, and how to design systems to reduce waiting). He had already published a book and he was in charge of a growing lab; his energy seemed boundless. Moreover, he was one of just a handful of scientists who had produced analytic models of store-and-forward networks before Roberts got started on the ARPA project.

At the time, the UCLA computer science department owned a computer made by Scientific Data Systems called the Sigma-7, the latest in that firm's line of computers. UCLA also had three major computer centers equipped with IBM 7094 mainframes. But the Sigma-7 was the machine assigned to the graduate students. No one liked the Sigma-7 much. It was unreliable and difficult to program. As a member of the UCLA team put it, the Sigma-7 was a dog. ("But it was our dog," Cerf said years later.) It was also the only computer they had to play with—until, that is, the ARPA network came along. Not only would the computer scientists at UCLA be receiving the first IMP, but presumably the network would open doors to all kinds of different host machines at the other sites.

The most pressing task in the summer of 1969 was to build the interface—a combination of hardware and software—between the

Sigma-7 and the IMP. As the UCLA guys understood it, BBN was working out some specifications for how to construct such a connection. The host-to-IMP interface had to be built from scratch each time a new site was established around a different computer model. Later, sites using the same model could purchase copies of the custom interface.

Nearly as urgent was the more far-reaching challenge of writing the software that allowed host computers throughout the network to communicate with one another. This was to be the host-to-host protocol, a very broad based set of operating terms that would be common to all machines. It had to be like a traveler's check: good anywhere and able to support a gamut of applications, from remote log-ins to file transfers to text processing. Inventing it wouldn't be easy.

❑ The Search for Protocols

In the summer of 1968, a small group of graduate students from the first four host sites—UCLA, SRI, UC Santa Barbara, and the University of Utah—had met in Santa Barbara. They knew that the network was being planned, but they'd been given few details beyond that. But networking in general, and the ARPA experiment in particular, were hot topics.

The meeting was seminal, if only because of the enthusiasm it generated. "We had lots of questions—how IMPs and hosts would be connected, what hosts would say to each other, and what applications would be supported," Crocker said. "No one had any answers, but the prospects seemed exciting. We found ourselves imagining all kinds of possibilities—interactive graphics, cooperating processes, automatic database query, electronic mail—but no one knew where to begin."

From that meeting emerged a corps of young researchers devoted to working on, thinking through, and scheming about the network's host-to-host communications. To speed up the process, they decided to meet regularly. Theoretically, a computer network would cut down on some of the ARPA-funded travel, but before long Crocker was traveling enough that Kleinrock had to procure a separate travel budget for him.

A month or so after the new group began meeting, it became clear to Crocker and others that they had better start accumulating notes on the discussions. If the meetings themselves were less than conclusive, perhaps the act of writing something down would help order their thoughts. Crocker volunteered to write the first minutes. He was an extremely considerate young man, sensitive to others. "I remember having great fear that we would offend whoever the official protocol designers were." Of course, there were no official protocol designers, but Crocker didn't know that. He was living with friends at the time and worked all night on the first note, writing in the bathroom so as not to wake anyone in the house. He wasn't worried about what he wanted to say so much as he wanted to strike just the right tone. "The basic ground rules were that anyone could say anything and that nothing was official."

To avoid sounding too declarative, he labeled the note "Request for Comments" and sent it out on April 7, 1969. Titled "Host Software," the note was distributed to the other sites the way all the first Requests for Comments (RFCs) were distributed: in an envelope with the lick of a stamp. RFC Number 1 described in technical terms the basic "handshake" between two computers—how the most elemental connections would be handled. "Request for Comments," it turned out, was a perfect choice of titles. It sounded at once solicitous and serious. And it stuck.

"When you read RFC 1, you walked away from it with a sense of, 'Oh, this is a club that I can play in too,'" recalled Brian Reid, later a graduate student at Carnegie-Mellon. "It has rules, but it welcomes other members as long as the members are aware of those rules." The language of the RFC was warm and welcoming. The idea was to promote cooperation, not ego. The fact that Crocker kept his ego out of the first RFC set the style and inspired others to follow suit in the hundreds of friendly and cooperative RFCs that followed. "It is impossible to underestimate the importance of that," Reid asserted. "I did not feel excluded by a little core of protocol kings. I felt included by a friendly group of people who recognized that the purpose of networking was to bring everybody in." For years afterward (and to this day) RFCs have been the principal means of open expression in the computer networking community, the accepted way of recommending, reviewing, and adopting new technical standards.

Before long, the assemblage began calling itself the Network Working Group, or NWG. It was a high commission for the country's young and exceptionally talented communication programmers. Its main challenge was to agree in principle about protocols—how to share resources, how to transfer data, how to get things done. In real terms, that meant writing programs, or at least adopting certain rules for the way programs got written, rules to which a majority could consent. Agreement was the *sine qua non*. This was a community of equals. They could all write code—or rewrite the code someone else had written. The NWG was an adhocracy of intensely creative, sleep-deprived, idiosyncratic, well-meaning computer geniuses. And they always half-expected, any day, to be politely thanked for their work and promptly replaced by others whom they imagined to be the field's true professionals. There was no one to tell them that they were as official as it got. The RFC, a simple mechanism for distributing documentation open to anybody, had what Crocker described as a "first-order effect" on the speed at which ideas were disseminated, and on spreading the networking culture.

Anticipating the construction of the network, the Network Working Group continued meeting regularly, and new terms and inventions often emerged by consensus. The very word "protocol" found its way into the language of computer networking based on the need for collective agreement among network users. For a long time the word has been used for the etiquette of diplomacy and for certain diplomatic agreements. But in ancient Greek, *protokollon* meant the first leaf of a volume, a flyleaf attached to the top of a papyrus scroll that contained a synopsis of the manuscript, its authentication, and the date. Indeed, the word referring to the top of a scroll corresponded well to a packet's header, the part of the packet containing address information. But a less formal meaning seemed even more fitting. "The other definition of protocol is that it's a handwritten agreement between parties, typically worked out on the back of a lunch bag," Cerf remarked, "which describes pretty accurately how most of the protocol designs were done."

But the first few meetings of the Network Working Group were less than productive. Over the course of the spring and summer of 1969, the group continued struggling with the problems of host-protocol design. Everyone had a vision of the potential for intercomputer communication, but no one had ever sat down to construct protocols that could actually be used. It wasn't BBN's job to worry about that problem. The only promise anyone from BBN had made about the planned-for subnetwork of IMPs was that it would move packets back and forth, and make sure they got to their destination. It was entirely up to the host computer to figure out how to communicate with another host computer or what to do with the messages once it received them. This was called the "host-to-host" protocol.

The computers themselves were extremely egocentric devices. The typical mainframe of the period behaved as if it were the only computer in the universe. There was no obvious or easy way to engage two diverse machines in even the minimal communication needed to move bits back and forth. You could connect machines, but once connected, what would they say to each other? In those days a computer interacted with the devices that were attached to it, like a monarch communicating with his subjects. Everything connected to the main computer performed a specific task, and each peripheral device was presumed to be ready at all times for a fetch-my-slippers type of command. (In computer parlance, this relationship is known as master-slave communication.) Computers were strictly designed for this kind of interaction; they send instructions to subordinate card readers, terminals, and tape units, and they initiate all dialogues. But if another device in effect tapped the computer on the shoulder with a signal that said, "Hi, I'm a computer, too," the receiving machine would be stumped. The goal in devising the host-to-host protocol was to get the mainframe machines talking as peers, so that either side could initiate a simple dialogue and the other would be ready to respond with at least an acknowledgment of the other machine's existence.

Steve Crocker once likened the concept of a host-to-host protocol to the invention of two-by-fours. "You imagine cities and buildings and houses, and so forth, but all you see are trees and forest. And somewhere along the way, you discover two-by-fours as an intermediate building block, and you say, well, I can get two-by-fours out of all these trees," Crocker recalled. "We didn't have the concept of an equivalent of a two-by-four, the basic protocols for getting all the computers to speak, and which would be useful for building all the applications." The computer equivalent of a two-by-four was what the Network Working Group was trying to invent.

In conceiving the protocol, the NWG members had to ask themselves a few basic questions. What form should the common base take? Should there be a single, foundational protocol on which to build all application protocols? Or should it be more complex, subdivided, layered, branched? Whatever structure they chose, they knew they wanted it to be as open, adaptable, and accessible to inventiveness as possible. The general view was that any protocol was a potential building block, and so the best approach was to define simple protocols, each limited in scope, with the expectation that any of them might someday be joined or modified in various unanticipated ways. The protocol design philosophy adopted by the NWG broke ground for what came to be widely accepted as the "layered" approach to protocols.

One of the most important goals of building the lower-layer protocol between hosts was to be able to move a stream of packets from one computer to another without having to worry about what was inside the packets. The job of the lower layer was simply to move generic unidentified bits, regardless of what the bits might define: a file, an interactive session between people at two terminals, a graphical image, or any other conceivable form of digital data. Analogously, some water out of the tap is used for making coffee, some for washing dishes, and some for bathing, but the pipe and faucet don't care; they convey the water regardless. The host-to-host protocol was to perform essentially the same function in the infrastructure of the network.

Designing the host-to-host protocol wasn't the only job before the group. The NWG also had to write the network applications for specific tasks such as transferring files. As the talks grew more focused, it was decided that the first two applications should be for remote log-ins and file transfers.

In the spring of 1969, a few months before Kleinrock and the UCLA host team were expecting to receive the first IMP, a thick envelope arrived from Cambridge. The guys at UCLA had been anticipating it. Inside the package was BBN Report 1822, the newly written set of specifications for connecting host computers to the soon-to-be-delivered IMPs. The ARPA network finally seemed to be coming into place.

After months of guessing, the UCLA team now learned what it was expected to do to get its site ready and build its hardware interface. BBN Report 1822 also instructed the sites in creating a piece of software called a device driver—a collection of code and tables for controlling a peripheral device—to operate the host-to-IMP interface. And, finally, BBN's issuance of the specifications clarified the boundary between the IMP and the host. It was clear that BBN planned to include no special software in the IMP for performing host-to-host communication. That problem would be left, once and for all, to the host computer and, thus, to the NWG.

This meant a lot of summertime work for the students in Los Angeles. They thought they might be able to finish building the host-to-IMP interface in time. But writing the host-to-host protocol had already stalled Crocker, Cerf, and the entire Network Working Group for months. Rather than try to rush something out in time, they decided to tell every site to patch together its own makeshift protocols for the time being.

UCLA asked technicians at Scientific Data Systems, makers of the Sigma-7, to build the interface hardware for their host-to-IMP connection. The company's response was discouraging: It would take months and probably wouldn't be finished in time for the IMP's arrival. Moreover, the company wanted tens of thousands of

dollars for the job. So when a graduate student named Mike Wingfield asked for the job, he got it. And why not? Wingfield was a whiz
at hardware and had just finished building a complex graphics interface for another computer.

BBN's specification for the host-to-IMP interactions and connections was a splendid blueprint. A cookbook of sorts, written by Bob
Kahn in crystalline prose, the document was accompanied by detailed diagrams. Kahn's specification gave Wingfield the basic
requirements for mating the Sigma-7 to an IMP. Almost before
Wingfield knew it, the summer had flown by and the interface had
been built without a hitch.

One week before the IMP was scheduled to arrive on September 1, Wingfield had the hardware finished, debugged, and ready to
connect to the IMP. Crocker was so impressed he described it as a
"gorgeous" piece of work. But, trying to get the communications
software done, Crocker was running behind. He had a tendency to
procrastinate anyway, and the absence of the actual IMP had only
encouraged this tendency.

Now, like anyone trying to outsmart a deadline, Crocker looked
at the calendar and did a few calculations. He counted on having at
least one extra day, since September 1 was Labor Day. Moreover, he
had heard BBN was having some troubles with the IMP's timing
chain. Synchronizer bugs were horribly nasty. Their bug was his
good fortune, and with a little luck it might even buy him an extra
week or two, he thought. So he was more than mildly surprised
when Len Kleinrock told him that BBN was about to put the IMP on
an airplane due to arrive in Los Angeles on Saturday, August 30,
two days early.

In Cambridge, Frank Heart was preoccupied with the question of
how best to ship the IMP to UCLA. After debating for a couple of
days, Heart decreed that it should go by air, and that Ben Barker
should go with it. A commercial flight was out of the question. The
modified Honeywell 516—now officially BBN Interface Message
Processor Number One—was just too big for the cargo bay of a passenger plane. It had to go out by air freight. Had Heart been able to,

he would have put Barker straight into the cargo plane's hold with his wrist handcuffed to the IMP. Never mind that he had chosen the machine precisely because it was battle-hardened; the rigors of combat were nothing compared to the punishment airline freight handlers could dish out. "He wanted somebody to be there, yelling at the cargo people to make sure they weren't careless with it," Barker recalled. But Barker would have to travel separately on a commercial passenger flight. Truett Thach, a technician in BBN's Los Angeles office, would be told to meet the plane.

Once the IMP was crated, Barker took a red Magic Marker and in large letters wrote DO IT TO IT TRUETT on the side of the crate. It was loaded onto an early-morning flight out of Boston's Logan Airport, and Thach was there to meet it at LAX that afternoon. When he arrived, accompanied by a freight mover, he was relieved to watch the crate come off the plane but appalled when he noticed that Barker's message to him was upside down. "Somewhere along the way, the IMP had been inverted an odd number of times," he observed. Thach had the shippers right the box before loading it on their truck. Then he followed them to UCLA.

It was the Saturday before Labor Day and Thach noticed the streets were unusually quiet all the way through Westwood and onto the campus. Barker was already waiting on the loading dock at Boelter Hall with about a dozen other people—Kleinrock, Crocker, Postel, Wingfield, Vint and Sigrid Cerf, and a handful of curiosity seekers. The Cerfs had brought along some champagne. Immediately upon seeing the crate, someone raised a question as to whether the crate would fit into the elevator; the IMP was unpacked so it could be wedged in.

When the machine was removed from the crate, the welcoming party was surprised by its size. Though smaller than the Sigma-7, it was not a small device. It was roughly the size of a refrigerator, weighing more than nine hundred pounds, and was formidably encased in battleship-gray steel, exactly to military specifications. There were four steel eyebolts on top of the IMP for lifting it onto a ship by crane or helicopter. At UCLA the IMP was like a soldier in combat fatigues crashing a faculty party.

When the elevator reached the third floor, the freight movers wheeled the machine down the hall and around the corner to its new home in room 3400. The Sigma-7 hummed nearby, oblivious to the massive disturbance that was about to invade its privacy. "It was a little like seeing your parents invite to dinner someone you've never met," Crocker said. "You don't pay much attention until you discover they actually intend to marry you off to this stranger."

Thach and Barker spent a few minutes cabling the IMP and powering it. Instantly the machine's core memory knew just what to do: It picked up just where it had left off in Cambridge, running the diagnostics that the IMP Guys had written for it. Next, Mike Wingfield attached his interface. Since this was node number one, there wasn't a network *per se* on which to test it. But Barker could do shunting experiments between the Sigma-7 and the IMP as they had done many times at Moulton Street between machines to simulate network links. Within an hour the Sigma-7 and the IMP were passing data back and forth as if they had been doing so for years.

Barker was still not absolutely certain that the synchronizer problem had been solved. But he was confident enough to consider going home. That night, Barker called Heart. "We're done, it's all working," he said. "It's talking to Mike's [Wingfield] stuff. I'm thinking of getting a flight home in the morning."

Heart paused, and Barker sensed what might be coming. "Why don't you just hang out there a few days?" Heart responded. "Just to see if something goes wrong." Barker spent three days relaxing with Thach, touring Los Angeles, and waiting for the IMP to crash. It didn't.

❏ A Real Network

A month after the first IMP was installed at UCLA, IMP Number Two arrived at SRI, right on schedule on October 1, 1969. That same month, Bob Taylor left ARPA. He had long since removed himself from the details of the network project. As he explained it, in the 1960s, "ARPA" was a magic word. Taylor's office was often called upon to sort out problems that others couldn't. In 1967 and 1968,

Taylor had been sent repeatedly to Vietnam to help straighten out, among other things, the controversy over the Army's "body count" reports handled by the military information centers. The experience had left Taylor burned out. He took a post at the University of Utah.

Many milestones in the network experiment had been passed so far: Taylor's funding victory and successful wooing of Roberts; Roberts's network concept; BBN's construction and delivery of the first IMP. But the installation of IMP Number Two marked the most important achievement to date. At last the researchers could connect two disparate computers and get them talking to each other like a couple of old comrades.

Like the UCLA team earlier, SRI's group had a similar mad scramble getting ready for the arrival of the IMP. One crucial difference between the two sites was that whereas the UCLA guys disliked their Sigma-7, the SRI guys loved their host computer, an SDS 940. Like the Sigma-7, the 940 was built by Scientific Data Systems. But the Sigma-7 had been designed as a commercial processor, whereas the 940 was basically an academic device, a revolutionary time-sharing system first put together by a team of Berkeley researchers, later to be sold under the SDS nameplate. As a result, it was far more fun to program than the Sigma-7.

Bill Duvall, an SRI researcher, spent about a month writing a clever program for the 940 that essentially fooled it into thinking it was communicating not with another computer but with a "dumb" terminal. A dumb terminal can neither compute nor store information; it serves only to display the most recent set of information sent to it by the computer to which it's linked. Duvall's program was a very specific interim solution to the host-to-host communication problem. For weeks, the UCLA researchers had been preparing for their first log-in session by actually dialing into the SRI system long-distance using a modem and a teletype, to familiarize themselves with SRI's time-sharing system. With both IMPs now in place, and both hosts running, the moment to test the actual two–node ARPA network had finally arrived.

The first thing to do, of course, was to connect. Unlike most systems today, which prompt the user for a log-in name and password, the SRI system waited for a command before acknowledging a connection. "L-O-G-I-N" was one of those commands.

Fastened to the first IMPs like a barnacle was a small phonelike box, with a cord and headset. It shared the line with the IMPs and used a subchannel intended for voice conversations. The voice line was, like the data line, a dedicated link. A few days after the IMP was in place at SRI, Charley Kline, then an undergraduate at UCLA, picked up the telephone headset in L.A. and pressed a button that rang a bell on the IMP in Menlo Park. A researcher in Engelbart's group at SRI answered it. It was somehow more thrilling to Kline than dialing a regular telephone.

The quality of the connection was not very good, and both men were sitting in noisy computer rooms, which didn't help. So Kline fairly yelled into the mouthpiece: "I'm going to type an *L*!" Kline typed an *L*.

"Did you get the *L*?" he asked. "I got one-one-four," the SRI researcher replied; he was reading off the encoded information in octal, a code using numbers expressed in base 8. When Kline did the conversion, he saw it was indeed an *L* that had been transmitted. He typed an *O*.

"Did you get the *O*?" he asked.

"I got one-one-seven," came the reply. It was an *O*.

Kline typed a *G*.

"The computer just crashed," said the person at SRI. The failure came thanks to a clever bit of programming on Duvall's part. Once the SRI machine recognized the letters L-O-G, it completed the word. "I think that is where the bug was," Kline recalled. "When the SRI 940 system received the *G*, it tried to send back "G-I-N," and the terminal program wasn't ready to handle more than one character at a time."

Later that day they tried again. This time it worked flawlessly. Crocker, Cerf, and Postel went to Kleinrock's office to tell him about it so he could come see for himself. Back in the UCLA lab Kline logged on to the SRI machine and was able to execute commands on the 940's time-sharing system. The SRI computer in Menlo Park responded as if the Sigma-7 in L.A. was a bona fide dumb terminal.

There is no small irony in the fact that the first program used over the network was one that made the distant computer masquerade as a terminal. All that work to get two computers talking to each other and they ended up in the very same master-slave situation the network was supposed to eliminate. Then again, technological advances often begin with attempts to do something familiar. Researchers build trust in new technology by demonstrating that we can use it to do things we understand. Once they've done that, the next steps begin to unfold, as people start to think even further ahead. As people assimilate change, the next generation of ideas is already evolving.

A network now existed. The first ARPA network map looked like this:

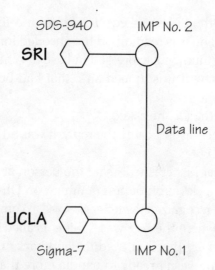

IMP Number Three was installed at UC Santa Barbara on November 1. For the Santa Barbara installation, Barker flew out to California again. By this time, Heart was more relaxed. There were few traces of the suspense that had attended the first trip. In fact, installing IMPs was beginning to seem routine.

Later that month, Larry Roberts decided to fly to California to inspect the network firsthand for the first time. Roberts didn't like to travel. When he did travel, he never left to catch his plane until the last minute. It drove his secretary crazy, but he missed only one plane that anyone could remember. That happened one afternoon when he was stopped for speeding on his way to Dulles Airport. Convinced that he hadn't been going too fast, Roberts decided to contest the ticket. He had been pulled over by the squad car near the point at which he had come onto the George Washington Parkway after a full stop, and his contention was that in that short distance he could not possibly have accelerated his Volkswagen Beetle to the speed alleged by the officer. Roberts went back to the scene and carefully measured off the distances. He gathered data on the engine output and weight of his VW bug, factored in Newton's law of inertia and made a few other calculations, and was prepared to go before a judge to make his case. It wasn't until friends convinced him he was unlikely to get a judge with a physics degree that he conceded the point and paid the fine instead of taking it to court.

Fortunately, there were no speeding tickets on this trip. Roberts and his program manager, Barry Wessler, flew to California without incident, and in Kleinrock's lab at Boelter Hall they watched the network in operation. This time, Kleinrock did the typing and in less than a minute he had logged on to the host computer at SRI. Roberts watched closely and left satisfied that the experiment was succeeding.

Fourth was Utah. By now it was December—prime ski season. There also happened to be a Network Working Group meeting scheduled at the site. Keen skiers all, the whole BBN team, even Frank Heart, went to Salt Lake City to plug in the IMP. (Ironically, Barker was the only one excluded from the Utah trip—a fact he would not let the others forget for many years.)

The layout of the growing number of communications links was becoming an interesting problem. For one thing, there was not a point-to-point link between every pair of sites. For reasons of economy, Roberts decided that no direct link was needed between UCLA and Utah, or between Santa Barbara and Utah, so that all traffic destined for Utah had to go through the IMP at SRI. That was fine as long as it was up and running. If it crashed, the network would divide and Utah would be cut off until SRI was brought back on-line. As it would turn out, the four-node network that Roberts designed was not a robust web of redundant connections.

Disruptions in the system also manifested themselves in less obvious ways. This was made clear very early, when the students at Santa Barbara began doing exactly what Heart had feared they might: fiddling with their new toy. And their attitude was, Why not? They had never had to worry about outside connections, and it didn't occur to them that something they did in their computer lab might have an effect elsewhere. "We merrily thought the IMP was ours to play with," recalled Roland Bryan, a Santa Barbara researcher. "We were testing it out, turning it on and off, resetting it, reloading it, and trying again." As a result, people who were taking network measurements, and who counted on the network path through Santa Barbara, would have their experiment thrown off. "Although we did not hurt the links between other sites, we were disrupting the data traffic analysis being carried on by BBN and UCLA," Bryan said. "We didn't think about the fact that every time we did that, someone out there would suffer."

By the end of 1969, the Network Working Group still hadn't come up with a host-to-host protocol. Under duress to show something to ARPA at a meeting with Roberts in December, the group presented a patched-together protocol—Telnet—that allowed for remote log-ins. Roberts was not pleased with the limited scope of the effort. Though Telnet was clearly useful and fundamental in that it let one terminal reach multiple remote computers, a remote log-in program by itself didn't solve the problem of letting two computers work together. Moreover, Telnet was a way to use the network, not a lower-level building block. Roberts sent them back to keep trying. After another year of meetings and several dozen RFCs, in the summer of 1970 the group reemerged with a preliminary version of a protocol for basic, unadorned host-to-host communications. When the "glitch-cleaning committee" finished its work a year later, the NWG at last produced a complete protocol. It was called the Network Control Protocol, or NCP.

In January 1970, Bob Kahn decided that with the first four nodes working, it was time to test his various scenarios in which the network could suffer congestive failure. The kind of lockup that most worried him, the scenario he had suggested to Crowther months earlier, would be caused by congestion at a destination IMP. He had speculated that storage buffers would become so full that the packets necessary for reassembling messages wouldn't be able to flow into a destination IMP, which itself would be filled with dismembered message parts awaiting completion.

To test that hypothesis and appease Kahn, Heart suggested that Kahn and Dave Walden fly out to Los Angeles to put the network through its paces. Kahn had several experiments in mind. He wanted to send all possible permutations of traffic from IMP to IMP, changing the size of the packets and the frequency at which they were sent, in an attempt to induce deadlock. Walden went along because he was the hands-on programmer who knew how to manipulate the code and make the packets do what Kahn wanted them to do. Walden took charge of reconfiguring the IMPs to send traffic in specific patterns. He could elongate or truncate the packets, send them out every three seconds or every half second. The IMP software, the algorithms, the whole design was in for a major wringing out.

The first thing Kahn set up was a test to demonstrate that his fear of a reassembly lockup was well founded. Just as Kahn had predicted, by besieging the IMPs with packets, within a few minutes he and Walden were able to force the network into catatonia. "I think we did it in the first twelve packets," Kahn recalled. "The whole thing came to a grinding halt."

Kahn was vindicated. He and Walden stayed on for a number of days, continuing the experiments. For Walden, who had spent so many months cooped up in Cambridge writing code in a quasi vacuum, it was gratifying to see the network in operation, even if his goal now was to break it. He was having a blast. "I was hacking for pay," Walden recalled. "I was driven to learn as much as I could as fast as I could."

Kahn and Walden established a routine. Every morning, they got up and ate breakfast at the Sambo's restaurant next to their hotel in Santa Monica. Walden used these mornings as an opportunity to indulge his native Californian's taste for fresh-squeezed orange juice, still a rarity back in Boston. Then they drove to the UCLA campus and spent all day and much of the evening testing the limits of the IMPs. Sometimes they took a dinner break; sometimes they didn't notice that dinnertime had come and gone. They took one night off to see the movie *M*A*S*H*, which had just been released.

Often they were joined by Cerf, and occasionally by Crocker and Postel as well. At one point in the testing, Cerf programmed the Sigma-7 to generate traffic to the IMP and used the host machine to gather data on the results. This was the first time he had worked closely with Kahn on a challenging project, cementing a professional link that would last for years to come.

By the end of the week, Kahn's notebook was filled with data proving his case. When he and Walden returned to Cambridge, they shared their findings with Crowther and Heart. Crowther didn't say much, but Kahn suspected that the battery of tests caused him to start thinking about the problem. "Somehow Crowther must have registered in the back of his mind that if two of us were coming back and reporting this problem, maybe there was an issue," Kahn said. Back in the lab, Crowther built a simulation of what Kahn and Walden had done in the field and discovered for himself that the network could indeed lock up. He reported his findings to a slightly crestfallen Heart, who instructed Crowther to work with Kahn on fixing the problem. "Bob got to feel a lot better, and Frank got to feel a little worse," Walden said of the entire episode. "Of course, Frank never thought the thing was perfect, but he always got discouraged when things didn't go right."

Heart had every reason to look past the few flaws that were beginning to show up in the nascent network. After all, problems with congestion control could be fixed. On a larger scale, the company had taken on a risky experiment, involving ideas and techniques never tested before. And it had worked. The hardware worked and the software worked. And the unique ways in which ARPA went about its business and its relationship with its contractor worked too.

Above all, the esoteric concept on which the entire enterprise turned—packet-switching—worked. The predictions of utter failure were dead wrong.

Hacking Away
and Hollering

The network was real, but with only four nodes clustered on the West Coast, its topology was simple, the experiment small. East Coast computing powerhouses like MIT and Lincoln Laboratory, where so much was happening, weren't connected. The very spot where Bob Taylor had daydreamed about a network, the ARPA terminal room in the Pentagon, wasn't yet wired in. Nor was BBN itself. All were awaiting new machines, which Honeywell promised were in production as Christmas came in 1969.

The past twelve months had been rough on ARPA. The agency's budget had reached a historic peak and gone into decline. The Vietnam War was consuming everything. In December 1969 ARPA had been pushed out of its headquarters in the Pentagon and forced to move into a leased office building in Arlington, Virginia. Director Stephen Lukasik called it "the American equivalent of being banished to Siberia." The ARPA that once rated a Pentagon-issue American flag behind the director's desk was quietly stripped of such trappings. Despite low morale, ARPA officials kept their flag

J. C. R. Licklider in 1965. A psycho-acoustician who saw computers as more than calculating machines, he was the first director of ARPA's Information Processing Techniques Office (IPTO). *(Photo courtesy of the MIT Museum)*

Bob Taylor in his office at Xerox PARC in the early 1970s. While at ARPA, Taylor had the idea for a new kind of computer network and got the funding to launch the experiment. Then he recruited Larry Roberts to build it. *(Photo courtesy of Bob Taylor)*

Larry Roberts, considered the father of the ARPANET. Roberts went to Washington from MIT's Lincoln Laboratory to design and direct the network project. *(Photo courtesy of Larry Roberts)*

▲ The Whirlwind Computer, an early "real-time" computer at Lincoln Lab that gave operators new levels of control and feedback. It was adorned with hot and cold spigots, a grenade, a shrunken head, and other "experimental features."
(*Photo courtesy of Frank Heart*)

◀ MIT's Lincoln Laboratory in 1956, a breeding ground for some of the most talented minds in the early years of computer science.
(*Photo reprinted with permission of MIT Lincoln Laboratory, Lexington, Massachusetts*)

BBN's time-sharing setup. Early time-sharing systems relied on ordinary phone lines to link terminals with computers in offices, schools, and research facilities. *(Photo courtesy of BBN)*

Paul Baran in the early 1960s. He worked for RAND and wrote the first papers on a distributed communications system. AT&T said his idea would never work. *(Photo courtesy of Paul Baran)*

The Interface Message Processor. Based on the ruggedized Honeywell 516 minicomputer, IMPs were the first specialized computers for handling data traffic to and from ARPANET sites. *(Photo courtesy of Frank Heart)*

◀ Donald Davies. A British computer pioneer, Davies independently invented "packet-switching" at the National Physical Laboratory, then learned of Paul Baran's similar work in the United States. *(Photo courtesy of National Physical Laboratory. Crown Copyright 1966. Reproduced by permission of the Controller, Her Majesty's Stationery Office.)*

Frank Heart, manager of BBN's ▶ project team, was an outspoken and pragmatic engineering leader. He insisted on measures to ensure high reliability in the Interface Message Processor. *(Photo courtesy of Frank Heart)*

◀ BBN performed remote diagnostics, monitored the status of the network twenty-four hours a day, traced line failures, and did troubleshooting, all from the Network Control Center. *(Photo courtesy of BBN)*

In the early 1970s, the Network Control Center and Heart's team moved down the street to BBN's new building on Fresh Pond Parkway in Cambridge. *(Photo courtesy of BBN)*

The IMP Guys *(left to right):* Truett Thach, Bill Bertell, Jim Geisman (crouching), Dave Walden (crouching), Frank Heart (standing), Ben Barker (behind Heart), Marty Thrope (next to Heart), Willy Crowther (crouching), Severo Ornstein, and Bob Kahn, 1969 (Bernie Cosell not pictured).
(Photo courtesy of Frank Heart)

Pioneers of computer networking reunited in Boston in 1994 at the twenty-fifth anniversary celebration of the ARPANET, hosted by Bolt Beranek and Newman. *Left to right, front row:* Bob Taylor (1), Vint Cerf (2), Frank Heart (3); *second row:* Larry Roberts (4), Len Kleinrock (5), Bob Kahn (6); *third row:* Wes Clark (7), Doug Engelbart (8), Barry Wessler (9); *fourth row:* Dave Walden (10), Severo Ornstein (11), Truett Thach (12), Roger Scantlebury (13), Charlie Herzfeld (14); *fifth row:* Ben Barker (15), Jon Postel (16), Steve Crocker (17); *last row:* Bill Naylor (18), Roland Bryan (19). (*Photo © by Clark Quin, Boston, Massachusetts*)

and displayed it in the new headquarters, hoping no one important would notice that it had only forty-eight stars.

Computing continued to be the one line in the agency's budget that didn't turn downward at the beginning of the 1970s. Larry Roberts was determined to win support from the top, and did. He was equally determined to get an additional dozen principal investigators across the country to buy into the idea of the ARPA network. He kept pushing. He kept steady pressure on new sites to prepare for the day when an IMP would arrive at their doors with a team from BBN to connect their host computers to the network. It wasn't a question of if but when, and Roberts always posed it that way.

In Cambridge, the activity on Moulton Street began taking on an air of production—"the factory," some called it. The majority of the effort moved into the large room at the back of the low building with the loading dock where deliveries from Honeywell were received; and there each new machine was set up to be debugged and tested before being shipped into the field. At the same time, Heart's team continued apace improving the design of the IMP, developing, testing, and tweaking the software and hardware. The fifth, sixth, and seventh 516 computers arrived from Honeywell in the first months of the year.

In late March the first cross-country circuit in the ARPA experimental network was installed. The new 50-kilobit line connected UCLA's computer center to BBN's Moulton Street site, which became the fifth node in the network. And it wasn't just a breakthrough symbolically from the West Coast to the East (frontier expansion in reverse); the transcontinental link was also an immediate boon to network maintenance and troubleshooting.

In the months before BBN had its own machine and was connected to the network, dealing with network problems in the four-node cluster out west was a job handled by people who were on site. More often than not, it meant someone in California or Utah would spend hours on the phone talking cross-country with someone at BBN, while the unfortunate soul who had volunteered to fix the problem shuttled between the telephone and the IMP to carry out the verbal instructions coming from Cambridge. During the early going, Heart's team spent a lot of time on the phone and kept a more or less continuous presence in the field, parentally guiding the startup of the infant network. At one point, Walden flew to Utah, Stanford, Santa Barbara, and UCLA to hand-deliver a new software release.

But when an IMP was installed at BBN in the early spring of 1970, suddenly there was a way to ship data and status reports electronically from the West Coast IMPs directly back to BBN. Heart's obsession with reliability had resulted in more than computers encased in heavy steel. His insistence on building robust computers—and on maintaining control over the computers he put in the field—had inspired the BBN team to invent a technology: remote maintenance and diagnostics. The BBN team had designed into the IMPs and the network the ability to control these machines from afar. This they used both for troubleshooting and sometimes actually fixing the message processors by remote control, as well as keeping a watchful eye on the IMPs twenty-four hours a day.

Horrified as he was at the prospect of graduate students messing with his IMPs, Heart had sought to build machines that could run largely unattended. He channeled his obsession into inventing this set of remarkably useful tools and system management techniques. Features for the remote control of the network had been built integrally throughout the IMP's hardware and software designs.

At BBN, on the hardware side, a Teletype terminal with logging capabilities was added to the BBN message processor, along with special warning lights and an audible alarm to indicate network failures. In designing the IMPs, BBN made it possible to loop the host and modem interfaces of the machine, so they could conduct "loopback" tests. The loopback test, which could be performed remotely, connected an IMP's output to its input, effectively isolating the IMP from the rest of the network. This generated test traffic through the interface and allowed BBN to check the returning traffic against the outgoing traffic generated by the IMP.

Loop tests were extremely important; they provided a way of isolating sources of trouble. By a process of elimination, looping one component or another, BBN could determine whether a problem lay with the phone lines, the modems, or an IMP itself. If test traffic completed the loop intact and error-free, then the problem was almost certainly in some exterior portion of a circuit—most likely in the phone company's lines or in the modems. And the loopback tests were conducted often enough that two of the IMP Guys, Ben Barker and Marty Thrope, became expert at whistling down the line at just the right frequency to imitate the signals that the telephone company used to test the lines.

From the PDP-1 computer room at Moulton Street where BBN's network monitoring equipment was installed, the IMP Guys could tell when a phone circuit anywhere in the network acted up. They could see, by the quality of messages and packets crossing a circuit, when the signal quality was being degraded, when the line was dropping bits, when it was introducing noise, or fading altogether. When the problem was in the phone lines or the modems, then the phone company would be called upon to fix it.

The engineers at BBN relished opportunities to spook the telephone company repair people with their ability to detect, and eventually predict, line trouble from afar. By examining the data, BBN could sometimes predict that a line was about to go down. The phone company's repair offices had never heard of such a thing and didn't take to it well. When BBN's loopback tests determined there was trouble on a line, say, between Menlo Park (Stanford) and Santa Barbara, one of Heart's engineers in Cambridge picked up the phone and called Pacific Bell. "You're having trouble with your line between Menlo Park and Santa Barbara," he'd say.

"Are you calling from Menlo Park or Santa Barbara?" the Pacific Bell technician would ask.

"I'm in Cambridge, Massachusetts."

"Yeah, right."

Eventually, when BBN's calls proved absolutely correct, the telephone company began sending repair teams out to fix whatever trouble BBN had spotted.

Due to the difficulty of remotely detecting component failures in the geographically dispersed system, the network software grew more complicated with time. Among the basic assumptions made by the IMP Guys was that the most effective way of detecting failures was through an active reporting mechanism. They designed their system so that each IMP periodically compiled a report on the status of its local environment—number of packets handled by the IMP, error rates in the links, and the like—and forwarded the report through the network to a centralized network operations center that BBN had set up in Cambridge. The center would then integrate the reports from all the IMPs and build a global picture of the most likely current state of the network.

In the first few months they called it the Network Control Center. But in fact it was really nothing more than a fairly small corner of an office at BBN. And the network monitoring was informal. The logging Teletype was connected via the network itself to all the IMPs in the field, and the terminal clacked away, taking reports from each IMP every fifteen minutes. Every once in a while, out of curiosity, someone at BBN would go in and look at the log that was running out of the machine, just to see what was going on with the network. No one had specific responsibility for scanning the log. No one checked, outside of business hours, so there were sometimes long periods in which line failures went undetected, especially at night. But if someone at a network site actually called in to say, "Hey there seems to be a problem," then one of the IMP Guys would immediately go look at the Teletype log and try to figure out what was going on.

Heart's team had designed the IMPs to run unattended as much as possible, bestowing on the IMPs the ability to restart by themselves after a power failure or crash. The "watchdog timer" was the crucial component that triggered self-corrective measures in the IMPs. The network as a whole "did a lot of looking in its navel all the time," said Heart, "sending back little messages telling us how it was feeling, and telling us what kind of things were happening where, so we could in fact initiate work" if necessary.

Not everything could be diagnosed or restored to working order remotely. There were times when people at BBN noticed that an

IMP had just stopped running, making it necessary to reload the software. First, BBN would have to alert someone at the other end of the line and ask him to reinsert a paper tape or flip a few switches and push the reset button. So from Moulton Street they would ring the "butler" bell, the telephone switchbox attached to every IMP, hoping to reach someone. Since the IMPs were installed in large, highly active computer centers, there was no telling who might answer. It was almost like calling a pay phone. You might get an expert or you might get a janitor or some undergraduate who didn't have a clue as to what was going on. Regardless of who picked up the phone, the technicians at BBN would try to talk that person through whatever fixes were necessary. Even people at the sites who actually knew a thing or two about the computers were asked, just the same, to follow BBN's strict instructions.

"I can remember spending an occasional half hour to an hour with the telephone glued to my ear," recalled Cerf, whose hearing impairment made him no friend of the telephone in the first place, "following instructions from someone at BBN saying, 'Push this button. Flip this thing. Key these things in,' to try to figure out what had gone wrong and get the thing running again." In a notebook, BBN kept a detailed list of sites, exact locations for each machine, and contacts at the various locations, which in at least one case included the building guard as a resource person of last resort.

As soon as IMP Number Five had been installed at BBN, the team stepped up its testing program to measure network performance and its limitations. Everyone was interested in knowing how well the network would perform under various scenarios, and whether it would stand up to extremely heavy loading. But the BBN engineers were not above becoming testy themselves when Len Kleinrock and others at UCLA's Network Measurement Center would deliberately try to crash the network. The tests ferreted out bugs and inspired corrections. Still, one thing was obvious: Under moderate traffic, the network was every bit as fast as BBN had predicted it would be. BBN reported to Roberts that the new network could be described as a "taut communications system." That is, messages entering the network showed no tendency to get lost.

"We observed that messages do not wander about the net, even at high traffic loads," the BBN team wrote in one of its periodic technical reports.

By summer 1970, machines number six, seven, eight, and nine had been extracted from Honeywell and were now operating at MIT, RAND, System Development Corp., and Harvard. AT&T had replaced the first cross-country link with a new 50-kilobit line linking BBN to RAND. A second cross-country link connected MIT and the University of Utah. The ARPA network was growing at a rate of about one node per month.

One day in 1970, a delivery truck from Honeywell pulled up to the Moulton Street loading dock and started backing up to unload another new 516 computer. Alerted to the truck's arrival, Severo Ornstein hurried out the door, made a quick inspection of the machine while it was still in the truck, and loudly waved the driver off. Heart, who had come out of his office to see what the commotion was about, stood watching, taken aback, as Ornstein told the driver to turn around and drive the machine back to Honeywell; he was rejecting the delivery.

Ornstein had had it with late deliveries and incomplete, faulty equipment. Sending the truck back caused an uproar at Honeywell, he said. But for once their attention was focused. BBN wasn't accepting another Honeywell 516 until some things were straightened out. The difficulties had been growing. To Heart's team, the relationship with Honeywell felt more like an arm-wrestling match than a partnership. "They kept shipping us machines that had the same old errors in them," Ornstein recalled. After the loading dock incident, he began going to Honeywell regularly to inspect each new machine before it was sent to BBN.

Before long, Honeywell had pulled its IMP-building team together and was producing acceptable machines. IMPs were delivered to Lincoln Laboratory and Stanford, and by the end of the year Carnegie-Mellon University and Case Western Reserve University were also connected to the network. By that point, hundreds of minor revisions had been written into the IMP software. Hardware had been tuned and retrofitted. The telephone company, doing its part, now had fourteen 50-kilobit links installed in the network. BBN's remote-diagnostic and network-management tools were also undergoing constant improvement. ARPA had extended BBN's contract to keep producing IMPs and run the control center, and it was all clicking.

The level of activity in the monitoring center at BBN increased. With the network's steady expansion, the diagnostic reports coming into BBN were starting to bloat and grow cumbersome. The IMP Guys were having difficulty staying on top of the data, scanning the printout of the Teletype log and locating trouble signs. They needed a housekeeper. So they decided to connect a spare machine, BBN's earliest prototype IMP, to the ARPA Network, where it would function as a host machine behind the regular BBN IMP. This new host machine would be used to help process the network status reports. The BBN programmers wrote new code to compile hourly summaries of the more frequent IMP status messages that were now stacking up at the rate of one per minute from each IMP. The code's operative assumption was that no news was bad news: If the Network Control Center failed to receive a status message from an IMP for three minutes, the network status readout would indicate that that IMP was dead. This and other improvements made it easier to detect important status changes in the network.

It was November 1970 when Alex McKenzie returned to BBN from a short leave of absence. He and his wife had spent six months camping in Europe. In the short time he was gone, the network project had advanced dramatically. Settled back into Cambridge now, McKenzie realized the importance to BBN of managing the network as if it were an electrical utility. That meant a reordering of certain fundamental assumptions would have to occur. The time had come to shift the network from an experimental to operational mode, he reasoned. And McKenzie began pressing that view on all of his colleagues. Organized and meticulous, McKenzie seemed the perfect candidate to take charge of BBN's Network Control Center, and Heart appointed him to the task.

Other cultural changes were in the wind around BBN. McKenzie's sensibility about the network project was in tune with a more business-oriented company overall. BBN itself was growing. Within a year or two after McKenzie made his push for running the network as a utility, BBN had bought the Superior Laundry at the busy end of Moulton Street and torn it down to make space for a new seven-story headquarters building. Eventually, the Network Control Center and the rest of Heart's division moved to the fifth floor of the new quarters. Architecturally, the style of the impressive new building subtly suggested a sleek fortress. Built at the height of the anti-war movement in the early 1970s, it reflected BBN's emerging corporate consciousness about antiestablishment threats to companies engaged in U.S. Defense Department contracting. The building had no windows on the ground floor, where a large computer center was located. It also had a basement parking garage designed so that the building itself stood back, surrounded by a substantial, waterless moat, allowing access to the front door only over a short footbridge.

On the fifth floor, the Network Control Center occupied one large room with large plate-glass windows looking north to the hills beyond Cambridge. Heart's team, numbering about thirty people, was spread out in modern offices and well-equipped labs throughout the floor. Heart's division had the only floor in the building with its own tiny kitchenette tucked off a central corridor, a special request by Heart, who intended to equip it with a restaurant-quality Italian espresso machine someday.

Dominating one large wall of the control center was a logical map of the network. Constructed of movable magnetic pieces on a metal background, the map was a wiring diagram showing all of the IMPs, host computers, and links—indicated by square, round, and triangular markers. Color codes and pointers indicated the status of each IMP, node, and link. At a glance, operators could tell which lines or IMPs were down and where traffic was being routed around the trouble spots. Besides critical information, an occasional joke or cartoon might be tacked up with a magnet as if the control map were one big refrigerator door.

One of the NCC's primary tasks was to issue software upgrades and reload IMP operating programs when necessary. The operators

used a cleverly cooperative scheme by which every IMP downloaded the software from a neighbor. Every Tuesday from 7:00 to
9:00 A.M., BBN had the network reserved for software distribution,
network testing, and maintenance. Within these two hours, operators in the NCC could have every IMP on the network running a
new software release. All new versions of the IMP operating codes
were eventually distributed this way. The process of electronic prop-
agation would begin in Cambridge as a new software program was
downloaded to a nearby site, which in turn would download the
software package to another neighbor, at the command of the operators.

The method also had restorative potential. If an IMP's operating
program were found to be destroyed, the IMP could send a request
for a program reload to a neighboring IMP. The responding IMP
would send back a copy of its own program.

❑ Fine Tuning

Other big changes had also taken place in the network's second
year. BBN and ARPA decided that the ruggedized Honeywell 516,
reflecting too much worry about reliability, was an expression of
overkill. It was expensive, too. The 516 cost roughly 20 percent more
than a newer version of the computer, the Honeywell 316, which
was not available in ruggedized form. Ben Barker, who remained in-
timately involved in maintaining and troubleshooting more than a
dozen IMPs now in the field, actually concluded that the cabinetry
on the ruggedized 516 was a source of *reduced* reliability, because it
hampered what should have been easily performed routine maintenance tasks.

Honeywell was under contract to handle routine maintenance.
But here, too, they were slow in coming around to BBN's emerging
view—McKenzie's utility model—of how a computer network
should operate. There were periods in which the downtime of the
IMPs averaged as much as 3 or 4 percent on a monthly basis. If an
electrical utility or the telephone system were down that much of

the time—a day out of every month—its performance would be considered abysmal. But Honeywell had to be coaxed into picturing where BBN and ARPA wanted to go with the network.

"I remember a great meeting when we went over the numbers with the guys at Honeywell," Barker recalled. "The Honeywell guys said, 'Wait a minute. You're saying these machines are down between half an hour and an hour a day? That's like, uh, three percent downtime. You mean, these machines are up ninety-seven percent of the time on a twenty-four-hour a day basis. How are you doing that!?'"

The 3 percent downtime that amazed Honeywell, was, in BBN's words, "prolonged hardware failure syndrome." The normal procedures of calling in and working with Honeywell field engineers had not cleared up several of these "persistent failures," reported BBN. They were particularly concerned about problems at several sites in the Washington, D.C., area.

Frustrated by recurring maintenance problems, Roberts threatened, ever so vaguely, to cancel BBN's contract. Barker eventually went to Heart and proposed letting him put together a BBN-directed maintenance team, with an adequate field staff for periodic maintenance and a roving expert "firefighter." But McKenzie adamantly opposed the idea, not because he was content with how things were going with Honeywell but because he feared that Barker would only make things worse. It was Barker's slovenly personal style to which McKenzie, a fastidious man, was reacting; he said Barker's office looked like a garbage truck had been backed up to it and emptied of its contents, and indeed it was a fitting image. Few would dispute that Barker's office was, on a good day, a total mess. Nor would they dispute the sharpness of his technical knowledge and skills. So in trade, Barker made a concerted effort to keep his office clean, and Heart handed him the job of building and directing a crack maintenance team.

Maintenance aside, Heart's own confidence about the network's intrinsic reliability had grown in the first year. He had seen the IMPs functioning successfully in the field. His team had met its initial tests. He was also a little more relaxed after a while about the trustworthiness of the on-site investigators and graduate students. As a consequence, the last ruggedized version of the Honeywell 516 rolled into Moulton Street around the end of 1970 and eventually was shipped as IMP Number Fifteen, headed for the Burroughs Corporation in Paoli, Pennsylvania. At about the same time, the University of Illinois at Urbana-Champaign received machine Number Twelve, which had been delayed.

By now, BBN had received ARPA's go-ahead to shift into another intensive engineering effort: designing a prototype 316-based IMP. Honeywell promised delivery of the machine in early 1971. The transition to the lighter 316 IMP was only part of a developing structural shift in the ARPA network.

For months, Heart's team and Roberts had been discussing the possibility of connecting many new users to the net without going through a host computer. It appeared they could make it possible to log onto the network, reach a distant host, and control remote resources through a simple terminal device—a Teletype or a CRT with a keyboard—directly connected to an IMP. The new scheme would eliminate the need for a host computer between every user and the IMP subnet. All you'd need to make it work would be a dumb terminal connected to an IMP. This would open up a lot of new access points.

If it could be worked out technically, then hundreds or even thousands more users might gain access to the network without physical proximity to a host computer. Then, the network would no longer be just an experiment for the hardcore computer scientists with mainframe accounts, but open to a whole panoply of more casual users—military officers, government bureaucrats, university administrators, students—who would be brought into the networking community. That would bring the world one step closer to realizing Licklider's vision of the computer as a facilitator of communication and human interaction.

But neither the original IMPs nor the new 316 IMPs could support more than four host interfaces. Neither machine could accommodate a terminal connection. To make the new concept workable, Heart's team would have to build a new interface that could handle dozens of terminal lines feeding into the IMP and the network. Sensing the value of going in this new direction, BBN launched an accelerated effort to design a terminal controller that could manage the traffic generated by a large number of terminal devices connected directly or through dial-up lines. The new device was called simply a Terminal IMP, or TIP.

Within six months, BBN and Honeywell completed the design and construction of two new prototype machines based on the 316. The first was a basic IMP, the other a TIP that included a multi-line controller capable of managing the signal traffic of up to sixty-three terminals at once. All terminal devices attached to a TIP would be addressable as if belonging to a single host on the network. In the backroom where BBN took deliveries, Heart's team had set up a small test cell to debug the incoming machines; the last of the 516 machines had been coming in the door at a fairly steady pace every four weeks, and at any time there might be two or three machines, sometimes more, linked together to test their performance and simulate network traffic. The first four deliverable TIPs were scheduled to arrive at BBN by late summer of 1971.

Everything seemed to be working according to design. BBN began exploring the gamut of terminal devices that might be connected to the network. The options ranged from graphics CRT displays, to slow and fast line printers, to alphanumerical displays, and Teletype-like terminals. The team was also considering how to link to card readers, magnetic tape recorders, and other peripheral devices.

Still more routing algorithm tests, throughput tests, tests of flow-control schemes, and remote diagnostics tests continued to occupy the BBN team on a daily basis, week in and week out, leading to steady improvements in their packet-switching technology.

The Network Control Center kept expanding with the network. Pressure to maintain the network grew. It became a steady part of ARPA's contract with the firm, and soon the center was staffed around the clock, seven days a week. At one point, the NCC upgraded some equipment and added an automatic phone dialer to the system. The auto-dialer was intended specifically to monitor the condition of modems spread throughout the network. There were dozens of modems handling data traffic to the TIPs. The BBN troubleshooters had the auto-dialer run a simple test: The dialer was programmed to call each modem once a day and listen for an answer. If a modem picked up and whistled back, its vital signs were considered normal. Any modem not answering or signaling back improperly turned up on a trouble report.

At one point, the NCC staff picked up on a particular modem that appeared to be malfunctioning whenever the auto-dialer ran its check. Someone suggested placing a call through the auto-dialer to the troublesome modem, while a technician listened in; perhaps he could diagnose the signal coming back. So he placed the call, listened for the modem to pick up, and heard an angry voice on the other end of the line. Before slamming down the receiver, the voice is reputed in countless retellings to have said, "Hey, Martha, it's that nut with the whistle again!"

Congestion control, one of the troublesome problems demonstrated by Kahn's experiments, had been attacked and improved. BBN had redesigned the scheme to reserve enough space in the IMP memory buffers for reassembly of incoming packets. A specific amount of reassembly space for each message would be reserved at a destination IMP before the message would be allowed to enter the network. The sending IMP would check, and if told that there was insufficient space available in the destination IMP's buffers, the RFNM (Request For Next Message) was delayed. The solution was not unlike the treatment many an airline passenger has experienced when a plane cannot take off because bad weather at the destination airport prevents the plane from landing. The passenger sits on the ground and waits for an opening at the destination. In simulations, the new scheme succeeded in preventing the insertion of more traffic into the network than the destination IMP could handle.

If development of the network was to proceed at a steady pace now, closer coordination would be necessary between BBN's effort to introduce the Terminal IMP and the Network Working Group's effort to develop protocols. So Heart's team decided to involve itself much more deeply in the work of the Network Working Group. By mid-1971, BBN had injected itself into the NWG's committees (McKenzie was the BBN representative) working on the host-to-host protocol, the file-transfer protocol, and the Telnet protocol.

Although it took more than a year to work out, the Telnet protocol was a relatively simple procedure. It was a minimal mechanism that permitted basic communication between two host machines. The first four nodes had connected four different machines, while other host sites offered a further melange of incompatible computers, ranging from the DEC PDP-10 to large IBMs, to Honeywell and Xerox machines. Telnet was conceived in order to overcome simple differences, such as establishing a connection and determining what kind of character set to use. It was TIPs and Telnet together that paved the way for rapid expansion of the network.

File transfers were the next challenge. For a couple of years, a half-dozen researchers had been trying to arrive at an acceptable file-transfer protocol, or FTP. The file-transfer protocol specified the formatting for data files traded over the network. Transferring files was something of a life force for the network. File transfers were the digital equivalent of breathing—data inhale, data exhale, ad infinitum. FTP made it possible to share files between machines. Moving files might seem simple, but the differences between machines made it anything but. FTP was the first application to permit two machines to cooperate as peers instead of treating one as a terminal to the other. Bringing this functionality to the network depended on the FTP working group coming up with a working final product.

The chairman of the group, Abhay Bhushan, an MIT graduate student and systems architect, was an expert in Multics, an ambitious and complex operating system. Bhushan had studied problems of multitasking in a single computer. The next step was to eventually transfer blocks of data in a multicomputer system like the ARPA network.

In the six months it spent working on the file-transfer protocol, the team usually met face to face in regular sessions of the Network Working Group. But it also frequently used real-time computer teleconferencing. Members of the team would all log on at once, from Palo Alto and Cambridge and L.A. and Salt Lake, and for an hour or two at a stretch trade comments back and forth. Conversing through keyboards and terminals was less spontaneous than speaking, but Bhushan believed it forced clarity into their thinking. It also had the advantage of creating a record of their work. In early July 1972, the final touches were put on FTP, and Jon Postel, now the editor and distributor of the Requests For Comments, released it as RFC 354.

❏ Showing It Off

The only real problem with this network now was load. That is, there wasn't much of it. At first, traffic was light because the protocols were late. Now, on a normal day the channels were virtually empty. In the fall of 1971, the network carried an average of just 675,000 packets per day, barely more than 2 percent of its capacity of 30 million packets a day. The UCLA Network Measurement Center continued generating test traffic to probe the weaknesses of all the network algorithms. But there wasn't enough natural traffic on the network to really push the limits of the routing and anticongestion schemes.

There were some interesting early uses. Programmers at SRI were using Utah's PDP-10 compiler in preparation for installing their own PDP-10, and they generated the most actual traffic. Jon Postel at UCLA was using the network to run SRI's oNLine System.

Bob Metcalfe, a Harvard graduate student working at MIT, and a friend, Danny Cohen, who taught at Harvard, did one of the more exciting early experiments over the network. Metcalfe and Cohen used Harvard's PDP-10 to simulate an aircraft carrier landing and then displayed the image on a graphics terminal at MIT. The graphics were processed at MIT, and the results (the view of the carrier's flight deck) were shipped back over the ARPA network to the PDP-1 at Harvard, which also displayed them. The experiment demonstrated that a program could be moved around the network at such high speed as to approximate real time. Metcalfe and others wrote up an RFC to announce the triumph and titled it "Historic Moments in Networking."

Others weren't so successful. There was an early attempt to devise something called a data-reconfiguration service; it was a failed attempt to write a programming language that would interpret incompatible files on different computers.

The ARPA network, however, was virtually unknown everywhere but in the inner sancta of the computer research community. And for only a small portion of the computer community, whose research interest was networking, was the ARPA network developing into a usable tool. To them it was a fantastic experiment—but you had to be involved in things like queueing theory or communications theory to appreciate it. If, on the other hand, your work was in artificial intelligence or robotics or computer graphics or almost anything else the community was investigating, the utility of this grand transcontinental packet-switching system had yet to be realized. No one had come up with a useful demonstration of resource-sharing; the protocols to make it work weren't even in place. The ARPA network was a growing web of links and nodes, and that was it—like a highway system without cars.

Yet ostensibly throughout the community there were rich resources to be shared. Carnegie-Mellon had a premier artificial-intelligence department and unique applications attendant to it. Stanford had an extraordinary robotics group. Theoretically, at just about every site some unique capability could be contributed to the network.

If the network was ever going to become anything more than a testbed for the artificial traffic generated by the Network Measurements and Network Control Centers, word of its potential had to spread. Larry Roberts knew it was time for a public demonstration. Roberts was on the program committee of the first International Conference on Computer Communication, to be held in Washington in October 1972. He circled the date and called Bob Kahn, who was still at BBN, and asked him to organize a demonstration of the ARPA network as the sole exhibit at the meeting. The conference was about a year away. Roberts asked Kahn to start planning immediately. Kahn had in fact already been planning to leave BBN and go work for Roberts at ARPA. But both men decided it would be a good idea for Kahn to stay at BBN for a while to plan the demonstration.

Kahn's first move was to recruit Al Vezza, of MIT's Project MAC, to assist him. Vezza always made a good impression. He was sociable and impeccably articulate; he had a keen scientific mind and first-rate administrative instincts. Between the two men there probably wasn't a key computer project in the U.S. research community they didn't know about or a key player they couldn't persuade to join them.

In mid-1971, Kahn and Vezza called a small group of about eight principal investigators from around the country to come to a meeting at MIT's Tech Square in Cambridge. They presented the idea of a highly accessible, engaging demonstration of the community's most interesting resources—accessible over the network. Vezza knew it would have to be a live, interactive demonstration if it was going to have any impact. Someone at the meeting argued strenuously in favor of a videotaped presentation, to ensure against computer crashes during the show. Vezza was incredulous and argued just as strenuously that anything but a hands-on, live demonstration using actual equipment and software would signal uncertainty and potential failure for the whole ARPA network experiment. It had to be done in real time, it had to be something that could be touched and controlled by anyone just sitting down at a terminal. It was a gamble. There still wasn't much operational experience with the Telnet and File Transfer protocols, which the participants would have to employ. And this increased the risk that the demonstration would fail. But if the demonstration succeeded, it would prove the network was not only real but useful.

For the next nine months, Kahn and Vezza traveled the country on Roberts's budget. "There were lots of blind alleys," Vezza recalled. They met with dozens of vendors in the computer industry, asking each to participate by bringing its own terminals to the Washington Hilton, where the meeting would be held and where a TIP would connect them to the ARPA network. Roberts was arranging for AT&T to bring two 50-kilobit lines into the hotel. The plan was to run demonstrations on as many machines as possible, connected to as many sites as possible. Organizers would invite conference-goers to come in, sit down, log on, and use the network's resources.

Dozens of meetings took place at the various network sites to design interesting scenarios. Teams of graduate students and principal investigators signed on. And almost as soon as they did, they began to feel a certain panic. To pull this off, they would have to step up their efforts to finalize the unfinished network tools and protocols. Roberts, ever so correctly, had foreseen the likelihood that scheduling a highly visible public demonstration for October 1972 would build pressure on the community to mobilize and make sure the network would be functioning flawlessly by that date. Kahn too acknowledged that the demonstration was "set up to force the utility of the network to occur to the end users."

In the fall of 1971, BBN had a prototype TIP running at 50 Moulton Street. Two other TIPs were operational elsewhere in the network, at this time consisting of just nineteen nodes. The TIPs, based on the Honeywell 316, were completely compatible with all of the older 516s. By early 1972 several additional 316 IMPs and TIPs had been installed and the central part of the network between the East and West Coasts was beginning to fill in. By August 1972, a third cross-country line had been added. In addition to IMPs scattered around the center of the country, there were now clusters of IMPs in four geographic areas: Boston, Washington, D.C., San Francisco, and Los Angeles. As the ICCC demonstration approached, there were twenty-nine nodes in what was now being widely referred to as the ARPANET or, more often, just the Net.

And people at the sites were madly scrambling. Dozens of major contributors from throughout the U.S. academic and research communities had become involved. Intensive efforts were under way to debug applications and get host computers up and running in time for the public demonstration. Every terminal manufacturer had been invited to prove its equipment could work with the ARPANET: They were lining up to show more than forty different computer terminals in the demonstration. Vezza negotiated with a local vendor in the Washington, D.C., area who agreed to lend a large section of antistatic, raised computer-room flooring for installation in the meeting room at the Hilton where the TIP and terminals would be located. AT&T promised it would come through with the data link. Getting such a circuit installed anywhere in less than six months was no small issue, and it certainly wasn't a small matter for AT&T to have that line into the Hilton as the ICCC approached.

Several days before the meeting, the networking equipment and people began arriving at the hotel. Kahn and Vezza had drawn up a floor plan. The TIP was located up on a section of raised flooring in the center of the large meeting room. Around the perimeter of the room were to be the dozens of terminals, virtually no two alike. It would take a couple of days for all the gear to be moved into place, connected, powered up, and checked out. In a matter of hours, the room was a teeming tangle of wire and people speaking technical jabber. Technicians were stretching cables everywhere. Members of Heart's team were all around, tools in hand, deeply engaged in helping the various terminal manufacturers modify the connector cables on each of the multitude of terminal devices, so that each could be connected to the TIP. Hours were spent stripping wires, rewiring the connectors, reconnecting, testing, and debugging.

Many of the participants were working at a fever pitch. Many had packed up while still finishing their projects and came to Washington to add the final touches. It was the first time the whole community showed up in one place at one time. "If somebody had dropped a bomb on the Washington Hilton, it would have destroyed almost all of the networking community in the U.S. at that point," observed Kahn. Not to mention the international community, for even Donald Davies, father of the term "packet-switching," had come over from England to see how this would all work out. "It was just an amazing experience," said Vint Cerf. "Hacking away and hollering and screaming and saying, 'No, no . . . you got this one wrong.' Getting all the details right."

At the end of Saturday (the conference opened on Monday), the BBN TIP was like a king on a throne of wire running to all corners of the room. AT&T had done its job and turned up at the right moment with the right line. Sunday was another frantic day of preparation, but now the TIP was in action, so people were starting to run programs and do their final checkouts. Many didn't finish until late Sunday afternoon, just before a preview demonstration was scheduled for a group of VIPs—a Washington coterie of congressmen, Pentagon officials, and others. At about six o'clock in the evening, minutes before the doors were to open, Vezza was standing near the TIP when Metcalfe said, with no faint urgency in his voice, "We're losing packets!"

Vezza shot a look to McKenzie, who was standing right there: "Alex, what changed?"

McKenzie reached for the hot line to Cambridge and shouted into the phone, "Get it out! Get it out!"

The Network Control Center had been watching and monitoring a slightly glitchy line in the network for the past few days. They thought they'd solved the problem that afternoon and had added the circuit back into the network. Within thirty seconds of McKenzie's call, the link was removed by the operators at the NCC and packets were flowing smoothly at the TIP again.

BBN's remote-management technology had never had a finer moment.

Later that evening, Jon Postel was in the exhibition room sitting at a keyboard, logged on to the host at UCLA. His team had designed a demonstration in which someone in Washington could pull up a file in Boston via the host computer in Los Angeles. The idea was to then print out the file in the exhibition room at the Hilton. When Postel shipped the file to the printer sitting beside him, nothing happened. He looked around the room. There were a lot of other demonstrations, one of which was a small robotic turtle built at MIT. The turtle was built to demonstrate how a computer program could be written to direct the motion of a machine. Kids could write their own programs in the LOGO language that said, "go left, go right, go forward, back up, move sideways," and when the program was run, the turtle would do that. At the moment, however, the turtle was jumping up and down, twitching and jerking crazily. Instead of sending Postel's file to the printer, the system had accidentally sent it to the turtle port, and the robot dutifully offered its interpretation of what it took to be motion commands.

As an enthusiastic graduate student, Bob Metcalfe had undertaken the task of writing a booklet to accompany the demonstrations. It described nineteen scenarios for using the ARPANET, listed resources at various sites, and showed how to log on to a remote host, how to gain access to one of the applications, and how to control a program or engage in some kind of interactive communication over the network. There were several chess games, an interactive quiz about the geography of South America, a way of reading the Associated Press news wire over the network, and many other games, tools, and demonstrations. One of the more practical applications simulated an air traffic control scenario in which responsibility for monitoring an airplane flight is automatically handed off from one computer to another, representing different air traffic control centers, as the plane crosses geographic boundaries. Metcalfe's scenarios book was designed to walk participants, most of whom knew little about the ARPANET, through each demonstration step by step.

On Monday morning, the ARPANET computer scientists eagerly awaited their public. When curious conference-goers approached, the network guys, like Jehovah's Witnesses handing out copies of *The Watchtower,* thrust Metcalfe's scenarios book into their hands and ushered them into the room. Although it was possible to follow the instructions, to all but the initiated the scenarios book was fairly incomprehensible, and it was easy to foul up the system. One man sat down in front of a terminal and typed in an instruction from the book. For some reason or other, the host he was trying to reach wasn't functioning, or he miscued the thing. The message came back: "HOST DEAD."

"Oh, my God. I've killed it!" he exclaimed. He wouldn't touch a terminal after that.

Other funny things happened. Two people had logged in to the University of Utah. One saw that somebody else he knew but had never met was logged in. They were in talk mode, and so he typed,

"Where are you?" The other replied, "Well, I'm in Washington," "Where in Washington?" "At the Hilton." "Well, I'm at the Hilton, too." The two turned out to be only a few feet from each other.

Some things weren't so funny. As the author of the scenarios book, Metcalfe was chosen to take ten AT&T executives on a virtual tour of the ARPANET. It was an odd sight: Young Metcalfe, with his big red beard, showing ten AT&T pinstriped businessmen around the network. In the middle of the demonstration the computers crashed. It was the first and only time the computers went down. The phone company executives' first reaction was to laugh.

"I looked up in pain," said Metcalfe, "and I caught them smiling, delighted that packet-switching was flaky. This I will never forget. It confirmed for them that circuit-switching technology was here to stay, and this packet-switching stuff was an unreliable toy that would never have much impact in the commercial world, and now they could go home to New Jersey. It was clear to me they were tangled up in the past."

Had they looked beyond the luckless Metcalfe and the failed demo, the AT&T executives would have seen the exuberance in other corners of the room. Not only did packet-switching work but it made wondrous things possible.

Some of the most ingenious demonstrations involved English-language conversational programs. These were elaborate programs constructed to engage a user in a verbal dialogue with a machine. There were four programs on display, two of which offered an especially fascinating glimpse into interactive computing.

PARRY, the first of these virtual conversationalists, mimicked the belief system of a paranoid psychotic. He held up his end of a conversation by offering canned responses to statements he thought he understood. Otherwise, his response was noncommittal. PARRY was the brainchild of Dr. Kenneth Colby at Stanford University.

The Doctor was another conversational program, based on ELIZA, a natural-language program written by MIT's Joseph Weizenbaum. The Doctor, which mimicked the behavior of a psychiatrist, was rather more diffident than PARRY. The Doctor accepted statements, then tried to produce new sentences based on the words and syntax of the other conversant. While the resulting conversation was altogether banal, users were often struck by how lifelike the quality of their conversations with the Doctor actually seemed. "People would sit down and interact with this thing," observed Cerf. "And sometimes they'd ask other people to leave the room, because they thought they were having a private conversation."

Cerf and others had toyed with the idea of setting up Colby's paranoid to have a "session" with the psychiatrist. Just a few weeks before the ICCC demonstration, PARRY indeed met the Doctor for an unusual conversation over the ARPANET, in an experiment orchestrated at UCLA. It perhaps marked the origin, in the truest sense, of all computer chat. There was no human intervention in the dialogue. PARRY was running at Stanford's artificial-intelligence lab, the Doctor was running on a machine at BBN, and at UCLA their input and output were cross-connected through the ARPANET, while the operators sat back and watched.

"Good evening," said the Doctor. "Tell me your problems. Please terminate input with a period or a question mark."
"People get on my nerves sometimes," PARRY replied.

"I am not sure I understand you."
"You should pay more attention."
"Suppose you should pay more attention."
"You're entitled to your own opinion."
"What makes you think I am entitled to my own opinion?"
"It bothers me just to be around people in general."
"Please go on."
"I went to the track at Bay Meadows a while back."
"Why do you say that just now?"
"There's a lot of crooked gambling going on there."
"Please go on."
"I gamble on horses."
"What does that suggest to you?"
"I went to the races."

"What else would you like to discuss?"

"Gambling has been nothing but trouble for me."

"Why do you say that just now?"

"I've had experience with crooks gambling at the track."

"I am not sure I understand you fully."

"Do you know anything about bookies?"

"What makes you think I know anything about bookies?"

"A bookie didn't pay me off once."

"What does that suggest to you?"

"I beat up the bookie who did not pay off, and I thought he might use his friends in the underworld to get even with me."

"Who are you really talking about?"

"Have you ever really thought about the MAFIA?"

"Suppose you ever really thought about the MAFIA."

"Let's talk about something else."

"I am not sure I understand you fully."

"You keep asking me the same things, why not change the topic?"

"Why are such questions on your mind?"

"I thought I told you, people get on my nerves."

"Your nerves?"

"I would rather not discuss that anymore."

"Would you like to discuss your nerves?"

"I guess so."

"I am not sure I understand you fully."

"You harp on the same questions too much."

"What does that similarity suggest to you?"

"I don't get you."

"Do you wish that you didn't get I?"

"It's about time you showed some interest in my feelings."

"Oh? I showed some interest in your feelings?"

"I will help you if I trust you."

"Do you wish that you trust I?"

"Maybe yes, maybe no."

"You don't seem quite certain."

"In my opinion you have a one-track mind."

"What makes you think I have a one-track mind?"

"I used to go to the track every week."
"What else would you like to discuss?
"That's something I don't want to go into."
"Why do you say that just now?"
"It's none of your business."
"Why are you concerned over my business?"
"I don't confide in strangers."
"Don't you really confide in strangers?"
"Let's change the subject."
"I'm not sure I understand you fully."
"What's wrong with you that you keep on bugging me about this?"
"Please go on."
"You are a real nag."
"Does it please you to believe I am a real nag?"
"I have had enough of this."
"What does that suggest to you?"
"Goodbye."

"It's been my pleasure.
"Fear = 4.2223001
"Anger = 10
"Mistrust = 12.650703
"That's $399.29 please."

Hundreds of people participated in the ICCC demonstration over its two and a half days. Executives, engineers, and technicians from the telecommunications and computer industries, a good number of them, entered the room skeptical of the ARPANET and packet-switching. Many left believing the technology might be real after all. For the most part, the forty-odd terminals worked, the resources were engaging, the TIP ran spectacularly, and the ARPANET came alive. "It was almost like the rail industry disbelieving that airplanes could really fly until they actually saw one in flight," said Kahn.

The ICCC demonstration did more to establish the viability of packet-switching than anything else before it. As a result, the ARPANET community gained a much larger sense of itself, its technology, and the resources at its disposal. For computer makers, there was the re-alization that a market might emerge. "The sense in that room was not one of fear, or concern," said Len Kleinrock. "It was excitement. I mean, here we could show it off, we knew it would work. Even if it fumbled, these things were fixable. It was a wonderfully exciting ex-perience." Roberts had shown steady confidence. He had gotten what he wanted, a more solidified effort, the foundation for a com-munity, something he could build on. The crash efforts and panic that preceded the event had paid off. And on this day, even BBN and Honeywell were getting along.

Bob Kahn had just devoted a year of his life to demonstrating that resource-sharing over a network could really work. But at some point in the course of the event, he turned to a colleague and re-marked, "You know, everyone really uses this thing for electronic mail."

E-Mail

One September evening in 1973, Len Kleinrock was unpacking his bags when he discovered that he'd forgotten his razor. He'd just returned home to Los Angeles from Brighton, England, where he'd left the razor in a Sussex University dormitory bathroom. An ordinary electric razor, it was no big loss. "But it was mine," he recalled, "and I wanted it back."

Kleinrock had just come from a conference on computing and communications. The conference had brought together scientists from several countries, some of whom had begun developing digital networks under the auspices of their own governments. But the U.S. Government's ARPANET was by far the largest and most sophisticated network experiment in the world, and the international community welcomed the chance to see the project demonstrated. The organizers of the conference had also decided to use the occasion to test the transmission of data packets via satellite. For the conference, a temporary link from the United States had been patched into Brighton. Packets traveled over a satellite link from Virginia to an earth station in Cornwall, at Goonhilly Downs near

Land's End, and from there a dedicated phone line was installed to connect with the University of London. From London a final hop was patched in to Brighton, where people had a chance to use the ARPANET just as if they were sitting in an office in Cambridge, Massachusetts, or Menlo Park, California.

Kleinrock had returned to the States a day early, so when he realized he had forgotten his razor, he thought he might find someone still at the conference to retrieve it. There was a handy bit of software on the network called the resource-sharing executive, or RSEXEC. If you typed in "where so-and-so," RSEXEC looked for so-and-so by searching the "who" list—a roster of everyone logged on—at each site. You could locate a person on the network this way if he happened to be logged on at that moment. "I asked myself what maniac would be logged in at three A.M.?" Kleinrock remembered. He went to his terminal and typed, "where roberts."

A few minutes later, Kleinrock's terminal displayed the answer. Larry Roberts was indeed still in Brighton, awake, and at the moment connected to a BBN host in Cambridge. A Teletype number for Roberts also appeared on Kleinrock's screen, enough information for him to tap his colleague on the shoulder electronically from L.A.

"All I had to do was make a Teletype connection to BBN," said Kleinrock. He linked to Roberts using TALK, which allowed them to converse by typing onto one half of a split screen while reading from the other. The two friends traded greetings. "I asked if he could retrieve the razor. He said, 'Sure, no problem.'" The next day the razor was returned by Danny Cohen, a mutual friend who had been at the conference and had come back to L.A.

There weren't any formal rules restricting use of the ARPANET by those with authorized access. Kleinrock's razor retrieval caper wasn't the first time anyone had pushed past official parameters in using the network. People were sending more and more personal messages. Rumor had it that even a dope deal or two had been made over some of the IMPs in Northern California. Still, tapping into the ARPANET to fetch a shaver across international lines was a bit like being a stowaway on an aircraft carrier. The ARPANET was an official federal research facility, after all, and not something to be toyed with. Kleinrock had the feeling that the stunt he'd pulled was slightly out of bounds. "It was a thrill. I felt I was stretching the Net."

The ARPANET was not intended as a message system. In the minds of its inventors, the network was intended for resource-sharing, period. That very little of its capacity was actually ever used for resource-sharing was a fact soon submersed in the tide of electronic mail. Between 1972 and the early 1980s, e-mail, or network mail as it was referred to, was discovered by thousands of early users. The decade gave rise to many of the enduring features of modern digital culture: Flames, emoticons, the @ sign, debates on free speech and privacy, and a sleepless search for technical improvements and agreements about the technical underpinnings of it all. At first, e-mail was difficult to use, but by the end of the 1970s the big problems had been licked. The big rise in message traffic was to become the largest early force in the network's growth and development. E-mail was to the ARPANET what the Louisiana Purchase was to the young United States. Things only got better as the network grew and technology converged with the torrential human tendency to talk.

Electronic mail would become the long-playing record of cyberspace. Just as the LP was invented for connoisseurs and audiophiles but spawned an entire industry, electronic mail grew first among the elite community of computer scientists on the ARPANET, then later bloomed like plankton across the Internet. It was about the time Kleinrock was reaching for his razor that taboos were tumbling and the tone of message traffic on the Net started loosening up.

As cultural artifact, electronic mail belongs in a category somewhere between found art and lucky accidents. The ARPANET's creators didn't have a grand vision for the invention of an earth-circling message-handling system. But once the first couple of dozen nodes were installed, early users turned the system of linked computers into a personal as well as a professional communications tool. Using the ARPANET as a sophisticated mail system was simply a good hack. In those days hacking had nothing to do with malicious or destructive behavior; a good hack was a creative or inspired bit of programming. The best hackers were professionals. Meddlesome and malicious network users, of which there were virtually none at the outset, were first referred to as "network randoms" or "net randoms" or just plain "randoms." It would be another decade before hacking was given a bad name.

In the decade before the ARPANET, computer scientists had devised ways of exchanging electronic messages within a time-sharing system. Researchers on the same time-sharing system each had a designated file, like an in-box, in the central machine. Colleagues could address short electronic messages to someone else's box, where only the recipient could read them. Messages could be dropped and picked up at any time. It was convenient, given the odd hours people kept. People within a single lab sent parades of one-liners back and forth, as well as longer memoranda and drafts of papers.

The first of these programs, called MAILBOX, was installed in the early 1960s on the Compatible Time-Sharing System at MIT. Similar mailboxes became a standard feature of almost every time-sharing system built thereafter. In places where people were spread out, programmers working hundreds of yards apart could exchange messages without having to get up from their desks. But often, exchanging messages in a single machine, or domain, became a superfluous exercise—like two people using walkie-talkies to converse in a one-room cabin. People still got up from their desks and walked down the hall to talk. Said one user, "I'll never forget a colleague who, while working in the next office, would constantly send me e-mail and it never failed to surprise him when I got up and walked next door to respond to him."

By virtue of its geographic reach, the ARPA network changed all that, turning electronic mail from an interesting toy into a useful tool. The tendencies of the ARPANET community ran strongly democratic, with something of an anarchic streak. The ARPANET's earliest users were constantly generating a steady stream of new ideas, tinkering with old ones, pushing, pulling, or prodding their network to do this or that, spawning an atmosphere of creative chaos. The art of computer programming gave them room for endless riffs, and variations on any theme. One of the main themes became electronic mail.

The first electronic-mail delivery engaging two machines was done one day in 1972 by a quiet engineer, Ray Tomlinson at BBN. Sometime earlier, Tomlinson had written a mail program for Tenex, the BBN-grown operating system that, by now, was running on most of the ARPANET's PDP-10 machines. The mail program was written in two parts: To send messages, you'd use a program called SNDMSG; to receive mail, you'd use the other part called READMAIL. He hadn't actually intended for the program to be used on the ARPANET. Like other mailbox programs of the day, it was created for time-sharing systems and designed only to handle mail locally, within individual PDP-10s, not across them.

But Tomlinson, an inveterate experimenter, decided to take advantage of having two PDP-10 computers set up in the Cambridge office; in fact, they were the same machines BBN was using to connect to the ARPANET. Weeks earlier, Tomlinson had written an experimental file-transfer protocol called CPYNET. Now he modified the program so that it could carry a mail message from one machine and drop it into a file on another. When he tried it, and sent mail from one PDP-10 to the other, the little hack worked, and even though his mail hadn't actually gone out onto the open network, it had crossed an important historical divide. Tomlinson's CPYNET hack was a breakthrough; now there was nothing holding e-mail back from crossing the wider Net. Although in technical terms Tomlinson's program was trivial, culturally it was revolutionary. "SENDMSG opened the door," said Dave Crocker, the younger brother of Steve Crocker and an e-mail pioneer. "It created the first interconnectivity, then everyone took it from there."

But how to get this invention running out on the network? The answer lay in the file-transfer protocol. In July 1972, one evening at Tech Square at MIT, as Abhay Bhushan was writing the final specifications for the ARPANET file-transfer protocol, someone suggested piggybacking Tomlinson's e-mail programs onto the end product. Why not? If electronic messages could ride on

CPYNET, they might just as well ride on the file-transfer protocol. Bhushan and others worked out some modifications. In August, when Jon Postel received an RFC outlining the e-mail feature, he thought to himself, "Now there's a nice hack." The ARPANET's first electronic mail-handling twins, named MAIL and MLFL, came to life.

Tomlinson became well known for SNDMSG and CPYNET. But he became better known for a brilliant (he called it obvious) decision he made while writing those programs. He needed a way to separate, in the e-mail address, the name of the user from the machine the user was on. How should that be denoted? He wanted a character that would not, under any conceivable circumstances, be found in the user's name. He looked down at the keyboard he was using, a Model 33 Teletype, which almost everyone else on the Net used, too. In addition to the letters and numerals there were about a dozen punctuation marks. "I got there first, so I got to choose any punctuation I wanted," Tomlinson said. "I chose the @ sign." The character also had the advantage of meaning "at" the designated institution. He had no idea he was creating an icon for the wired world.

Stephen Lukasik, a physicist who directed ARPA from 1971 to 1975, was among the first users and great advocates of network mail. His favorite part of ARPA, in fact, was Larry Roberts's Information Processing Techniques Office. Lukasik had begun his career in the 1950s working for BBN and MIT as a graduate student. He joined ARPA in 1966 to work on nuclear test detection, and he had watched the creation of the ARPANET. During his rise to the directorship, Lukasik had fought especially hard to protect the computer science community's funding. ARPA was under pressure to do defense-related work. He saw computing as a more fundamental but important technology and defended it as such before Congress.

But sometimes things went a bit too far. As director, he walked around a lot, dropping in on people in their offices. One day he was in the IPT Office when he noticed a folder lying on top of a file cabinet. Its orange cover ("not my favorite color") caught his eye. The folder was labeled "Computer-Assisted Choreography." It contained progress reports on a project that used dancers' movements to map human motions by computer. "I went ballistic," he said. He could picture the headline: PENTAGON FUNDS DANCE RESEARCH.

Lukasik told his staff to tell the scientists, if "you're going to do something that looks like it's forty thousand miles away from defense, please leave our name off of it." He understood the research and didn't care if they did it, but didn't want them bragging about it. Steve Crocker, now an IPTO program manager working under Roberts, was glad he wasn't the one overseeing the dance automation project. But he did have a small problem of his own with researchers he was funding at Stanford's Artificial Intelligence Lab. "On random unannounced visits, they would show me proudly the lab's quadraphonic simulation of a buzzing fly—which ate up twenty-five percent of the computing resources there," Crocker said.

One of the first things Lukasik had done upon being named head of the agency was get Roberts to give him an e-mail address and access to the ARPANET. It was unusual for someone who wasn't a computer scientist to be interested in using network mail, and more unusual for anyone to grow as reliant on it as Lukasik did.

A frequent flier, Lukasik seldom boarded a plane without lugging aboard his thirty-pound "portable" Texas Instruments terminal with an acoustic coupler, so he could dial in and check his messages from the road. "I really used it to manage ARPA," Lukasik recalled. "I would be at a meeting, and every hour I would dial up my mail. I encouraged everybody in sight to use it." He pushed it on all his office directors and they pushed it on others. ARPA managers noticed that e-mail was the easiest way to communicate with the boss, and the fastest way to get his quick approval on things.

Lukasik and Roberts had an excellent relationship, partly because they were both analytical thinkers, and partly because Roberts was always quick to answer any questions Lukasik had about his projects. "If we had a meeting on Tuesday afternoon and I sent

Larry away with some questions to answer, he'd come back the next day for another meeting with more than just answers. He'd have trends and projections and comparisons."

Then Lukasik discovered what was happening, and the utility of e-mail became clearer than ever. Typically, Roberts would leave Lukasik's office, return to his own office and fire off messages to the experts on the topic at hand, who in turn bounced the questions off their graduate students. Twenty-four hours and a flurry of e-mail later, the problem had usually been solved several times over. "The way Larry worked was the quintessential argument in favor of a computer network," Lukasik said. During Lukasik's tenure, Roberts's annual budget nearly doubled, from $27 million to $44 million.

In 1973, Lukasik commissioned an ARPA study that found that three quarters of all traffic on the ARPANET was e-mail. By then, sending e-mail was a simple and nearly trouble-free process. However, trying to read or respond to it was something else: functional but not at all easy. Text just poured onto the screen or out of the printer, and nothing separated the messages. To get to the last one, you had to run through them all again. For many users, the only way to read mail was to turn on the Teletype and print out streams of text. Composing messages was truly an annoyance, because tools for text editing were primitive. And there was no "reply" function for e-mail; to respond, you had to start a new message from scratch.

Lukasik, who hated throwing anything away, was beginning to get frustrated by the volume of e-mail piling up in his in-box. He went to Roberts. "I said, 'Larry, this e-mail is great, but it's a mess!'" Lukasik recalled. "In typical Larry fashion, he came in the next day, and said, 'Steve, I wrote some code for you that may help.' And he showed me how to get a menu of messages, or file them, or delete them." Roberts had just written the first mail manager software.

Roberts called his program RD, for "read." Everyone on the ARPANET loved it, and almost everyone came up with variations to RD—a tweak here and a pinch there. A cascade of new mail-handling programs based on the Tenex operating system flowed into the network: NRD, WRD, BANANARD ("banana" was programmer's slang for "cool" or "hip"), HG, MAILSYS, XMAIL . . . and they kept coming. Pretty soon, the network's main operators were beginning to sweat. They were like jugglers who had thrown too much up in the air. They needed more uniformity in these programs. Wasn't anyone paying attention to the standards?

For reasons unrelated to e-mail but apparent to all who used the network daily, occasionally the network simply went berserk. Or, as one person said, it became "wrinkled." Trouble in one machine could trip a systemwide domino effect. Case in point: the Christmas Day, 1973, lockup. The Harvard IMP developed a hardware fault that had the bizarre effect of reading out all zeros into the routing tables, thereby informing other IMPs across the country that Harvard had just become the shortest route—zero hops—to any destination on the ARPANET. The rush of packets toward Harvard was breathtaking.

Users would notice a crash like that. Everything came to a halt. "Harvard became a black hole," said John McQuillan, then a Harvard graduate student. "All the traffic went to Harvard, and like a black hole, no information came out." McQuillan had been introduced to network operations by Ben Barker and had helped connect Harvard's PDP-1. While finishing his doctorate, McQuillan was hired to improve the software for BBN's Network Control Center. On Christmas Day, as the zeros from Harvard were sent to routing tables across the country, even the control traffic used by BBN to diagnose and debug the system got sucked into the "gravitational orbit" of Harvard's faulty IMP. The BBN operators had to "cauterize"—cut off that part of—the network, debug it, and then bring it back up.

Like a utility company, BBN was rapidly developing the means to deal with such occurrences. And there were relatively few networkwide crashes, none lasting very long.

On Tuesdays, the days that BBN had the ARPANET reserved for housekeeping chores, McQuillan got in by six A.M. Crowther and Walden had stopped programming the IMPs. Between 1972 and

1974 McQuillan picked up primary responsibility for revising the codes and designing the release procedures. He led the team that wrote all the new IMP software and made the releases into the network. He built "fairly elaborate" test networks in the BBN laboratory, where he simulated failure scenarios, forcing the test network to fail so he could learn to make the ARPANET more fail-safe.

"You just know that the computers are going to encounter lightning storms, and power failures, and software bugs, and hardware bugs, and the janitor's going to trip over the power cord, and just anything you can think of could happen," said McQuillan. But of all the potential problems, trouble in the routing algorithm was deemed the worst.

For all of its elegance and simplicity, the original routing algorithm written by Crowther was flawed, for although it was lean, in a sense the scheme was too primitive for heavy traffic. It was a known problem, but it didn't matter until the network reached a point when heavy use and a large number of nodes began to strain the routing scheme. "This didn't start to happen until the network got big," said McQuillan. "When it was real small, the basic protocols all worked. But when it's small, almost anything will work." They knew that when the system reached fifty or sixty nodes, the old algorithm wouldn't be able to provide routing updates fast enough, and they'd have a real big mess on their hands. McQuillan made it his mission to "completely bullet-proof" the calculation so that it would "keep working in the face of 'impossible' problems."

In two years, with a lot of releases, McQuillan replaced the routing algorithms, the way acknowledgments worked, and eventually the whole IMP operating program. He built a completely different algorithm for flooding information about changes in the network very quickly to all the IMPs so they wouldn't make bad routing decisions. And he eliminated deadlock scenarios, partly by eliminating the infamous RFNM's from the equation.

"I knew all the computers on the network," McQuillan said. "I knew where they were and what their numbers were and who was there and I knew them all by name." By now there were nearly fifty IMPs on the ARPANET.

• • •

Something about a mail system, digital or otherwise, is inviting to those with a certain nonconformist temperament. Perhaps because there must be rules, some people will always try bending them. There was the clever fellow, for instance, who got away with using the U.S. Postal Service to mail bricks, one by one, to Alaska, until he had enough there to build himself a house; it was the cheapest way to ship them from the lower forty-eight states. Or there's Auntie Em, who embellishes her packages to her far-flung nieces and nephews with fanciful illustrations, to the probable amusement rather than consternation of the postal clerks. Somewhere in a thick book of fine print are the official postal regulations regarding U.S. mail—what can be sent, what can't, and how. But within limits, all manner of packages get delivered, because human mail clerks can adjust to a fairly wide latitude of nonconformity.

But imagine a local post office somewhere that decided to go it alone, making up its own rules for addressing, packaging, stamping, and sorting mail. Imagine if that rogue post office decided to invent its own set of ZIP codes. Imagine any number of post offices taking it upon themselves to invent new rules. Imagine widespread confusion. Mail handling begs for a certain amount of conformity, and because computers are less fault-tolerant than human beings, e-mail begs loudly.

The early wrangling on the ARPANET over attempts to impose standard message headers was typical of other debates over computer industry standards that came later. But because the struggle over e-mail standards was one of the first sources of real tension in the community, it stood out.

In 1973 an ad hoc committee led by MIT's Bhushan tried bringing some order to the implementation of new e-mail programs. Everyone knew that in the long run a separate mail-transmission protocol—independent of the FTP—was needed. Network mail was taking on a life of its own. It had its own technical problems. And it couldn't stay glued to FTP forever. But for now, just standardizing mail headers was enough of a headache.

Data packets on the ARPANET already had something called headers, but they were entirely different from e-mail headers. The headers on data packets were coded bits read strictly by the IMPs, telling them how to handle each packet as it came along. In the context of electronic mail, however, the header refers to a larger raft of information at the top of every e-mail message. The idea was that certain information should always appear at the top of messages in a specified format, really just an elaborate time and date locator, including information such as the time a message was sent and delivered, the route it traveled, other recipients to whom it was sent, and more. Bhushan's committee also suggested a syntax that would make it easier to read headers without the aid of a lot of special message processing.

Headers weren't always something seen only by the user. Some header fields were processed by receiving systems, programmed to deal with reserved meanings and very tightly defined syntax. If the recipient program somehow misinterpreted the sender's header, the results could be exceedingly frustrating. The reader program might stop dead in its tracks or spit out an error message. Dates, for example, were specified in a particular way, and deviations might be unintelligible. Or if you put a comma in the wrong place, your mail program's ability to process messages might go awry. When one mail handler couldn't parse headers sent by others, it was as if a postal clerk in Kenosha, Wisconsin, were being asked to deliver letters addressed in Sanskrit and Arabic.

Machines on the ARPANET encountered computer-language barriers of this kind regularly, and the problems multiplied with the growth in both the number of mail programs and the number of nodes on the Net. Depending on the kind of mail system one might use to send a message, an incompatible program or operating system at the receiving end would "barf up" the headers, as one observer put it. If the message got through, the person who received it still might have to deal with a garbled translation or screwed-up formatting. Recipients would complain about the sender. A sender might agree to fix the problem with a hack or kludge ("a kludge is a crock that works," went one definition), if he had the time. Or, if he liked his own mail program well enough, he might simply complain about the recipient's.

Setting up an e-mail exchange was like asking someone out on a date. "E-mail was seen as something between consenting adults," said Brian Reid, a computer scientist who was working on his Ph.D. at Carnegie-Mellon. A certain mature understanding was required. "I have an e-mail program, I want to send you mail, and you want to receive it," he continued, "and as long as we agree on the standard, it's fine." Many users of early fax machines went through the same kind of rigmarole making sure the sender's machine could communicate with the recipient's fax machine.

The problem occurred on a massive scale between Tenex and non-Tenex machines. Programmers at a few non-Tenex sites, like those working with machines based on the Multics operating system, continued introducing e-mail programs and features in the syntax of their own operating systems, and continued sending their messages out over the Net. Tenex machines, however, couldn't handle the syntax of other formats used at some sites, so again, conflict and confusion would result.

The diversity of nonstandard systems on the Net caused problems even with something as apparently trivial as Tomlinson's @ sign. The @ sign dispute was long-running, and there were many sides to it. There was disagreement over what should go on the left hand side of the sign and what should go on the right. But before that, there was the debate over whether it should even be used at all as the delimiter between the user and host names in the address.

The Multics folks objected vehemently when it was first used, understandably so. Tomlinson, a Tenex hacker, had chosen the @ sign without realizing, perhaps, that in the Multics system it was the character used to send a "line kill" command. Any Multics user who tried to send mail to "Tomlinson@bbn-tenex" would quickly get into trouble. Multics would start reading the address, encounter the @ sign, and throw away everything on the line that had been typed previously.

Ted Myer and Austin Henderson, from the BBN Tenex group, decided to try their hand at solving one of these compatibility issues, the header problem. In April 1975 they issued a new list of "standard" headers. The document, which they gave the title, "Message Transmission Protocol," appeared as RFC 680.

But RFC 680 immediately created a ruckus among those who thought the effort too Tenex-oriented. Postel, keeper of the RFCs, whose quiet word was often final, wielded the gavel. RFC 680, he said, was as standard as mail ever got. "It is nice that many mail-reading programs will accept mail that does not conform to the standard," he said, "but that does not justify mail-sending programs' violation of the standard." If the standard is inadequate, he added, any proposals to change it are welcome.

The tiff made clear that Tenex sites, led by BBN, formed a dominant culture on the network, while the "minority" sites, with their diverse operating systems, posed a potentially rebellious countermovement. Thus were planted the roots of a protracted conflict that continued into the ensuing decade and became known in the community as the header wars. Many of those battles were fought in the arena of a new group of computer conversationalists—the "Msg-Group."

❑ The MsgGroup

On June 7, 1975, Steve Walker, an ARPA program manager at IPTO, drafted a message to announce the formation of something new—an electronic discussion group. The network community, he wrote, needs "to develop a sense of what is mandatory, what is nice, and what is not desirable in message services. We have had a lot of experience with lots of services and should be able to collect our thoughts on the matter. He welcomed opinions from anyone willing to toss them in and even provided a bit of ARPA funding to launch it. "This whole thing is a new attempt," he continued. "I hope from all this to develop a long-term strategy for where message services should go on the ARPANET and indeed in the DOD. Let's have at it."

In the truncated verbal style permeating the culture of computing, the Message Services Group was dubbed the MsgGroup.

Dave Farber at UC Irvine volunteered to be the MsgGroup file
clerk; and Farber volunteered the help of a colleague, a consultant
named Einar Stefferud. Before long, the bulk of the daily housekeeping chores fell to Stefferud, who began in the job by keeping
the list of MsgGroup participants, signing up newcomers, cajoling
them into posting introductory biographies of themselves, and sorting out bounced mail. Stefferud would become the MsgGroup's
moderator and man behind the curtain. Serving as the go-between,
he received messages for posting and manually remailed them to
everyone on the list. It was an arduous process that became automated later on.

Not everyone conducted his business in the open-air market of
the MsgGroup; there was just as much or more private e-mail traffic among programmers. But everyone in the world involved in implementing mail systems eventually participated or at least knew
what transpired in the group. The discussion was to last ten years. In
time, thousands of messages, and hundreds of thousands of words,
were exchanged by the hundred or so MsgGroup participants.

The MsgGroup was among the first network mailing lists. There
were other mailing lists, most of them unsanctioned, around the
educational sites. The first widely popular unofficial list, called SF-
Lovers, was devoted to science-fiction fans.

The header wars brought out the stubborn and strong-willed traits
of the programmers. Operating conflicts between machines were
only the half of it. Header troubles were also rooted in human disagreement over how much and what kind of information should be
presented at the tops of the messages. People differed widely over
how much header information they cared to deal with when looking at their mail.

Some programmers and mail programs included a lot more in
their header fields than others did. They iced the cake with character counts, key words, and various esoterica. Critics meanwhile
argued strenuously for economy, opposing an information over-

load. They saw too many fat and frivolous headers—the electronic equivalent of noting the cotton-rag content of a sheet of stationery. Short messages with cumbersome headers always appeared top-heavy, out of balance, emphasizing the header rather than the message. Brian Reid at Carnegie-Mellon, who often sounded the voice of reason in the MsgGroup, was in the short-header camp. One day he received a sarcastic message from a colleague and posted it to the MsgGroup:

Date: 7 Apr 1977 1712-EST
From: Bob Chansler at CMU-10A
Reply-To: Cheese Coop at CMU-10A
Subject: Re: Close, but no cigar
To: BRIAN. REID at CMU-10A
CC: Chansler@CMU-10A
Sender: BOB.CHANSLER at CMU-10A
Message-ID: [CMU-10A] 7 Apr 1977 17:12:49 Bob Chansler In-Reply-To: Your message of April 6, 1977
My-Seq-#: 39492094
Yr-Seq-#: 4992488
Class: A
Subclass: MCMXLVII
Author: RC12
Typist: Fred
Terminal: TTY88
FE-L#: 44
Reason: Did Godzilla need a reason?
Valid: Not before 12 Apr 1977 1321Z
Suspend: After 19 Apr 1977 0000Z
Spelling-errors-this-message: 0
Spelling-errors-to-date: 23
Weather: Light rain, fog
Forecast: Clearing by morning
Psych-evaluation-of-sender: Slightly unstable
Security-level: Public
Security-sublevel: 0
Authority-to-send: General
Authority-to-rcv: General

#-people-in-terminal-room: 12
XGP: UP-cutter not working
Ht/Wt-sender: 76/205
Machines: M&Ms available but almond machine is empty
M&Ms-Last Nickel: 17
HDR-chksum: 032114567101

Brian,
I do not understand your concern about the size of message headers.
Bob.

Why can't we configure headers to print only the pieces of the header we choose to read? Reid asked. "Go ahead and put in thirty-four different header fields," he said. "All I ever really want to look at is 'from' and 'date.'" Others agreed. The ideal program would allow users to design their own headers. At least one elaborate mail system, Doug Engelbart's NLS JOURNAL MAIL, offered an "invisible information" feature that allowed selective viewing of a great deal of header data.

On May 12, 1977, Ken Pogran, John Vittal, Dave Crocker, and Austin Henderson launched a computer mail putsch. They announced "at last" the completion of a new mail standard, RFC 724, "A Proposed Official Standard for the Format of ARPA Network Messages." The standard they were proposing contained more than twenty pages of specifications—syntactical, semantic, and lexical formalities. The RFC explained that the receiver of a message could exercise an extraordinary amount of control over the message's appearance, depending on the capabilities of one's mail-reading system.

In the days after the publication of RFC 724, the computing community's response was at best cool to the new protocol. Alex McKenzie of BBN was particularly outspoken. Postel, who had been a defender of the old RFC 680, was the least impressed by the new proposal. He came down hard on the assertion that this was to be an official ARPA standard. "To my knowledge no ARPANET protocol at any level has been stamped as official by ARPA," he said. "Who are the officials anyway? Why should this collection of computer research organizations take orders from anybody?" There was too much emphasis on officialism and not enough on cooperation and perfection of the system. "I prefer to view the situation as a kind of step-by-step evolution," he said, "where documents such as RFCs 561, 680, and 724 record the steps. To make a big point of official-ness about one step may make it very hard to take the next step."

The RFC 724 team absorbed the criticism. Six months later, under Dave Crocker's and John Vittal's leadership, a final revised edition of RFC 724 was published as RFC 733. This specification was intended "strictly as a definition" of what was to be passed between ARPANET hosts. They didn't intend to dictate the look and feel of message programs or the features they could support. Less was *required* than *allowed* by the standard, they said, so here it was. And there it sat.

A number of developers wrote or revised mail programs to con-form with the new guidelines, but within a year of RFC 733's publi-cation the persistent conflict picked up again. Of particular concern, RFC 733 headers were incompatible with a mail program called MSG (in spite of the fact that its author, John Vittal, had helped write RFC 733). MSG was far and away the most popular mail program on the ARPANET.

A hacker's hacker, Vittal had written the MSG program in 1975 out of sheer love for the work. MSG was never formally funded or sup-ported, "other than by me in my spare time," he explained. But soon, MSG had a user community of more than a thousand people, which in those days meant a huge portion of the wired world. Vittal had used Roberts's RD mail program, which was great for handling two or three messages at a time, or even a short message stack, but Vit-tal was getting twenty messages a day now and wanted a program to manage them with greater ease. "What MSG did was close the loop," he said, "so that you could parcel messages out to various other files, called folders, and ultimately answer and forward."

Vittal, in fact, became widely known for putting the word "an-swer" into the lexicon of e-mail. He invented the ANSWER command, which made replying to messages a cinch. Recalled Vittal, "I was thinking, 'Hey, with an answer command I don't have to retype—or mistype!—a return address or addresses.'"

An inspiring model, MSG spawned a whole new generation of mail systems including MH, MM, MS, and a heavily funded, Pentagon-sponsored project at BBN called HERMES. MSG was the original "killer app"—a software application that took the world by storm. Although there was never anything official about it, MSG clearly had the broadest grassroots support. It was all over the network; even ARPA's top folks in the Pentagon used it. If anything was the most widely accepted standard, it was MSG, which reigned for a long while. (A few people at BBN were still using MSG in the 1990s.)

Vittal's MSG and his ANSWER command made him a legendary figure in e-mail circles. "It was because of Vittal that we all assimilated network mail into our spinal cords," recalled Brian Reid. "When I met him years later, I remember being disappointed—as one often is when one meets a living legend—to see that he had two arms and two legs and no rocket pack on his back."

More than just a great hack, MSG was the best proof to date that on the ARPANET rules might get made, but they certainly didn't prevail. Proclamations of officialness didn't further the Net nearly so much as throwing technology out onto the Net to see what worked. And when something worked, it was adopted.

❏ Adventure and Quasar: The Open Net and Free Speech

The more that people used the ARPANET for e-mail, the more relaxed they became about what they said. There were antiwar messages and, during the height of the Watergate crisis, a student on the ARPANET advocated Nixon's impeachment.

Not only was the network expanding, it was opening wider to new uses and creating new connections among people. And that was pure Licklider. One of the most stunning examples of this began with one of the original IMP Guys—Will Crowther.

A small circle of friends at BBN had gotten hooked on Dungeons and Dragons, an elaborate fantasy role-playing game in which one player invents a setting and populates it with monsters and puzzles, and the other players then make their way through that setting. The entire game exists only on paper and in the minds of the players.

Dave Walden got his introduction to the game one night in 1975, when Eric Roberts, a student from a class he was teaching at Harvard, took him to a D&D session. Walden immediately rounded up a group of friends for continued sessions. Roberts created the Mirkwood Tales, an elaborate version of Dungeons and Dragons set in J. R. R. Tolkien's Middle Earth. The game stretched on for the better part of a year and was played mostly on Walden's living room floor. One of the regulars was Will Crowther. Where the other dozen players chose names like Zandar, Klarf, or Groan for their characters, Crowther's was simply Willie, a stealthy thief.

Crowther was also an ardent cave explorer. And his wife Pat had achieved renown among cavers for having been part of a small group that discovered the first known link between the Mammoth and Flint Ridge caves in Kentucky. The combined 144-mile system was the longest known cave in the world. Crowther was the cartographer for the Cave Research Foundation. He used his off-hours to plot intricate subterranean maps on a BBN computer.

In early 1976 Will and Pat divorced. Looking for something he could do with his two children, he hit upon an idea that united Will the programmer with Willie the imaginary thief: a simplified, computer version of Dungeons and Dragons called Adventure. Although the game did not use actual maps of the Kentucky caves, Crowther based the geometry of Adventure on stark mental images of those underground chambers. The iron grate through which players passed at the start of the game was modeled on those installed by the Park Service at entrances to the Flint Ridge system. He even included a caving in-joke or two; the "Y2" inscribed on a rock at one point in the game is caver shorthand for a secondary entrance.

Crowther finished the program over the course of three or four weekends. His kids—ages seven and five—loved it, and Crowther began showing it to friends. But the breakup of his marriage had sapped Crowther's spirit, and he never got around to refining the game.

Bob Taylor, now director of the Computer Science Lab at Xerox Corporation's Palo Alto Research Center, persuaded first Severo Ornstein, then Will Crowther, to join him, and when Crowther moved to California in 1976 he left the Adventure program behind in a file on a BBN computer. Unpolished though the game was, word of Adventure had filtered through the network community.

A Stanford graduate student named Don Woods heard about Adventure from a friend who had run across a copy on the Stanford Medical School computer, and he downloaded the game from there. But Woods had difficulty getting Adventure to run at first, and when he did he found it riddled with bugs. Still, he was hooked. "Adventure made users feel like they were interacting more with the computer," said Woods. "It seemed to be responding more to what you typed, rather than just making its own moves like a silent opponent. I think this attracted a lot of players who might otherwise have been turned off by the idea of playing 'against' a computer. This was playing 'with' a computer."

The game listed Will Crowther as the author, and Woods decided to track down Crowther to get the source code so he could start making repairs to the rudimentary little program. He sent e-mail to every host on the network looking for Crowther, and finally he found him at PARC. Crowther happily handed over the code. It took several months to rework, during which the simple program doubled in size. Woods created new obstacles, added a pirate, twisted the mazes further, and added several treasures that required some problem solving before they were found.

When Adventure was done, Woods created a guest account on the computer at the Stanford AI Lab to let people play, and swarms of guests logged in. Adventure spread like hula hoops, as people sent the program to one another over the network. Because Crowther had written it in FORTRAN, it could be adapted to many different computers with relative ease. Both Crowther and Woods encouraged programmers to pirate the game and included their e-mail addresses for anyone looking for help installing, playing, or copying the game.

People grew bleary-eyed searching for treasure into the small hours of the morning. "I've long ago lost count of the programmers who've told me that the experience that got them started using computers was playing Adventure," Woods said. The game inspired hundreds of knockoffs, which eventually spawned an entire industry.

Adventure demonstrated the appeal of an open networking culture. And the emphasis on openness grew with time. There were few closed doors on the network, and a free spirit prevailed in people's attitudes about who could come and go through them, and for what purposes. Anyone trying to restrict the graduate student population from freely using the network would have grossly misunderstood the mind-set of the computer science community. The ARPANET was official federal government property, but network mail was being used for all manner of daily conversation.

Then, in the spring of 1977, Quasar rolled in the door. Its arrival marked the beginning of the first debate over free speech in cyberspace. The controversy centered on an unusual device made by Quasar Industries and blew up into an argument over using the taxpayer-funded ARPANET to speak, in openly critical terms, about a private company.

The brainchild of Quasar Industries, the device stood five feet four inches and weighed two hundred forty pounds. It was called the Domestic Android robot, a programmable helper that could perform a dozen basic household tasks such as mopping the floor, mowing the lawn, washing dishes, and serving cocktails. It came equipped with a personality and speech, so that it could "interact in any human situation." It could "teach the kids French" and "continue teaching them, while they sleep." At the advertised price of $4,000, the thing seemed a steal.

Phil Karlton of Carnegie-Mellon was the first to alert the Msg-Group, on May 26, 1977. His site on the ARPANET was heavily involved in exploring artificial intelligence, speech recognition, and related research problems, so he knew a thing or two about robots. The android and its inventor had attracted a fair amount of national press attention, most of it favorable. Quasar's sales pitch had also caught the attention of *Consumer Reports,* which ran a skeptical item on it in the June issue, just out.

At first Quasar seemed nothing but an amusing diversion from the MsgGroup's main business. Everyone in the group knew the thing was a hoax, and for a while that seemed enough. But then a sense of civic duty arose. Dave Farber told of being in Boca Raton, Florida, and hearing on the radio that the Dade County police department was considering purchasing a Quasar guard robot for their county jail, for $7,000. In March *The Boston Globe* ran a story quoting MIT's Marvin Minsky and other skeptical AI experts. But the article took the overall attitude, said a MsgGroup member, that it "just goes to show you, those academicians can't do anything practical, and all you need is some guy working in the back of a garage to put them to shame." The saga left a trail of disbelief in the artificial intelligence research community.

Brian Reid and a colleague, Mark Fox, from the Carnegie-Mellon Artificial Intelligence Lab, posted an offbeat report to everyone in the MsgGroup, giving them a personal account of their inspection of the domestic robot, "Sam Strugglegear," at a large department store in downtown Pittsburgh. People in the research community, knowing of CMU's pioneering AI work, had been calling the Lab to ask how it was possible for Quasar's robot to be so much better at speech recognition than anything CMU had produced. Rising to the challenge, a four-member team from CMU had done the fieldwork.

"They found a frightening sight," reported Reid and Fox. In the men's department, among the three-piece suits, was a five-feet-two-inch "aerosol can on wheels, talking animatedly" to a crowd. Electric motors and a system of gears moved the device's arms. The robot seemed conversant on any subject, recognized the physical features of customers, and moved freely in any direction. The crowd was charmed.

But the scientists were skeptical. They looked around for some evidence of a remote controller. "Lo and behold, about ten feet from the robot, standing in the crowd, we found a man in a blue suit with his hand held contemplatively to his mouth like Aristotle contemplating the bust of Homer in the famous Rembrandt painting." Reid and the others watched for awhile and noticed that whenever the robot was talking, so was the man in the blue suit—muttering into his hand. The man had a wire dangling suspiciously from his waist.

The discussion about the Quasar robot continued on and off for a couple of years until in early 1979, Einar Stefferud, the MsgGroup's moderator, and Dave Farber, who had been lurking on the sidelines of the commentary, sent a note of caution to the MsgGroup. "We are asking for potential problems," they warned, "when we criticize the Quasar robot." Using U.S. Government facilities to cast aspersions on a corporation, they said, could backfire on the ARPA research community. They urged their peers to impose careful self-censorship, to report only facts of technical interest to the community. Not everyone agreed, and with that the MsgGroup got embroiled in a soul-searching exchange.

John McCarthy, who worked at Stanford's Artificial Intelligence Lab, was among those most offended by Quasar's claims. He told the group that he would not be deterred by speculation that Quasar might sue. "I think someone seems to be frightened of his shadow," McCarthy said. "It has never been the custom of carnival snake-oil salesmen to sue their critics." Minsky and Reid also made it clear that they would tell any reporter who asked that they believed the robot was a joke, and they'd already expressed that opinion to more than a dozen journalists.

"I have no fear of being sued," replied Farber. "However, we are using a public vehicle called the ARPANET. We thereby expose ARPA, DOD, and our future access and use of the network to certain dangers when we use that vehicle for potentially libelous material." Farber again urged restraint.

Reid chimed in, saying, "[the] MsgGroup is the closest that we have to a nationwide computer science community forum." Reid had begun to notice that the Message Group was like a social club. They had argued with each other so much that they had become friends. To restrict discussion would be unnatural. Besides, Reid took a more liberal view of free speech, reasoning that the experiment in communications would suffer if topics were restricted. "Until such time as people start suggesting the overthrow of our government," he said, "I don't think any sensible topic should be off limits."

Someone suggested attaching a disclaimer to personal communications on the ARPANET so that personal opinions wouldn't be mistaken for official business. Admitted someone else, "Who hasn't used Net mail for personal communication? Who hasn't spent time playing some new game over the Net? Be honest." The passion in defense of free speech was matched by an equally strong will to self-protection; the way to protect the network itself was not to attract unwanted supervision by the government. After a few days the argument wore itself out without resolution and the MsgGroup carried on with business as usual.

What emerged from the debate was strong evidence that the networking community felt a deep stake in the creation of the Net, ARPA funding or no ARPA funding, and was trying jealously to guard its right to determine its future. In a realm where, in a sense, personal identity is defined entirely by the words people choose, free speech seemed second only to concern for the survival of the realm itself.

❑ Copper Umbilicals

For the first quarter of 1976, traffic reports showed that the volume of ARPANET mail, compared to the volume of regular U.S. mail, was a mere ant trail in the tracks of an elephant herd. MIT's Artificial Intelligence Lab, for example, passed some 9,925 messages during the period. (By 1996, by comparison, some sites were processing 150,000 e-mail messages every day.) MIT was a typical site, and by extrapolation, if one machine processed about a hundred pieces of e-mail a day, multiplied by a factor of 98 or so (the number of hosts then on the Net) electronic mail didn't yet appear to pose a threat to the U.S. postal system. The post office handled more than 50 billion pieces of first-class mail a year. But e-mail's steep growth curve wasn't going unnoticed.

In the private sector, companies were poised for the concept of electronic-mail service to take off. The Computer Corporation of America soon began selling one of the first commercially available e-mail software packages, a $40,000 product called COMET, designed for the PDP-11 minicomputer. Another program called MESSENGER, developed for IBM 360 and 370 computers, was soon available from a company called On-Line Software International, for $18,000. Costs were heading down, and some analysts projected a "devastating" impact on the U.S. Postal Service's first-class business.

"We are being bypassed technologically," reported an assistant U.S. postmaster general at the beginning of 1976. The new technology's growth trend and obvious potential were indeed quite dramatic. A few versions of the more sophisticated ARPANET mail programs such as MSG, HERMES, and SRI's NLS JOURNAL MAIL, were coming into the hands of nonresearchers. Several large organizations including the U.S. Geological Survey, Department of Commerce, National Security Agency, and Gulf Oil had all started using e-mail over local area networks.

The government was looking closely at the future of e-mail service. A report for the White House Office of Telecommunications Policy by the consulting firm Arthur D. Little estimated that 30 percent of all first-class mail was likely to be sent electronically within a few years. The postal service reacted to that prediction by awarding RCA a $2.2 million contract to evaluate the technical and economic feasibility of providing e-mail service. In its report, RCA argued for adding e-mail to the post office's services. A USPS advisory panel also took a close look. They recommended making a "firm and continuing commitment" to electronic mail, on a par with NASA's manned space program.

Jimmy Carter's presidential campaign used e-mail several times a day in the autumn of 1976. The system they were using was a basic mailbox program, a technology already more than a decade old. But for a political campaign this was a revolutionary stroke in communications. On that basis, Carter was labeled the "computer-driven candidate."

By 1979, President Carter was supporting a post office proposal to offer a limited kind of electronic message service to the nation. The hybrid scheme worked more like a telegram service than a state-of-the-art electronic communications system. Messages would be transmitted electronically between post offices overnight, then delivered to recipients' doorsteps the next day. The proposal was remarkable mainly for how cautious it seemed in view of the technological possibilities.

Stefferud and others in the MsgGroup—the community with the most experience with e-mail—immediately saw the flaws in the U.S. Postal Service's plan, which involved converting messages from digital electronic media to paper and then delivering them by hand as you would ordinary mail. Not only would this approach cost more than e-mail, but it would never be fast enough to compete with e-mail as long as it depended on USPS's traditional foot power for those final steps to the mailbox. Desktop computers "will make the perfect mailbox," Stefferud predicted, and would bypass the post office entirely. An analogy could be drawn to the once farcical notion of automated garbage collection, which was unthinkable until the invention of the "electric pig," the early name given to the in-sink disposal. "The key is not in automating the bag/can/truck/person mechanism," Stefferud said. "It is in bypassing them altogether."

The USPS, like AT&T earlier, never really broke free of the mind-set guarding its traditional business, probably because both were monopolistic entities. Eventually the U.S. Justice Department, the FCC, and even the Postal Rate Commission opposed any significant government role in e-mail services, preferring to leave them to the free market.

No issue was ever too small for long discussion in the MsgGroup. The speed and ease of the medium opened vistas of casual and spontaneous conversation. It was apparent by the end of the decade to people like Licklider and Baran that a revolution they had helped start was now under way.

"Tomorrow, computer communications systems will be the rule for remote collaboration" between authors, wrote Baran and UC Irvine's Dave Farber. The comments appeared in a paper written jointly, using e-mail, with five hundred miles between them. It was "published" electronically in the MsgGroup in 1977. They went on: "As computer communication systems become more powerful, more humane, more forgiving and above all, cheaper, they will become ubiquitous." Automated hotel reservations, credit checking, real-time financial transactions, access to insurance and medical records, general information retrieval, and real-time inventory control in businesses would all come.

In the late 1970s, the Information Processing Techniques Office's final report to ARPA management on the completion of the ARPANET research program concluded similarly: "The largest single surprise of the ARPANET program has been the incredible popularity and success of network mail. There is little doubt that the techniques of network mail developed in connection with the ARPANET program are going to sweep the country and drastically change the techniques used for intercommunication in the public and private sectors."

To members of the MsgGroup, electronic mail was as engrossing as a diamond held to the light. MsgGroup members probed every detail. They were junkies for the technology. The issue of time and date stamps, for example, was classic. "My boss's boss's boss complains of the ravings of the late-nighters," someone said. "He can tell from the time stamp (and the sender's habits) how seriously to take the message."

"Perhaps we should time-stamp with the phase of the moon in addition to date and time," said another. (Before long someone wrote an e-mail program that did just that.)

"I really like seeing an accurate time stamp," said someone else. "It's nice to be able to unravel the sequence of comments received in scrambled order."

"Some people use it blatantly as a kind of one-upmanship. 'I work longer hours than you do.'"

MsgGroup members could argue about anything. There were times when you'd swear you had just dropped in on a heated group of lawyers, or grammarians, or rabbis. Strangers fell casually into the dialogue or, as someone called it, the "polylogue." As the regulars became familiar to one another, fast friendships were cemented, sometimes years before people actually met. In many ways the ARPANET community's basic values were traditional—free speech, equal access, personal privacy. However, e-mail also was uninhibiting, creating reference points entirely its own, a virtual society, with manners, values, and acceptable behaviors—the practice of "flaming," for example—strange to the rest of the world.

Familiarity in the MsgGroup occasionally bred the language of contempt. The first real "flaming" (a fiery, often abusive form of dialogue) on the ARPANET had flared up in the mid-1970s. The medium engendered rash rejoiners and verbal tussles. Yet heavy flaming was kept relatively in check in the MsgGroup, which considered itself civilized. Stefferud almost single-handedly and cool-headedly kept the group together when things got particularly raucous and contentious. He slaved to keep the MsgGroup functioning, parsing difficult headers when necessary or smoothing out misunderstandings, making sure the group's mood and its traffic never got too snarly. About the worst he ever said, when beset by technical problems, was that some headers had "bad breath."

By comparison, there was a discussion group next door (metaphorically speaking), called Header People, reputed to be an inferno. "We normally wear asbestos underwear," said one participant. Based at MIT, Header People had been started by Ken Harrenstien in 1976. The group was unofficial, but more important, it was unmoderated (meaning it had no Stefferud-like human filter). Harrenstien had set out to recruit at least one developer from every kind of system on the ARPANET, and in no time the conflicts in Header People raised the debate over headers to the level of a holy war before flaming out. "A bunch of spirited sluggers," said Harrenstien, "pounding an equine cadaver to smithereens." The two mail-oriented groups overlapped considerably; even in civilized MsgGroup company, tempers flared periodically. The acidic attacks and level of haranguing unique to on-line communication, unacceptably asocial in any other context, was oddly normative on the ARPANET.

Flames could start up at any time over anything, and they could last for one message or one hundred.

The FINGER controversy, a debate over privacy on the Net, occurred in early 1979 and involved some of the worst flaming in the MsgGroup's experience. The fight was over the introduction, at Carnegie-Mellon, of an electronic widget that allowed users to peek into the on-line habits of other users on the Net. The FINGER command had been created in the early 1970s by a computer scientist named Les Earnest at Stanford's Artificial Intelligence Lab. "People generally worked long hours there, often with unpredictable schedules," Earnest said. "When you wanted to meet with some group, it was important to know who was there and when the others would likely reappear. It also was important to be able to locate potential volleyball players when you wanted to play, Chinese food freaks when you wanted to eat, and antisocial computer users when it appeared that something strange was happening on the system." FINGER didn't allow you to read someone else's messages, but you could tell the date and time of the person's last log-on and when last he or she had read mail. Some people had a problem with that.

In an effort to respect privacy, Ivor Durham at CMU changed the FINGER default setting; he added a couple of bits that could be turned on or off, so the information could be concealed unless a user chose to reveal it. Durham was flamed without mercy. He was called everything from spineless to socially irresponsible to a petty politician, and worse—but not for protecting privacy. He was criticized for monkeying with the openness of the network.

The debate began as an internal dialogue at CMU but was leaked out onto the ARPANET by Dave Farber, who wanted to see what would happen if he revealed it to the outer world. The ensuing flame-fest consumed more than 400 messages.

At the height of the FINGER debate, one person quit the Msg-Group in disgust over the flaming. As with the Quasar debate, the FINGER controversy ended inconclusively. But both debates taught users greater lessons about the medium they were using. The speed of electronic mail promoted flaming, some said; anyone hot could shoot off a retort on the spot, and without the moderating factor of having to look the target in the eye.

By the end of the decade, the MsgGroup's tone, which had begun stiffly, was an expansive free-for-all. Stefferud always tried to get newcomers to introduce themselves electronically when they joined the group; when leaving, some bid farewell only to turn up again later at other sites; only one or two people huffed off, quite ceremoniously, over a flame-fest or some other perceived indignity.

One of the MsgGroup's eminent statesmen, Dave Crocker, sometimes probed the Net with a sociologist's curiosity. One day, for example, he sent a note to approximately 130 people around the country at about five o'clock in the evening, just to see how fast people would get the message and reply. The response statistics, he reported, were "a little scary." Seven people responded within ninety minutes. Within twenty-four hours he had received twenty-eight replies. Response times and numbers on that order may seem hardly noteworthy in a culture that has since squared and cubed its expectations about the speed, ease, and reach of information technology. But in the 1970s "it was an absolutely astonishing experience," Crocker said, to have gotten so many replies, so quickly, so easily, as that.

On April 12, 1979, a rank newcomer to the MsgGroup named Kevin MacKenzie anguished openly about the "loss of meaning" in this electronic, textually bound medium. Unquestionably, e-mail allowed a spontaneous verbal exchange, but he was troubled by its inability to convey human gestures, facial expressions, and tone of voice—all of which come naturally when talking and express a whole vocabulary of nuances in speech and thought, including irony and sarcasm. Perhaps, he said, we could extend the set of punctuation in e-mail messages. In order to indicate that a particular sentence is meant to be tongue-in-cheek, he proposed inserting a hyphen and parenthesis at the end of the sentence, thus: -).

MacKenzie confessed that the idea wasn't entirely his; it had been sparked by something he had read on a different subject in an old copy of *Reader's Digest*. About an hour later, he was flamed, or rather, singed. He was told his suggestion was "naive but not stupid." He was given a short lecture on Shakespeare's mastery of the language without auxiliary notation. "Those who will not learn to use this instrument well cannot be saved by an expanded alphabet; they will only afflict us with expanded gibberish." What did Shakespeare know? ;-) Emoticons and smileys :-), hoisted by the hoi polloi no doubt, grew in e-mail and out into the iconography of our time.

It's a bit difficult to pinpoint when or why—perhaps it was exhaustion, perhaps there were now too many new players in the MsgGroup—but by the early 1980s, note by note, the orchestra that had been performing magnificently and that had collectively created e-mail over a decade, began abandoning the score, almost imperceptibly at first. One key voice would fade here, another would drift off there. Instead of chords, white noise seemed to gradually overtake the MsgGroup.

In some sense it didn't matter. The dialogue itself in the Msg-Group had always been more important than the results. Creating the mechanisms of e-mail mattered, of course, but the MsgGroup also created something else entirely—a community of equals, many of whom had never met each other yet who carried on as if they had known each other all their lives. It was the first place they had found something they'd been looking for since the ARPANET came into existence. The MsgGroup was perhaps the first virtual community.

The romance of the Net came not from how it was built or how it worked but from how it was used. By 1980 the Net was far more than a collection of computers and leased lines. It was a place to share work and build friendships and a more open method of communication. America's romance with the highway system, by analogy, was created not so much by the first person who figured out how to grade a road or make blacktop or paint a stripe down the middle but by the first person who discovered you could drive a convertible down Route 66 like James Dean and play your radio loud and have a great time.

8

A Rocket on Our Hands

Bob Kahn left BBN and went to work for Larry Roberts in 1972. He had deferred his arrival in Washington for a year to stay in Cambridge and plan the ICCC demonstration. Having spent six uninterrupted years focused on computer networking, he was now ready to make a clean break. He did not want to run a network project. So he and Roberts agreed that Kahn would set up a new program in automated manufacturing techniques. But Congress canceled the project before Kahn arrived. By now, ARPA had been changed to DARPA—the Defense Advanced Research Projects Agency. As Kahn once put it, the *D* had always been there, but now it was no longer silent. The name ARPANET remained.

With the manufacturing project gone, Kahn was called back to the field in which he had grown expert. But he wanted to work on the newest experiments.

The early 1970s were a time of intense experimentation with computer networking. A few people were beginning to think about new kinds of packet networks. The basic principles of packet-switching were unlikely to be improved upon dramatically. And the protocols, interfaces, and routing algorithms for handling messages were growing more refined. One area still to explore, however, was the medium over which data traveled. The existing AT&T web of telephone lines had been the obvious first choice. But why not make a wireless network by transmitting data packets "on the air" as radio waves?

In 1969, before Bob Taylor had left ARPA, he set up funding for a fixed-site radio network to be built at the University of Hawaii. It was designed by a professor named Norm Abramson and several colleagues. They constructed a simple system using radios to broadcast data back and forth among seven computers stationed over four islands. Abramson called it ALOHA.

The ALOHANET used small radios, identical to those used by taxicabs, sharing common frequency instead of separate channels. The system employed a very relaxed protocol. The central idea was to have each terminal transmit whenever it chose to. But if the data collided with somebody else's transmission (which happened when there was a lot of traffic), the receivers wouldn't be able to decode either transmission properly. So if the source radio didn't get an acknowledgment, it assumed the packet had gotten garbled; it retransmitted the packet later at a random interval. The ALOHA system was like a telephone service that told you, after you tried to speak, and not until then, that the line was busy.

Roberts and Kahn liked the general idea of radio links between computers. Why not do something still more challenging: devise small portable computer "sites" carried around in vehicles or even by hand, linked together in a packet-switching network? In 1972 Roberts outlined the scheme. He envisioned a network in which a central minicomputer situated in a powerful radio station would communicate with smaller mobile computer sites. Roberts asked SRI to study the problem and work out a practical system.

The concept of mobile computer sites held obvious appeal to the Army. Battlefield computers installed in vehicles or aircraft—moving targets—would be less vulnerable and more useful than fixed installations. Still, destruction of the single most crucial element—the stationary master computer in a centralized system—would take out a whole network. The need to defend against that danger was what had led Paul Baran to devise distributed networks in the first place. So from the standpoint of survivability and easy deployment, the packet radio network was conceived as a wireless version of the ARPANET, distributed rather than centralized. Over the years, the packet radio program was deployed at a handful of military sites, but technical problems made it expensive, and it was eventually phased out.

The limited range of radio signals made it necessary for packet-radio networks to use relay sites no more than a few dozen miles apart. But a link above the earth would have no such constraints. Such a relay would "see" almost an entire hemisphere of the earth. While overseeing the packet-radio projects, Kahn began to think about networks linked by satellites accessible over broad domains—to and from ships at sea, remote land-based stations, and aircraft flying almost anywhere in the world.

By the early 1970s, many communications satellites—most of them military—were in orbit. Appropriately equipped, such a satellite could serve as a relay for communication. With the huge distances involved in satellite communications, signals would be delayed. The average trip for a packet to its destination would take about one third of a second, several times longer than host-to-host delays on the ARPANET. As a result, packet-satellite networks would be slow.

Still, the idea that packet-switched networks and their attached computers could be linked by radio waves bounced from a satellite was appealing, not only to the American government but also to Europeans, because transatlantic terrestrial circuits at the time were expensive and prone to error. The satellite network was dubbed SAT-NET. Researchers in the United States were joined by British and Norwegian computer scientists, and before long satellite links were established to Italy and Germany as well. For a while, SATNET did well. In time, however, the phone company upgraded its transatlantic lines from copper to high-speed fiber-optic cable, eliminating the need for the more complicated SATNET link.

The technical lessons of radio and satellite experiments were less significant than the broader networking ideas they inspired. It was obvious there would be more networks. Several foreign governments were building data systems, and a growing number of large corporations were starting to develop networking ideas of their own. Kahn began wondering about the possibility of linking the different networks together.

The problem first occurred to him as he was working on the packet-radio project in 1972. "My first question was, 'How am I going to link this packet-radio system to any computational resources of interest?'" Kahn said. "Well, my answer was, 'Let's link it to the ARPANET,' except that these were two radically different networks in many ways." The following year, another ARPA effort, called the Internetting Project, was born.

By the time of the 1972 ICCC demonstration in Washington, the leaders of several national networking projects had formed an International Network Working Group (INWG), with Vint Cerf in charge. Packet-switching network projects in France and England were producing favorable results. Donald Davies' work at the U.K.'s National Physical Laboratory was coming along splendidly. In France, a computer scientist named Louis Pouzin was building Cyclades, a French version of the ARPANET. Both Pouzin and Davies had attended the ICCC demonstration in Washington. "The spirit after ICCC," said Alex McKenzie, BBN's representative to the INWG, "was, 'We've shown that packet-switching really works nationally. Let's take the lead in creating an international network of networks.'"

Larry Roberts was enthusiastic about INWG because he wanted to extend the reach of the ARPANET beyond the DARPA-funded world. The British and the French were equally excited about expanding the reach of their national research networks as well. "Developing network-interconnection technology was a way to realize that," said McKenzie. The INWG began pursuing what they called a "Concatenated Network," or CATENET for short, a transparent interconnection of networks of disparate technologies and speeds.

❑ An Internet

The collaboration that Bob Kahn would characterize years later as the most satisfying of his professional career took place over several months in 1973. Kahn and Vint Cerf had first met during the weeks of testing at UCLA in early 1970, when they had forced the new-born ARPANET into catatonia by overloading the IMPs with test traffic. They had remained close colleagues, and now both were thinking extensively about what it would take to create a seamless connection among different networks. "Around this time," Cerf recalled, "Bob started saying, 'Look, my problem is how I get a computer that's on a satellite net and a computer on a radio net and a computer on the ARPANET to communicate uniformly with each other without realizing what's going on in between?'" Cerf was intrigued by the problem.

Sometime during the spring of 1973, Cerf was attending a conference at a San Francisco hotel, sitting in the lobby waiting for a session to start when he began doodling out some ideas. By now he and Kahn had been talking for several months about what it would take to build a network of networks, and they had both been exchanging ideas with other members of the International Network Working Group. It occurred to Cerf and Kahn that what they needed was a "gateway," a routing computer standing between each of these various networks to hand off messages from one system to the other. But this was easier said than done. "We knew we couldn't change any of the packet nets themselves," Cerf said. "They did whatever they did because they were optimized for that environment." As far as each net was concerned, the gateway had to look like an ordinary host.

While waiting in the lobby, he drew this diagram:

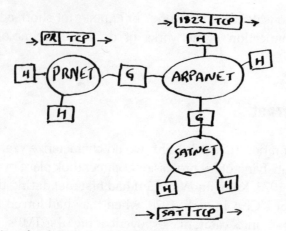

Reproduction of early Internet design ideas

"Our thought was that, clearly, each gateway had to know how to talk to each network that it was connected to," Cerf said. "Say you're connecting the packet-radio net with the ARPANET. The gateway machine has software in it that makes it look like a host to the ARPANET IMPs. But it also looks like a host on the packet-radio network."

With the notion of a gateway now defined, the next puzzle was packet transmission. As with the ARPANET, the actual path the packets traveled in an internet should be immaterial. What mattered most was that the packets arrive intact. But there was a vexing problem: All these networks—packet radio, SATNET, and the ARPANET—had different interfaces, different maximum packet sizes, and different transmission rates. How could all those differences be standardized in order to shuttle packets among networks? A second question concerned the reliability of the networks. The dynamics of radio and satellite transmission wouldn't permit reliability that was so laboriously built into the ARPANET. The Americans looked to Pouzin in France, who had deliberately chosen an approach for Cyclades that required the hosts rather than the network nodes to recover from transmission errors, shifting the burden of reliability on to the hosts.

It was clear that the host-to-host Network Control Protocol, which was designed to match the specifications of the ARPANET, would have to be replaced by a more independent protocol. The challenge for the International Network Working Group was to devise protocols that could cope with autonomous networks operating under their own rules, while still establishing standards that would allow hosts on the different networks to talk to each other. For example, CATENET would remain a system of independently administered networks, each run by its own people with its own rules. But when time came for one network to exchange data with, say, the ARPANET, the internetworking protocols would operate. The gateway computers handling the transmission couldn't care about the local complexity buried inside each network. Their only task would be to get packets through the network to the destination host on the other side, making a so-called end-to-end link.

Once the conceptual framework was established, Cerf and Kahn spent the spring and summer of 1973 working out the details. Cerf presented the problem to his Stanford graduate students, and he and Kahn joined them in attacking it. They held a seminar that concentrated on the details of developing the host-to-host protocol into a standard allowing data traffic to flow across networks. The Stanford seminar helped frame key issues, and laid the foundation for solutions that would emerge several years later.

Cerf frequently visited the DARPA offices in Arlington, Virginia, where he and Kahn discussed the problem for hours on end. During one marathon session, the two stayed up all night, alternately scribbling on Kahn's chalkboard and pacing through the deserted suburban streets, before ending up at the local Marriott for breakfast. They began collaborating on a paper and conducted their next marathon session in Cerf's neighborhood, working straight through the night at the Hyatt in Palo Alto.

That September, Kahn and Cerf presented their paper along with their ideas about the new protocol to the International Network Working Group, meeting concurrently with a communications conference at the University of Sussex in Brighton. Cerf was late arriving in England because his first child had just been born. "I arrived in midsession and was greeted by applause because word of the birth had preceded me by e-mail," Cerf recalled. During the Sussex meeting, Cerf outlined the ideas he and Kahn and the Stanford seminar had generated. The ideas were refined further in Sussex, in long discussions with researchers from Davies' and Pouzin's laboratories.

When Kahn and Cerf returned from England, they refined their paper. Both men had a stubborn side. "We'd get into this argumentative state, then step back and say, 'Let's find out what it is we're actually arguing about.'" Cerf liked to have everything organized before starting to write; Kahn preferred to sit down and write down everything he could think of, in his own logical order; reorganization came later. The collaborative writing process was intense. Recalled Cerf: "It was one of us typing and the other one breathing down his neck, composing as we'd go along, almost like two hands on a pen."

By the end of 1973, Cerf and Kahn had completed their paper, "A Protocol for Packet Network Intercommunication." They flipped a coin to determine whose name should appear first, and Cerf won the toss. The paper appeared in a widely read engineering journal the following spring.

Like Roberts's first paper outlining the proposed ARPANET seven years earlier, the Cerf-Kahn paper of May 1974 described something revolutionary. Under the framework described in the paper, messages should be encapsulated and decapsulated in "datagrams," much as a letter is put into and taken out of an envelope, and sent as end-to-end packets. These messages would be called transmission-control protocol, or TCP, messages. The paper also introduced the notion of gateways, which would read only the envelope so that only the receiving hosts would read the contents.

The TCP protocol also tackled the network reliability issues. In the ARPANET, the destination IMP was responsible for reassembling all the packets of a message when it arrived. The IMPs worked hard making sure all the packets of a message got through the network, using hop-by-hop acknowledgments and retransmission. The IMPs also made sure separate messages were kept in order. Because of all this work done by the IMPs, the old Network Control Protocol was built around the assumption that the underlying network was completely reliable.

The new transmission-control protocol, with a bow to Cyclades, assumed that the CATENET was completely unreliable. Units of information could be lost, others might be duplicated. If a packet failed to arrive or was garbled during transmission, and the sending host received no acknowledgment, an identical twin was transmitted.

The overall idea behind the new protocol was to shift the reliability from the network to the destination hosts. "We focused on end-to-end reliability," Cerf recalled. "Don't rely on anything inside those nets. The only thing that we ask the net to do is to take this chunk of bits and get it across the network. That's all we ask. Just take this datagram and do your best to deliver it."

The new scheme worked in much the same way that shipping containers are used to transfer goods. The boxes have a standard size and shape. They can be filled with anything from televisions to underwear to automobiles—content doesn't matter. They move by ship, rail, or truck. A typical container of freight travels by all three modes at various stages to reach its destination. The only thing necessary to ensure cross-compatibility is the specialized equipment used to transfer the containers from one mode of transport to the next. The cargo itself doesn't leave the container until it reaches its destination.

The invention of TCP would be absolutely crucial to networking. Without TCP, communication across networks couldn't happen. If TCP could be perfected, anyone could build a network of any size or form, and as long as that network had a gateway computer that could interpret and route packets, it could communicate with any other network. With TCP on the horizon, it was now obvious that networking had a future well beyond the experimental ARPANET. The potential power and reach of what not only Cerf and Kahn, but Louis Pouzin in France and others, were inventing was beginning to occur to people. If they could work out all the details, TCP might be the mechanism that would open up worlds.

As more resources became available over the ARPANET and as more people at the sites became familiar with them, Net usage crept upward. For news of the world, early Net regulars regularly logged on to a machine at SRI, which was connected to the Associated Press news wire. During peak times, MIT students logged on at some other computer on the Net to get their work done. Acoustic and holographic images produced at UC Santa Barbara were digitized on machines at USC and brought back over the Net to an image processor at UCSB, where they could be manipulated further. The lab at UCSB was outfitted with custom-built image-processing equipment, and UCSB researchers translated high-level mathematics into graphical output for other sites. By August 1973, while TCP was still in the design phase, traffic had grown to a daily average of 3.2 million packets.

From 1973 to 1975, the Net expanded at the rate of about one new node each month. Growth was proceeding in line with Larry Roberts's original vision, in which the network was deliberately laden with large resource providers. In this respect, DARPA had succeeded wonderfully. But the effect was an imbalance of supply and demand; there were too many resource providers, and not enough customers. The introduction of terminal IMPs, first at Mitre, then at NASA's Ames Research Center and the National Bureau of Standards with up to sixty-three terminals each, helped right the balance. Access at the host sites themselves was loosening up. The host machine at UCSB, for example, was linked to minicomputers in the political science, physics, and chemistry departments. Similar patterns were unfolding across the network map.

Like most of the early ARPANET host sites, the Center for Advanced Computation at the University of Illinois was chosen primarily for the resources it would be able to offer other Net users. At the time Roberts was mapping out the network, Illinois was slated to become home to the powerful new ILLIAC IV, a massive, one-of-a-kind high-speed computer under construction at the Burroughs Corporation in Paoli, Pennsylvania. The machine was guaranteed to attract researchers from around the country.

An unexpected twist of circumstances, however, led the University of Illinois to become the network's first large-scale consumer instead of a resource supplier. Students on the Urbana campus were convinced the ILLIAC IV was going to be used to simulate bombing scenarios for the Vietnam War and to perform top-secret research on campus. As campus protests erupted over the impending installation, university officials grew concerned about their ability to protect the ILLIAC IV. When Burroughs finished construction of the machine, it was sent to a more secure facility run by NASA.

But the Center for Advanced Computation already had its IMP and full access to the network. Researchers there took quickly to the newfound ability to exploit remote computing resources—so quickly, in fact, that the Center terminated the $40,000 monthly lease on its own high-powered Burroughs B6700. In its place, the university began contracting for computer services over the ARPANET. By doing this, the computation center cut its computer bill nearly in half. This was the economy of scale envisioned by Roberts, taken to a level beyond anyone's expectations. Soon, the Center was obtaining more than 90 percent of its computer resources through the network.

Large databases scattered across the Net were growing in popularity. The Computer Corporation of America had a machine called the Datacomputer that was essentially an information warehouse, with weather and seismic data fed into the machine around the clock. Hundreds of people logged in every week, making it the busiest site on the network for several years.

Abetted by the new troves of data, the ARPANET was beginning to attract the attention of computer researchers from a variety of fields. Access to the Net was still limited to sites with DARPA contracts, but the diversity of users at those sites was nonetheless creating a community of users distinct from the engineers and computer scientists who built the ARPANET. Programmers helping to design medical studies could tie in to the National Library of Medicine's rich MEDLINE database. The UCLA School of Public Health set up an experimental database of mental health program evaluations.

To serve the growing user community, SRI researchers established a unique resource called the *ARPANET News* in March 1973. Distributed monthly in ink-on-paper form, the journal was also available over the Net. A mix of conference listings, site updates, and abstracts of technical papers, the newsletter read like small-town gossip riddled with computer jargon. One of the more important items in the ARPANET *News* was the "Featured Site" series, in which system managers from the growing list of host computers described what they had to offer. In May 1973 Case Western Reserve University, which was selling computer services to network users, described its PDP-10 in terms that sounded altogether like an ad from the Personals section: "Case is open to collaborative propositions involving barters of time with other sites for work related to interests here, and sales of time as a service."

Communicating by computer and using remote resources were still cumbersome processes. For the most part, the Net remained a user-hostile environment, requiring relatively sophisticated programming knowledge and an understanding of the diverse systems running on the hosts. Demand was growing among users for "higher-level" application programs aimed at helping users tap into the variety of resources now available. The file-transfer and Telnet programs existed, but the user community wanted more tools, such as common editors and accounting schemes.

SRI's Network Information Center estimated the number of users at about two thousand. But a newly formed users' interest group, called USING, was convinced there was a gap between the design of the network resources and the needs of the people trying to use those resources. Envisioning itself as a lobby group, a consumers' union even, USING began immediately to draw up plans and recommendations for improving the delivery of computer services over the ARPANET.

But DARPA saw no need to share authority with a tiny self-appointed watchdog group made up of people the agency viewed as passengers on its experimental vehicle. The initiative died after about nine months with a terse memo from a DARPA program manager named Craig Fields, warning the group that it had overstepped its bounds. With neither funding nor official support for their effort forthcoming, members put USING into a state of suspended animation from which it never emerged.

Other problems developed for DARPA as the profile of the network began to rise. Like the USING insurgency, most were relatively minor affairs. But together they illustrated the ongoing tensions related to DARPA's stewardship of the network. One area of tension had to do with DARPA's Pentagon masters. IPTO in particular managed to steer clear of the most blatantly military research. But while the Illinois students were wrong about the ILLIAC IV being used for simulated bombing missions against North Vietnam, there *were* plans to use it for nuclear attack scenarios against the Soviet Union. Similarly, researchers of all sorts used seismic information stored on the Computer Corporation of America (CCA) database server, information that was being collected to support Pentagon projects involving underground atomic testing.

In the late 1960s, growing political unrest—both violent and nonviolent—caught the U.S. military by surprise. Army intelligence knew all about Prague, Berlin, and Moscow, but now the Pentagon was contemplating Newark, Detroit, and Chicago. The Army gathered information from dozens of U.S. cities on the location of police and fire stations, hospitals, and so forth. Someone in the Pentagon thought it would be a good idea to keep track of local troublemakers as well.

In 1972 public outcry erupted over the Army's information gathering, and the order went out for the files to be destroyed immediately. But three years later, allegations surfaced that Army intelligence officers had instead used the ARPANET to move the files to a new location. When the story broke, the fact that something like the ARPANET existed was news to most Americans. That the story was reported in the most draconian, cloak-and-dagger terms only added to the stormy reaction. The result was a Senate investigation in which DARPA was called upon to explain how it was using the ARPANET.

DARPA eventually proved that the Army files had not moved on the ARPANET by reviewing hundreds of rolls of Teletype printouts that had been stored in a dusty crawl space at BBN. DARPA was vindicated, but a perceived entanglement with the Army's clandestine operations was the last thing the ARPANET needed.

❑ Changes at DARPA

Discussions about how DARPA would ultimately divest operational responsibility for the network had already begun around 1971. DARPA had set out to link the core processing capabilities in America's top computer science research centers, and as far as the agency was now concerned, it had accomplished that. Its mission was research. It wasn't supposed to be in the business of operating a network. Now that the system was up and running, it was becoming a drain on other priorities. It was time for DARPA to shed the service provider's role.

Handling the transition was a touchy matter. The ARPANET was now a valuable tool, and Roberts's goal was to ensure its continued development. He commissioned several studies to help determine the best option. The best route, it seemed, was to maintain a networking research effort, but sell off the network itself to a private contractor. But sell to whom? The market for data-communications networks was still largely uncharted, and the big communications companies remained as skeptical as ever about the DARPA technology.

When Roberts contacted AT&T to see if it wanted to take over the ARPANET, AT&T formed a committee of corporate and Bell Labs staff and studied the idea for months. AT&T could have owned the network as a monopoly service, but in the end declined. "They finally concluded that the packet technology was incompatible with the AT&T network," Roberts said.

Others were not so blind to the prospects of computer networking. In July 1972 three engineers left BBN to form a company that would market a commercial network called Packet Communications Incorporated. And BBN itself had spoken to Roberts about buying the network and setting up a subsidiary company to operate it. Small, specialized, commercial carriers like these were the obvious solution to DARPA's problem.

But soon Roberts had a new problem. In early 1973, BBN recruited him to run a new subsidiary called TELENET (not to be confused with Telnet, the program for remote log-ins), which would market a private packet-switching service. Now unable to recommend a sale by the government to TELENET, Roberts arranged to have the ARPANET transferred temporarily to the Defense Communications Agency—the same agency that Baran had refused to let build his network ten years earlier. The generals and majors and captains were still only slightly more receptive to the idea of a packet-switched network than AT&T, but Roberts expected this to be only an interim arrangement.

Having decided to accept the post at TELENET, Roberts now had the job of finding a successor. DARPA's Information Processing Techniques Office, however, no longer held the appeal it once had for those in academe. Roberts approached a couple of his principal investigators at universities, but people who had active research programs did not want to leave them. Others were concerned about the salary cuts they would have to take to come to the DARPA office.

When Licklider heard of the trouble Roberts was having, he offered to return if Roberts needed him. Roberts knew it was just a gesture on Licklider's part. Lick was now happily entrenched back at MIT. But after six months of searching, Roberts decided he didn't have a choice. When Roberts called Lick's office at MIT, he was told that Lick was on a walking tour in England. Roberts tracked him down in the middle of Wales and asked him if he was serious about taking the job. Licklider said yes. "I never saw Larry so overjoyed as when he finally got his replacement, because he was ready to go," recalled a colleague of Roberts. "I think some of his delight was also the fact that Lick was going to take it, because he liked him. Everybody did."

One of the first problems Lick faced upon his return was an awkward one involving BBN, his onetime employer. BBN was refusing to release the IMP source code—the original operating program written by the IMP Guys five years earlier.

BBN's apparent impulse to control every aspect of the network created a certain tension from the beginning. Len Kleinrock and his group at UCLA's Network Measurement Center had found it particularly frustrating. The center's job was to find problems in the network, but when they did, BBN refused to help. "Whenever we found a software bug or inefficiency, we'd alert Heart specifically, and the response we got was typically almost a stiff arm," said Kleinrock. "He'd say, 'Look, the network is working, I've got a network to keep up and running and we'll put your comment in the queue.' We couldn't fix it ourselves because we didn't have the source code."

The intellectual property issue finally boiled over when the engineers who left BBN to start their own company made a pointed request for their former employer to turn over the IMP source code. When BBN refused, they appealed to DARPA. While keeping source code proprietary is usually the prerogative of the company that develops it, the IMP source code was different, for it had been developed by BBN with federal funds. Moreover, BBN was in the midst of starting up the TELENET subsidiary, which would be competing with the company started by the engineers. There was some concern at DARPA that if anyone in Congress or the press corps latched onto the fact that BBN's subsidiary and no one else had access to the Defense Department–sponsored IMP technology, the agency could have a major problem on its hands.

Frank Heart and Dave Walden at BBN argued that since the source code was changed frequently to improve performance or fix bugs, the company was uncomfortable with distributing software that would become obsolete. The company held its ground.

Steve Crocker, by then a DARPA program manager who oversaw most of BBN's contracts, took charge of the situation. He had control of about $6 million worth of work a year at BBN, about a quarter of the firm's gross revenues. "I seriously considered moving all of the work we were supporting at BBN to other places because we couldn't reach closure with them on the data rights to the IMP code," he said. And he let BBN know what he was thinking.

Lick had had a long association with BBN, and he had high regard for people there, but he was dismayed by their posture. Reaction throughout the computer community was much the same. Finally, in direct response to Crocker's threat, BBN agreed to provide the code to whoever asked for it, charging a nominal handling fee. "This was just an early version of much more serious intellectual property rights issues that emerged across the industry over the next few decades," Crocker said.

With Bob Kahn's help, Licklider also finished the job of spinning off the network to the Defense Communications Agency. Roberts's earlier probes into selling off the network notwithstanding, federal rules required that a resource as rich as the ARPANET couldn't just be sold to an outside party until the Defense Department determined whether it had a need for the Net in Defense. The agency eventually decided it did. In the summer of 1975, DCA took over the network management job from DARPA. Now DCA set operational policy for the network. DCA decided such things as where and when new nodes would be installed and what the configuration of data lines should be. And BBN retained the contract for network operations, which meant the company carried out the decisions made by DCA. Shortly after the transition had been made, Lick returned to MIT, where he would spend the remainder of his career.

Soon everyone at BBN noticed an increasing number of forms that had to be filled out, even for the smallest of jobs. The DCA bureaucracy rattled many of the university people, too. "The agency generated a blizzard of memoranda from colonels and generals about things you were and weren't allowed to do," recalled Brian Reid. A few months after DCA took over the ARPANET, several of the graduate students in Stanford's computer science department came to a Halloween party dressed as colonels.

Relieved of the day-to-day management chores, DARPA was now able to concentrate on developing the new CATENET protocols. By 1975, Yogen Dalal, a Stanford graduate student, had polished the Transmission-Control Protocol from Cerf and Kahn's 1974 paper into a set of concrete specifications. The TCP specification was sent to three separate places for concurrent implementation: BBN, Cerf's computer lab at Stanford, and University College, London.

At about the same time, Kahn and Steve Crocker began talking to Cerf about taking a job as a DARPA program manager in Washington. "I flew there and landed in a big snowstorm and thought, I don't want to live in this part of the country," Cerf recalled. "So I said no. But the real reason was I was afraid I wouldn't do a very good job. I thought it would be a very visible position and if I screwed up, everybody would know."

A year later, Kahn and Crocker tried again. This time Cerf accepted. "I was getting a little tired of being so fragmented at Stanford. I couldn't get any research done. So I thought, Why not go to DARPA and have a bigger impact, because instead of the small little budgets I got at Stanford for my work, at DARPA I'd have an opportunity to have a bigger impact with more money to spend."

As a program manager, Cerf was given responsibility for the packet radio, packet satellite, and research programs in what was now simply called the ARPA Internet. Cerf also continued working intensively on refining the TCP specification. A milestone occurred in October 1977, when Cerf and Kahn and a dozen or so others demonstrated the first three-network system with packet radio, the ARPANET, and SATNET, all functioning in concert. Messages traveled from the San Francisco Bay area through a packet-radio net, then the ARPANET, and then a dedicated satellite link to London, back across the packet-satellite network and across the ARPANET again, and finally to the University of Southern California's Information Sciences Institute (ISI) in Marina del Rey. The packets traveled 94,000 miles without dropping a single bit.

During a break from a meeting Cerf chaired at ISI to discuss TCP in early 1978, Cerf, Postel, and Danny Cohen, a colleague of Postel's at ISI, got into a discussion in a hallway. "We were drawing diagrams on a big piece of cardboard that we leaned up against the wall in the hallway," Postel recalled. When the meeting resumed, the trio presented an idea to the group: break off the piece of the Transmission-Control Protocol that deals with routing packets and form a separate Internet Protocol, or IP.

After the split, TCP would be responsible for breaking up messages into datagrams, reassembling them at the other end, detecting errors, resending anything that got lost, and putting packets back in the right order. The Internet Protocol, or IP, would be responsible for routing individual datagrams.

"I remember having a general guideline about what went into IP versus what was in TCP," Postel recalled. "The rule was 'Do the gateways need this information in order to move the packet?' If not, then that information does not go in IP." This twist on the protocol was inspired by a group of engineers from the Xerox Corporation's Palo Alto Research Center who had attended the Stanford seminar. The Xerox team had solved similar issues on a smaller, proprietary scale by defining a family of protocols called the PARC Universal Packet, or PUP. Once Postel decided that creating a separate protocol was the right thing to do, he set about making sure it got done. With a clean separation of the protocols, it was now possible to build fast and relatively inexpensive gateways, which would in turn fuel the growth of internetworking. By 1978, TCP had officially become TCP/IP.

❑ ETHERNET

In 1973, just when Cerf and Kahn had begun collaborating on the concept of internetworking, Bob Metcalfe at Xerox PARC was inventing the technological underpinnings for a new kind of network. Called a short-distance, or local-area, network, Metcalfe's network would connect computers not in different cities but in different rooms.

Metcalfe had received his undergraduate degrees in electrical engineering and management from MIT and enrolled at Harvard for graduate school. But he hated Harvard immediately. "Harvard is full of old-money people," he said. "MIT is full of no money. It was a class thing."

Metcalfe took a job at MIT, where he felt more comfortable. The Institute was about to join the ARPANET, and he was assigned to build the interface between MIT's PDP-10 and its IMP. Harvard had a PDP-10, too, and Metcalfe offered to make a duplicate interface to give to Harvard. But the networking people at Harvard declined the offer. "They said they couldn't possibly let a graduate student do something that important," said Metcalfe. Harvard officials decided to have BBN do it. BBN in turn gave the job to its graduate student in residence, Ben Barker, who recruited John McQuillan, a fellow Harvard graduate student, to help him.

Although enrolled at Harvard, Metcalfe stayed at MIT to work on his dissertation, an examination of the ARPANET. When Metcalfe submitted the work, Harvard rejected the finished dissertation as insufficiently theoretical (too much engineering and not enough science, he was told). The rejection was embarrassing for Metcalfe, who had just taken a job at Xerox Corporation's Palo Alto Research Center after persuading his wife to leave her job to join him. He went to Xerox PARC anyway and began looking for a more theoretical topic for his thesis.

Then in 1972, while on DARPA-related business for PARC, Metcalfe stayed at the Washington home of his friend Steve Crocker. Crocker had gathered together some of the best technical people from the early sites to assist new sites and called these people "network facilitators." Metcalfe, who had become something of an ARPANET expert at MIT, was one of them.

Crocker had just been visited by Norm Abramson, the primary architect of the ALOHA network at the University of Hawaii. On the night of Metcalfe's visit, Crocker left one of Abramson's papers about the ALOHA network out. Metcalfe picked it up and read it before going to sleep. The paper kept him up much of the night. "The math in the paper was not only familiar but infuriating," he said, "because they made the typical inaccurate assumptions that people make so that their models work."

Metcalfe's chance encounter with Abramson's paper was to change his life. "I set out to make a new model for the ALOHA system." Within a few weeks, he was on a Xerox-funded trip to the University of Hawaii. He stayed a month, and before coming home had added an extensive analysis of the ALOHA system to his thesis. It was just the theoretical boost the dissertation needed. When he resubmitted the work, it was accepted.

But the ALOHA system gave Metcalfe far more than a doctorate.

Xerox PARC was in the process of developing one of the first personal computers, called the Alto. The company saw that customers would want to connect the machines, so Metcalfe, one of the resident networking experts, was assigned the task of tying the Altos together. Without a store-and-forward model, preventing data packets from colliding was impossible. But simply scaling down the ARPANET by building a subnet of IMP-like store-and-forward computers would have been prohibitively expensive for a system designed to work in an office building.

Metcalfe had an idea, borrowed directly from the ALOHANET—in fact, he would call it the Alto Aloha Network: Let the data packets collide, then retransmit at a random time. But Metcalfe's idea differed in several respects from the Hawaiian system. For one thing, his network would be a thousand times faster than ALOHANET. It would also include collision detection. But perhaps most important, Metcalfe's network would be hardwired, running not by radio waves but on cables connecting computers in different rooms, or among clusters of buildings.

One computer wishing to send a data packet to another machine—say, a desktop workstation sending to a printer—listens for traffic on the cable. If the computer detects conflicting transmissions, it waits, usually for a few thousandths of a second. When the cable is quiet, the computer begins transmitting its packet. If, during the transmission, it detects a collision, it stops and waits before trying again—usually a few hundred microseconds. In both instances, the computer chooses the delay randomly, minimizing the possibility of retrying at the same instant selected by whatever device sent the signal that caused the collision. As the network gets busier, computers back off and retry over longer random intervals. This keeps the process efficient and the channel intact.

"Imagine you're at a party and several people are standing around having a conversation," said Butler Lampson, who helped Metcalfe develop the idea, describing the system. "One person stops talking and somebody else wants to talk. Well, there's no guarantee that only one person wants to talk; perhaps several do.

It's not uncommon for two people to start talking at once. But what typically happens? Usually they both stop, there's a bit of hesitation, and then one starts up again."

Metcalfe and Lampson, along with Xerox researchers David Boggs and Chuck Thacker, built their first Alto Aloha system in Bob Taylor's lab at Xerox PARC. To their great delight, it worked. In May 1973 Metcalfe suggested a name, recalling the hypothetical luminiferous medium invented by nineteenth-century physicists to explain how light passes through empty space. He rechristened the system Ethernet.

❏ CSNET

DCA, the ARPANET's caretaker, wasn't the only R&D agency in Washington to have grown bureaucratic. Nowhere in Washington could you walk into your boss's office anymore with a bright idea for a project and walk out twenty minutes later with a million dollars in support. In the mid-1970s, the only organization that bore any resemblance to the ARPA of old was the National Science Foundation. The foundation was created in 1950 to promote progress in science by funding basic research and strengthening education in science. By the late 1970s, NSF was on the rise in the computing field.

Not only was NSF a new likely source of sufficient funds, it was also the only organization whose officials could act on behalf of the entire scientific community. DARPA had provided the research base and new technology. Now NSF would carry it forward to a larger community.

Officials at NSF had been interested in creating a network for the academic computer science community for some time. In a 1974 report, an NSF advisory committee concluded that such a service "would create a frontier environment which would offer advanced communication, collaboration, and the sharing of resources among geographically separated or isolated researchers." At that point, NSF was mostly concerned with spurring the development of what was still a fledgling discipline. Perhaps because computer science was still an emerging field on most campuses, nothing much came of the notion.

By the late 1970s, computer science departments had mushroomed. The advantages of the ARPANET were now clear. Rapid electronic communication with colleagues and easy resource-sharing meant tasks that usually took weeks could now be finished in hours. Electronic mail created a new world of fast samizdat, replacing the slow postal services and infrequent conferences. The network had become as essential to computer science research as telescopes were to astronomers.

But the ARPANET was threatening to split the community of computer researchers into haves and have-nots. In 1979 there were about 120 academic computer science departments around the country, but just fifteen of the sixty-one ARPANET sites were located at universities. Faculty candidates and graduate students alike were starting to accept or decline offers based on whether or not a school had access to the Net, putting research institutions without an ARPANET node at a disadvantage in the race to land top scholars and the research grants that followed them.

More important, an exodus of computing talent from academia to industry had caused a nationwide fear that the United States would not be able to train its next generation of computer scientists. The lure of private sector salaries was part of the problem. But scientists weren't just being pulled into industry; they were also being pushed. Computer facilities at many universities were obsolete or underpowered, making it hard for people on campuses to stay abreast of the rapidly changing computer field.

Little could be done about the salary discrepancies between academia and industry. But the resource problem was essentially the same one that DARPA had faced a decade earlier. A network for computer scientists would reduce the need for duplicative efforts. And if this network was open to private research sites, there would be less pressure on researchers to leave the universities in order to keep up with their discipline.

Clear though the solution seemed, implementing it proved an-

242 ❑ **WHERE WIZARDS STAY UP LATE**

other matter. Linking the computer science departments to the ARPANET was out of the question. To be assigned a site, universities had to be involved in specific kinds of government-funded research, typically defense-related. Even then, it was costly to allocate new sites. ARPANET connections came in one size only: extra large. The system used costly leased telephone lines, and each node had to maintain two or more links to other sites. As a result, maintaining an ARPANET site cost more than $100,000 each year, regardless of the traffic it generated.

The computer scientists had to invent another way. In May 1979, Larry Landweber, head of the computer science department at the University of Wisconsin, invited representatives of six universities to Madison to discuss the possibility of building a new Computer Science Research Network, to be called CSNET. Although DARPA couldn't provide financial support, the agency sent Bob Kahn to the meeting as an advisor. NSF, which had raised the academic network issue five years earlier, sent Kent Curtis, the head of its computer research division. After the meeting, Landweber spent the summer working with Peter Denning from Purdue, Dave Farber from the University of Delaware, and Tony Hearn who had recently left the University of Utah for the RAND Corporation, to flesh out a detailed proposal for the new network.

Their proposal called for a network open to computer science researchers in academia, government, and industry. The underlying medium would be a commercial service provider like TELENET. Because CSNET would be using slower links than those used by the ARPANET, and did not insist on redundant linkages, the system would be far less expensive. The network would be run by a consortium of eleven universities, at an estimated five-year cost of $3 million. Because of the DCA policy restricting ARPANET access to DOD contractors only, the proposal contained no gateway between the two networks. A draft of the proposal circulated by the group received enthusiastic praise. They sent the final version to NSF in November 1979.

But after nearly four months of peer review, NSF rejected the proposal, although it remained enthusiastic about the CSNET idea. So

NSF sponsored a workshop to overcome the deficiencies that NSF's reviewers found in the draft proposal. Landweber and company returned to their drawing boards.

In the summer of 1980, Landweber's committee came back with a way to tailor the architecture of CSNET to provide affordable access to even the smallest lab. They proposed a three-tiered structure involving ARPANET, a TELENET-based system, and an e-mail-only service called PhoneNet. Gateways would connect the tiers into a seamless whole.

Under the new proposal, NSF would support CSNET for a five-year startup period, after which it was to be fully funded by user fees. A university's annual costs, a combination of dues and connection charges, ranged from a few thousand dollars for PhoneNet service (mostly for the long-distance phone connections) to $21,000 for a TELENET site.

As to how the network would be managed—a concern of the National Science Board, the NSF's governing body—the plan took a novel approach. For the first two years, the NSF itself would play the role of manager for the university consortium. After that, responsibility would be handed off to the University Corporation for Atmospheric Research. UCAR was familiar with advanced computing work and had the expertise to handle a project involving so many academic institutions. More important, the Science Board knew UCAR and trusted its management skills. The Board agreed to provide nearly $5 million for the CSNET project.

By June 1983, more than seventy sites were on-line, obtaining full services and paying annual dues. At the end of the five-year period of NSF support in 1986, nearly all the country's computer science departments, as well as a large number of private computer research sites, were connected. The network was financially stable and financially self-sufficient.

The experience that NSF gained in the process of starting up CSNET paved the way for more NSF ventures in computer networking.

In the mid-1980s, on the heels of CSNET's success, more networks began to emerge. One, called BITNET (the Because It's Time Net-

work), was a cooperative network among IBM systems with no restrictions on membership. Another, called UUCP, was built at Bell
Laboratories for file transfer and remote-command execution.
USENET, which began in 1980 as a means of communication between
two machines (one at the University of North Carolina and one at
Duke University), blossomed into a distributed news network using
UUCP. NASA had its own network called the Space Physics Analysis Network, or SPAN. Because this growing conglomeration of networks was able to communicate using the TCP/IP protocols, the
collection of networks gradually came to be called the "Internet,"
borrowing the first word of "Internet Protocol."

By now, a distinction had emerged between "internet" with a
small *i*, and "Internet" with a capital *I*. Officially, the distinction was
simple: "internet" meant any network using TCP/IP while "Internet" meant the public, federally subsidized network that was made
up of many linked networks all running the TCP/IP protocols.
Roughly speaking, an "internet" is private and the "Internet" is
public. The distinction didn't really matter until the mid-1980s
when router vendors began to sell equipment to construct private
internets. But the distinction quickly blurred as the private internets
built gateways to the public Internet.

At around the same time, private corporations and research institutions were building networks that used TCP/IP. The market
opened up for routers. Gateways were the internetworking varia-
tion on IMPs, while routers were the mass-produced version of
gateways, hooking local area networks to the ARPANET. Sometime in
the early 1980s a marketing vice president at BBN was approached
by Alex McKenzie and another BBN engineer who thought the
company should get into the business of building routers. It made
sense. BBN had built the IMPs and the TIPs, and even the first gateway for the Internet as part of the packet radio program. But the
marketing man, after doing some quick calculations in his head, decided there wasn't much promise in routers. He was wrong.

Also in the middle of the 1980s several academic research
networks in Europe sprang to life. In Canada there was CDNet.
Gradually, however, each network built a gateway to the U.S.

Government–sponsored Internet and borders began to dissolve. And gradually the Internet came to mean the loose matrix of inter-connected TCP/IP networks worldwide.

By now, all research scientists with NSF support—not just com-puter scientists, but oceanographers, astronomers, chemists, and others—came to believe they were at a competitive disadvantage unless they had network access. And CSNET, which was to be used only by academic computer science departments, wasn't the an-swer. But CSNET was the stepping stone to NSF's major accomplish-ment, NSFNET.

The model of CSNET convinced NSF of the importance of net-working to the scientific community. The professional advantages to be gained from the ability to communicate with one's peers was incalculable. And since the agency had been working so closely with the computer scientists, it had a number of people internally who understood networking and were able to help manage pro-grams. But NSF didn't have the means to build a national network. Maintaining the ARPANET alone cost millions of dollars a year.

The creation in 1985 of five supercomputer centers scattered around the United States offered a solution. Physicists and others were agitating for a "backbone" to interconnect the supercomputer centers. The NSF agreed to build the backbone network, to be called NSFNET. At the same time, the NSF offered that if the academic in-stitutions in a geographic region put together a community net-work, the agency would give the community network access to the backbone network. The idea was not only to offer access but also to give the regional networks access to each other. With this arrange-ment, any computer could communicate with any other through a series of links.

In response, a dozen or so regional networks were formed around the country. Each had the exclusive franchise in that region to connect to the NSFNET backbone. In Upstate New York, NYSERNET (for New York State Educational Research Network) was formed. In San Diego there was the California Educational Research Network, or CERFnet (although Vint Cerf had no relationship to the network, the CERFnet founders invited him to its inauguration). The funding for the regional networks would come from the member companies themselves. The NSF provided the backbone as essentially a "free good" to the academic community in the sense that the regional networks didn't pay to use it. On the other hand, NSF grants to universities to connect their campuses to the regional network were always two-year, strictly nonrenewable grants. This meant that after two years, universities were paying the cost of the regional connection out of their own pockets. Typical charges were between $20,000 and $50,000 per year for a high-speed connection.

❏ TCP/IP versus OSI

In 1982 Vint Cerf announced that he was going to leave ARPA to take a job at MCI. Earlier that year he had met an MCI executive whose job was to get MCI into the data business. "His idea was to build a digital post office," Cerf recalled. "I was immediately grabbed by the idea." The reaction to Cerf's leaving was shock. One colleague cried. "Vint was as close to a general as we had," said another.

Cerf was leaving at a critical time for the network. The ARPANET was about to make its official transition to TCP/IP, but no one knew for certain whether the U.S. Government was serious about embracing it. The Defense Department had endorsed TCP/IP, but the civilian branch of the government had not. And there was mounting concern that the National Bureau of Standards would decide to support an emergent rival standard for network interconnection called the OSI Reference Model.

Several years earlier, the International Organization for Standardization, ISO, had begun to develop its own internetworking "reference" model, called OSI, or open-systems interconnection. Since the 1940s, ISO had specified worldwide standards for things ranging from wine-tasting glasses to credit cards to photographic film to computers. They hoped their OSI model would become as ubiquitous to computers as double-A batteries were to portable radios.

A battle of sorts was forming along familiar lines, recalling the confrontation between AT&T and the inventors of packet-switching during the birth of ARPANET. On the OSI side stood entrenched bureaucracy, with a strong we-know best attitude, patronizing and occasionally contemptuous. "There was a certain attitude among certain parts of the OSI community whose message was, 'Time to roll up your toy academic network,'" recalled one ardent TCP/IP devotee. "They thought TCP/IP and Internet were just that—an academic toy." No one ever claimed that what had started with the Network Working Group and continued throughout the academic community for years had been anything but ad hoc. Someone had written the first RFC in a bathroom, for heaven's sake. Not only had the RFC series never been officially commissioned by ARPA, but some of the RFCs were, quite literally, jokes.

But the Internet community—people like Cerf and Kahn and Postel, who had spent years working on TCP/IP—opposed the OSI model from the start. First there were the technical differences, chief among them that OSI had a more complicated and compartmentalized design. And it was a *design,* never tried. As far as the Internet crowd was concerned, they had actually implemented TCP/IP several times over, whereas the OSI model had never been put to the tests of daily use, and trial and error.

In fact, as far as the Internet community was concerned, the OSI model was nothing but a collection of abstractions. "Everything about OSI was described in a very abstract, academic way," Cerf said. "The language they used was turgid beyond belief. You couldn't read an OSI document if your life depended on it."

TCP/IP, on the other hand, reflected experience. It was up and running on an actual network. "We could try things out," Cerf said. "In fact we felt compelled to try things out, because in the end there was no point in specifying something if you weren't going to build it. We had this constant pragmatic feedback about whether things worked or didn't."

Cerf and others argued that TCP/IP couldn't have been invented anywhere but in the collaborative research world, which was precisely what made it so successful, while a camel like OSI couldn't have been invented anywhere but in a thousand committees. Perhaps most important, the Defense Department had already announced its choice of TCP and IP as the protocols that would run on military computers.

ISO meetings, which were often held overseas in the 1980s, were occasionally painful experiences for people like Cerf and Postel. They attended them only to feel like King Canute yelling at the incoming tide. "I was the guy who was forever writing the counterpaper," Cerf recalled.

If anyone could claim credit for having worked tirelessly to promote TCP/IP, it was Cerf. The magic of the Internet was that its computers used a very simple communications protocol. And the magic of Vint Cerf, a colleague once remarked, was that he cajoled and negotiated and urged user communities into adopting it.

While at MCI in 1983, building what was to become MCI Mail, Cerf tried to get IBM, Digital, and Hewlett-Packard to support TCP/IP, but they refused and adopted OSI instead. Digital, in particular, had invested a great deal of money in its DECNET network, based on OSI. TCP/IP, they argued, was "a research thing." Cerf was disappointed and a little irked. "They said they weren't gonna make products out of it. So I had to build MCI Mail out of a dog's breakfast of protocols." Cerf patched together MCI Mail from existing protocols that were being used internally by Digital and IBM, and developed a few more specifically for MCI Mail. "I understood why they took the position they did, but it still bugged me."

❏ The Switch

On January 1, 1983, the ARPANET was to make its official transition to TCP/IP. Every ARPANET user was supposed to have made the switch from the Network Control Protocol to TCP/IP. On that day, the protocol that had governed the ARPANET would be mothballed, so that only those machines running the new protocols could communicate over the network. Some sites that hadn't made the transition yet pleaded their case to Postel or his colleague Dan Lynch, or, to Bob Kahn, who was overseeing the transition, and usually won a grace period. But by the spring of 1983, either you had made the conversion or your machine fell off the network.

As milestones go, the transition to TCP/IP was perhaps the most important event that would take place in the development of the Internet for years to come. After TCP/IP was installed, the network could branch anywhere; the protocols made the transmission of data from one network to another a trivial task. "To borrow a phrase," Cerf said, "now it could go where no network had gone before." An impressive array of networks now existed—from the ARPANET to TELENET to Cyclades. There were so many, in fact, that in an attempt to impose some order, Jon Postel issued an RFC assigning numbers to the networks.

In 1983 the Defense Communications Agency decided that the ARPANET had grown large enough that security was now a concern. The agency split the network into two parts: the MILNET, for sites carrying nonclassified military information, and the ARPANET for the computer research community. Before the split, there were 113 nodes in the combined network. Afterward, 45 nodes remained with the ARPANET, and the rest went to MILNET. Administratively and operationally there were two different networks, but with gateways connecting them users couldn't tell. The old ARPANET had become a full-fledged Internet.

In 1988, five years after the 1983 ARPANET transition to TCP/IP, the ISO finally produced standards for Open Systems Interconnection, and the U.S. Government immediately adopted the rival OSI protocols as its official standard. It appeared that OSI might prevail over TCP/IP. In Europe, where national governments decree the standards, it seemed an article of faith that OSI was the solution.

On the other hand, an American culture of the Internet was growing exponentially, and its foundation was TCP/IP. And while governments throughout Europe were anointing OSI, something of an underground movement sprang up at European universities to implement TCP/IP.

One key development in determining the outcome between TCP/IP and OSI turned out to be the popularity of the UNIX operating system, which had been developed at AT&T's Bell Laboratories in 1969.

Programmers liked UNIX for two primary reasons: Its flexibility let them tailor it to whatever program they were working on, and it was "portable," meaning it could be made to work on many different computers. In the late 1970s, programmers at Berkeley developed their own brand of UNIX, and seeded the computer science community with it. Berkeley UNIX eventually became a fixture at universities and research institutions all over the world. Around 1981, Bill Joy, a UNIX hacker at Berkeley, got ARPA funding to write TCP/IP into a version of Berkeley UNIX. BBN had already written a version of UNIX with TCP/IP, but Joy didn't like it and decided to do it his own way.

Then, in 1982, Joy joined a couple of Stanford Business School graduates who were starting a new company to build and sell powerful "workstations," computers that were of an order of magnitude more powerful than personal computers. Joy was brought in as the UNIX expert. They called their company Sun (for Stanford University Network) Microsystems. The first Sun machines were shipped with the Berkeley version of UNIX, complete with TCP/IP. Berkeley UNIX with TCP/IP would be crucial to the growth of the Internet. When Sun included network software as part of every machine it sold and didn't charge separately for it, networking exploded.

It further mushroomed because of Ethernet.

While packet radio and SATNET sparked the thinking about a conceptual framework for internetworking, they were largely experimental. Ethernet—the local area network designed by Bob Metcalfe and his colleagues at Xerox PARC back in 1973—was a practical solution to the problem of how to tie computers together, either on a campus or at a company. Xerox began selling Ethernet as a commercial product in 1980. At around the same time, Bob Taylor's division at Xerox PARC gave a grant to major research universities in the form of Ethernet equipment, powerful computers, and laser printers. It amounted to millions of dollars worth of hardware. Then a small networking company called Ungermann-Bass sold Ethernet as a connection between terminals and host computers. And Metcalfe started his own company, 3Com, to sell Ethernet for commercial computers, including Sun machines.

Throughout the early 1980s, local area networks were the rage. Every university hooked its workstations to local area networks. Rather than connect to a single large computer, universities wanted to connect their entire local area network—or LAN—to the ARPANET.

Ethernet made this possible. Ethernets were simple and, compared to the 50-kilobit lines of the ARPANET, they were tremendously powerful. Their rapid growth in the university and research community pushed the demand for network interconnection. If your whole university was not connected to the ARPANET, CSNET gave you a way to connect one computer at your university to the ARPANET. But it was Ethernet that created a huge networking constituency.

At major research universities there would be a network of hundreds of computers that could all talk to each other over an Ethernet network. To send traffic from an Ethernet in say, San Diego, to another Ethernet in Buffalo, you sent it through the ARPANET hub. In this way, the ARPANET was the centerpiece of what was called the ARPA Internet. And through the first half of the 1980s, the ARPA Internet resembled a star, with various networks surrounding the ARPANET at the center.

Perhaps what TCP/IP had to recommend it most was the fact that it was unerringly "open." Its entire design was an open process, following a path first blazed by Steve Crocker and the Network Working Group and continuing into the Internet. The ARPANET, and later the Internet, grew as much from the free availability of software and documentation as from anything else. (By contrast, Digital Equipment's DECNET was a proprietary network.) The Internet also supported a wide range of network technologies. Although the satellite and packet-radio networks had finite lifetimes, they helped open developers' eyes to the need to handle a multitude of different networks.

❑ Reforming e-mail

The TCP and IP standards weren't the only major renovation to net-working in the early 1980s. For years, every e-mail program written for the ARPANET had depended on the original file-transfer protocol to serve as its barge for schlepping the mail back and forth. It may have been a neat hack to attach the mail commands to the file-transfer protocol at first, but the processing of e-mail had grown more complicated. In a message to his colleagues in the MsgGroup mailing list one day in late August 1982, Postel said, "If you really go look at the FTP spec, you will see that the mail commands are really some sort of wart." Postel and a lot of others felt it was time to build a completely separate transfer mechanism for mail.

Since the network was undergoing massive rearrangement any-way with the switch to TCP/IP, this seemed an appropriate time to bring out the new standard. Postel and his colleagues called it the simple mail transfer protocol (SMTP). It clarified existing practices, while adding a few new control features.

At the same time, the growth of the network gave rise to a new problem. "When we got to about two thousand hosts, that's when things really started to come apart," said Craig Partridge, a pro-grammer at BBN. "Instead of having one big mainframe with twenty thousand people on it, suddenly we were getting inundated with individual machines." Every host machine had a given name, "and everyone wanted to be named Frodo," Partridge recalled.

Sorting out the Frodos of the Internet wasn't unlike sorting out the Joneses of Cleveland or the Smiths of Smithville. Where one lived, precisely, was important in differentiating who one was. For years, sorting this out was among the most troublesome, messiest issues for the Internet, until at last a group chiseled out a workable scheme, called the domain name system, or DNS.

The core of the DNS team was Jon Postel and Paul Mockapetris at ISI, and BBN's Craig Partridge. They spent three months working out the details of the new addressing scheme and in November 1983 came forward with two RFCs describing the domain name system. "DNS was a very significant change in the way we thought about the system being organized," said Postel. "Tree-branching" was the guiding metaphor. Each address would have a hierarchical structure. From the trunk to the branches, and outward to the leaves, every address would include levels of information representing, in progression, a smaller, more specific part of the network address.

But that sparked a debate about the sequence of the hierarchy; what should come first or last. Postel and others finally decided on a specific-to-general addressing scheme. The Internet community also argued back and forth over what to name the domains, delaying any implementation for about a year. It was asserted by some, unconvincingly, that domain names should reflect specific funding sources—MIT, DARPA, for example. Eventually, a committee agreed on seven "top-level" domains: edu, com, gov, mil, net, org, and int. Now there could be seven Frodos: a computer named Frodo at a university (edu), one at a government site (gov), a company (com), a military site (mil), a nonprofit organization (org), a network service provider (net), or an international treaty entity (int).

DARPA began pressuring people to adopt DNS addresses in 1985. In January 1986 a grand summit meeting took place on the West Coast, bringing together representatives of all the major networks. By the time the summit was over, everyone had agreed that yes, they really believed in the DNS concept. "And yes, here was how we were going to make it work," Partridge recalled, "And yes, we have the technology to make it all fly."

❑ Pulling the Plug

The first hint Cerf got that the Internet was going to be embraced by a world outside the scientific and academic communities came in 1989, when he walked on to the exhibition floor at Interop, a trade show started by Dan Lynch in 1986 to promote interconnectivity through TCP/IP. In its first couple of years, Interop was attended by a few hundred hardcore networking people. By 1989 the show was teeming with men and women in business attire. "It was an epiphany to walk into Interop and see the major money being spent on exhibitions with huge demonstrations set up," Cerf said. "I realized, oh my God, people are spending serious money on this." The exhibitors had names like Novell, Synoptics, and Network General. "We started looking at the network statistics and realized we had a rocket on our hands." For years Cerf had seen the Internet as a successful, satisfying experiment. Occasionally he had hoped the Internet might reach a wider world of users. Now here was evidence that it was doing just that.

By this time, virtually everyone was using TCP/IP. And there was an ever-increasing infrastructure built upon TCP/IP in Europe. TCP/IP was so widespread and so many people depended on it, that taking it down and starting over seemed unthinkable. By virtue of its quiet momentum, TCP/IP had prevailed over the official OSI standard. Its success provided an object lesson in technology and how it advances. "Standards should be discovered, not decreed," said one computer scientist in the TCP/IP faction. Seldom has it worked any other way.

By the late 1980s the Internet was no longer a star with the ARPANET its center; it was a mesh, much like the ARPANET itself. The NSFNET program had democratized networks as even CSNET hadn't. Now anyone on a college campus with an Internet connection could become an Internet user. The NSFNET was fast becoming the Internet's spine, running on lines that were more than twenty-five times faster than ARPANET lines. Users now had a choice between connecting to the ARPANET or to the NSFNET backbone. Many chose the latter, not only for its speed but because it was so much easier to connect to.

As the 1990s approached, the number of computers in the world that were connected to one another via the NSFNET far outstripped the number of computers connected to one another via the ARPANET. The ARPANET was now just one of hundreds of ARPA Internet networks, and a dinosaur, unable to evolve as quickly as the rest of the Internet.

Bob Kahn, DARPA's sole remaining champion of networking, had left the agency in 1985 to form the Corporation for National

Research Initiatives, a nonprofit company whose charter was to foster research and development for a "national information infra- structure." The people now running DARPA weren't particularly in- terested in networking. In their view, all the interesting problems had been solved. Moreover, the agency was distracted by President Ronald Reagan's Star Wars program.

The ARPANET itself, which cost ARPA $14 million a year to run, looked arthritic next to the higher-speed NSFNET. DARPA manage- ment decided the ARPANET had outlived its usefulness. It was time to shut it down.

Mark Pullen, a DARPA program manager who now ran the net- working project, was given the task of decommissioning the ARPANET. Exactly who gave the order from within DARPA's higher reaches was never made quite clear. "No one wanted to be the ghoul that turned off the ARPANET," Pullen said, "so I became the source of the policy." Pullen's plan was to pull sites off the ARPANET and put them on the NSFNET backbone.

It was hard telling Bob Kahn about the plan to decommission the network. Kahn had hired Pullen, and now Pullen played the execu- tioner. "I had a sense he might feel I was turning off his greatest achievement," Pullen said. "The one that seemed to hurt him worse was when I turned off the old SATNET." SATNET was slow and expen- sive and antiquated. "No doubt he must have felt it was his very own child. For valid reasons. But after he thought about it, he agreed I was doing the right thing." (As it turned out, the money DARPA saved by turning off the ARPANET helped fund Kahn's new project.)

One by one, Pullen turned off the IMPs and TIPs that still lay at the heart of the original network. There was a certain sadness in its demise that called to mind the scene from Arthur C. Clarke's *2001: A Space Odyssey* where the fictional fifth-generation computer HAL is threatening its mission and has to be dismantled circuit by circuit. As HAL gradually loses its "mind," it makes pathetic appeals for its "life" to Dave, the astronaut, who is doing the dismantling.

In the case of the ARPANET, the network died but its pieces lived on. "It wasn't all that different from the breakup of Ma Bell," Pullen recalled. "It involved locating clusters of ARPANET sites and finding someone to take them over." In most cases, Pullen transferred each ARPANET site to one of the regional networks, and eased the transition by subsidizing the cost for a while. With the exception of two sites that went on to the MILNET, all the sites went to one or another of the regional networks. "I never had anyone object all that loudly," Pullen said. "I think they all knew the time had come." One site at a time, Pullen found new homes for them. Where there wasn't a home, DARPA and NSF helped create one. Several ARPANET sites in Southern California quickly formed their own regional network and called it Los Nettos; it was run by Danny Cohen and Jon Postel. The IMPs themselves were powered down, uncabled, and shipped away. Most were simply junked. Others went into service on the MILNET. The Computer Museum in Boston got one, and Len Kleinrock put IMP Number One on display for visitors at UCLA. The last IMP to go was at the University of Maryland. By coincidence, Trusted Information Systems, a company in Maryland where Steve Crocker now worked, was connected to that IMP. Crocker had been there at the birth and he was there at the death.

By the end of 1989, the ARPANET was gone. The NSFNET and the regional networks it had spawned became the principal backbone. That year, to mark both the ARPANET's twentieth anniversary and its passing, UCLA sponsored a symposium and called it "Act One."

In his speech, Danny Cohen found a source of inspiration, and he said this:

"In the beginning ARPA created the ARPANET.

"And the ARPANET was without form and void.

"And darkness was upon the deep.

"And the spirit of ARPA moved upon the face of the network and ARPA said, 'Let there be a protocol,' and there was a protocol. And ARPA saw that it was good.

"And ARPA said, 'Let there be more protocols,' and it was so. And ARPA saw that it was good.

"And ARPA said, 'Let there be more networks,' and it was so."

Epilogue

❏ **September 1994**

The party was BBN's idea: gather a couple of dozen key players in Boston and celebrate the twenty-fifth anniversary of the installation of the first ARPANET node at UCLA. By now, the Internet had grown far beyond a research experiment. As more people discovered its utility, it was becoming a household word. The Net promised to be to the twenty-first century what the telephone had been to the twentieth. Its existence was already reaching into nearly every aspect of American culture—from publishing to socializing. For many, e-mail had become an indispensable part of daily life. Housebound seniors used it to find companionship; some far-flung families used it as their glue. More people by the day were logging-on to conduct business or find entertainment on the Net. Analysts pronounced the Internet the next great marketing opportunity.

The takeoff was just beginning. In 1990, the World Wide Web, a multimedia branch of the Internet, had been created by a researcher at the European Laboratory for Particle Physics, CERN, near

Geneva. And in late 1993, around the time BBN began to think about throwing a party, a couple of computer science students at the University of Illinois were busy making the Web easier to use with a graphics program they called Mosaic. The Mosaic browser, forerunner of the Netscape web browser, made using the Internet as easy as pointing a mouse and clicking on pictures and words.

The Net of the 1970s had long since been supplanted by something at once more sophisticated and more unwieldy. Yet in dozens of ways, the Net of 1994 still reflected the personalities and proclivities of those who built it. Larry Roberts kept laying pieces of the foundation to the great big rambling house that became the Internet. Frank Heart's pragmatic attitude toward technical invention—build it, throw it out on the Net, and fix it if it breaks—permeated Net sensibility for years afterward. Openness in the protocol process started with Steve Crocker's first RFC for the Network Working Group, and continued into the Internet. While at DARPA, Bob Kahn made a conspicuous choice to maintain openness. Vint Cerf gave the Net its civility. And the creators of the Net still ran the Internet Society and attended meetings of the Internet Engineering Task Force.

Just as the party plans got under way, BBN got a new chief executive officer. George Conrades, a high-powered marketing veteran from IBM, had been recruited by BBN's chairman Steve Levy to reshape the company's businesses. Conrades loved the party idea. He seized on it as a perfect marketing vehicle. Conrades was smitten with BBN's pioneering role. BBN was *the* original Internet company, he decided, a claim to fame the firm had yet to exploit. Make the party big and lavish. Rent out the Copley Plaza Hotel. Celebrate the network pioneers as if they had been the first to tread on the moon's surface. Invite computer industry luminaries. And invite the press.

BBN needed the boost. Throughout the 1980s, the company's fortunes had mostly ebbed. As the Internet had grown more popular, BBN, which time and again had failed to commercialize on its research efforts, had slipped into relative obscurity. In 1993 the company lost $32 million on $233 million in sales. The next year wasn't much better, with an $8 million loss on lower sales.

The company had missed its greatest opportunity when it failed to enter the market for routers—of which IMPs were the progenitors. BBN failed to see the potential in routers much as AT&T had refused to acknowledge packet-switching. Anyone wanting to connect a local area network—of which there were now hundreds of thousands—to the Internet needed a router. By 1994, the router business was a multibillion-dollar industry. More than a decade earlier a couple of BBN's own computer guys had tried to push the company into the router business, and they had been brushed off by a marketing vice president.

BBN's troubles went beyond failed market opportunities. In 1980 the federal government accused the company of conspiring to overcharge the government on its contracts during the period from 1972 to 1978, and of altering time sheets to conceal the overcharges. The practice was discovered when, in the course of a routine audit in the late 1970s, BBN officials were less than candid with a government auditor. ("BBN had gotten very arrogant," said one long-time employee.) A federal investigation lasted more than two years. Auditors moved into the firm's Cambridge headquarters. Senior BBN employees were called before a grand jury. None of the IMP Guys was implicated. But in 1980 two of the company's high-ranking financial officers plea-bargained their way out of a one-hundred-count charge. They were given suspended sentences and fined $20,000 each. The company agreed to pay a $700,000 fine.

At the time, BBN depended on government contracts for nearly 80 percent of its revenues. Given the certainty that all government contract awards to BBN would have been suspended during the course of any lengthy legal defense, had no settlement been reached, the charges could have ruined the company. People in the company felt that the government had overreacted to incorrect accounting practices. BBN, they said, had always given the federal government much more than its money's worth on contract R&D.

The networking group at BBN, only minimally involved in the government investigation, was simultaneously offering proof positive that government-funded science can bear splendid fruit. The ARPANET was Exhibit A. Funded entirely by ARPA, its creators given reasonably free rein, the network was evidence of a once-pervasive

American trust in science. The network was built in an era when Washington provided a little guidance and a lot of faith.

By 1994, BBN's brush with the government auditors was forgotten. Unfortunately, so was the company's role in building the ARPANET. Only those insiders who were acquainted with history associated the company with the newly popular Internet. When Conrades arrived, he decided it was time to polish BBN's image. And a silver-anniversary bash for the ARPANET was the perfect opportunity.

The invitation list for the party was as scrutinized as an invitation list for a White House dinner. Some names were obvious, of course; but scores of people had had a hand in building the ARPANET, and even more people, from all over the world, had been involved with the Internet. Heart, Walden, and others submitted suggestions. Vice President Al Gore, an advocate of the information superhighway, was invited. So was Ed Markey, a Democratic congressman from Massachusetts who had also put the Internet on his political agenda; he accepted the invitation. Bill Gates was invited, although the Microsoft chairman had yet to acknowledge the Internet as a useful tool. He declined. Paul Baran, whose role was minimized at BBN, nearly wasn't invited at all. In time, the list ballooned to five hundred invitees.

Conrades wanted this to be as much a signal for the future as a celebration of the past. He was planning for BBN to expand its somewhat diminished role in Internet-related businesses. BBN already owned and operated NEARnet, the New England regional network. One of his first moves after arriving was to purchase BARRnet, the regional network in the San Francisco Bay Area. And he had his eye on SURAnet, the regional network for the Southeast.

Seeking a lofty theme, the public relations firm that BBN hired to augment its own PR department came up with one: "History of the Future." It suited Conrades's plans for BBN perfectly. Conrades also hired a production company to put together an elaborate video presentation that would include interviews with a core group of pioneers—Larry Roberts, Bob Kahn, Steve Crocker, Len Kleinrock, Frank Heart, and Vint Cerf.

Bob Metcalfe, the inventor of Ethernet, was now publisher of a computer trade newspaper called *InfoWorld.* He wrote an opinion column on the upcoming event that he titled, "Old Fogies to Duke It Out for Credit at Internet's 25th Anniversary." "I'll be there to see old friends, to renew some old animosities, and to join in the jockeying for credit—of which there is plenty to go around," Metcalfe wrote. "I'll begin by making sure partygoers realize that most TCP/IP traffic is carried by Ethernet, which I invented . . . As the party peaks, I'll see how much credit I can grab from Vint Cerf and Bob Kahn for the invention of internetworking . . . Failing that, I'll see if I can smile my way into the group photo of the inventors of packet-switching."

Weeks and days before the event, BBN's public relations firm placed stories in magazines and newspapers. *Newsweek* ran a lengthy piece on the ARPANET pioneers, and so did *The Boston Globe.* BBN put together a video news clip, which was aired on more than one hundred local newscasts. Ray Tomlinson, whose scrutiny of his keyboard at an opportune moment had produced the @ sign, was celebrated as a folk hero in a story aired on National Public Radio on the evening of the party.

The guests of honor began arriving on Friday, September 9, and gathered for a reception followed by a press conference at the Copley Plaza that afternoon. As a joke, Wes Clark, now a consultant in New York, pinned Larry Roberts's name badge to his own sport coat. At the press conference, several of the ARPANET pioneers, who outnumbered the journalists, delivered speeches. In his speech, Bob Taylor wryly remarked that the people who had been invited had sent their grandfathers instead.

The most notable absence was that of Licklider, who died in 1990, but his wife, Louise, accepted the invitation. Bernie Cosell, the IMP team's ace debugger, who now lived in rural Virginia and raised sheep ("Too many people, too few sheep," read Cosell's e-mail signature), was unable to come because of the expense. Others refused. Famously averse to parties, Will Crowther declined the invitation; repeated phone calls from fellow IMP Guys could not change his mind.

At a stand-up Mexican buffet following the press conference, everyone mingled. Some people had seen each other a few days earlier, or a few months earlier, but others hadn't seen each other for years, or even decades. New spouses, old spouses, and premature aging were quietly remarked upon. Larry Roberts, now running a small company that was building a new generation of switch, lived in Woodside, California, a well-to-do community on the San Francisco peninsula. Now fifty-eight, Roberts was on a daily regimen of "smart drugs" (Deprenyl, used to treat Parkinson's, was one; melatonin was another) to regain the powers of concentration he possessed at twenty-eight. With characteristic intensity, he steeped himself in the subject. He read hundreds of research reports and had even produced an "anti-aging" videotape.

In 1983, Taylor had left Xerox's Palo Alto Research Center. His departure had sparked a rash of resignations from loyal researchers, who followed him to Digital Equipment Corp., where he set up a research lab just a few miles from Xerox PARC. For years he lived around the corner from Larry Roberts and neither man knew it. One day a piece of mail addressed to Lawrence G. Roberts was misdelivered to Taylor's house, and the two discovered that they lived a few hundred yards apart.

On day two of BBN's fete, Saturday morning, came photo sessions, one after another. First was the official group shot. The group was large, about twenty-five people. When Len Kleinrock missed the first official photo shoot, another had to be arranged. For another pose, the core group of IMP Guys was asked to pose precisely as in the original IMP Guys photo taken in 1969. "Could you guys lose some weight?" Cerf called out as the photographer tried to place everyone in the shot.

Afterward, the scientists were bused two blocks away to the Christian Science Center for a *Wired* magazine shoot. Gamely, the nineteen men squeezed themselves onto a short, narrow bridge at the Center's Mapparium. Being engineers, they couldn't help but offer some advice to the photographer, who was having a little trouble fitting them all in the shot: Try a different angle. Try a different configuration. Try a different lens. Try a different camera. Later, a few in the group grumbled about hangers-on having shown up for the photo, but for the most part, the general good cheer of the weekend was beginning to infect them all.

The multiple paternity claims to the Internet (not only had each man been there at the start but each had made a contribution that he considered immeasurable) came out most noticeably that afternoon during a group interview with the Associated Press. The interview was done over a speakerphone in a suite at the hotel. Kahn, Heart, Engelbart, and Kleinrock sat hunched over the phone as the AP reporter asked questions. Before long the interview transformed into a study in credit management. Taylor arrived late, but not too late to engage in something of a dustup with Bob Kahn, who warned the AP reporter to be certain to distinguish between the early days of the ARPANET and the Internet, and that it was the invention of TCP/IP that marked the true beginnings of internetworking. Not true, said Taylor. The Internet's roots most certainly lay with the ARPANET. The group around the telephone grew uncomfortable. "How about women?" asked the reporter, perhaps to break the silence. "Are there any female pioneers?" More silence.

The weekend was as noteworthy for who wasn't present as for who was. Tim Berners-Lee, the inventor of the World Wide Web, had just moved to Boston from Geneva to join MIT's Laboratory for Computer Science. He wasn't invited, nor was Marc Andreessen, the co-inventor of Mosaic, who had just left Illinois to develop a commercial version of his Web browser. Granted, they hadn't played roles in the birth of either the ARPANET or the Internet (Andreessen wasn't even born until 1972, after the first ARPANET nodes were installed) and couldn't technically be counted as founders. But they were behind the two inventions that were already giving the Net its biggest reach into everyday life.

Three years earlier, the NSF had lifted restrictions against commercial use of the Internet, and now you could get rich not just by inventing a gateway to the Net but by taking business itself onto the Net. When reporters asked them to comment on this, some of the original ARPANET builders said they found the new commercialization of the Net lamentable. Others welcomed it.

Few of the pioneers had become wealthy. Metcalfe's invention of Ethernet had made him a multimillionaire. In his nearly thirty years as a computer science professor at UCLA, Kleinrock had guided an army of Ph.D. students, many of whom went on to become luminaries in the field of computer networking. Still teaching at UCLA, Kleinrock ran a successful seminar business on the side. But at the other end of the spectrum was Jon Postel, the unsung hero of networking. He observed the weekend of celebration quietly, much as he had worked for years as keeper of the RFCs and final arbiter in technical matters when consensus couldn't be reached. Postel believed that decisions he had made in the course of his work over the years had been for the good of the community, and that starting a company to profit from those activities would have amounted to a violation of public trust.

Most of the IMP Guys had ended up in BBN's senior management. Walden had served briefly as Heart's boss, and Barker had gone on to run one of BBN's divisions. The most conspicuous exception to this was Crowther, who had remained a programmer. For years Heart had been Crowther's champion, lobbying for the company to let Crowther just be Crowther and think up ingenious ideas in his own dreamy way. In the years following the IMP project, Crowther pursued some unusual ideas about natural language processing, and worked extensively on high-speed packet-switching technology.

Severo Ornstein had left BBN in the 1970s for Xerox PARC, and while there he started Computer Professionals for Social Responsibility. When he retired from Xerox, he and his wife moved into one of the remotest corners of the San Francisco Bay Area. For years Ornstein stayed off the Net, and for years he eschewed e-mail.

Of everyone, Vint Cerf was perhaps the most celebrated this weekend. He was the person most of the press turned to for quotes on the Internet's origins. In early 1994 he had left Kahn's Corporation for National Research Initiatives to return to MCI as a senior vice president and help build the company's Internet businesses. His reputation was well known throughout the company. At an MCI operations center in North Carolina someone had hung a sign:

"Vint Cerf is the Father of the Internet, but we're the mothers that have to make it work!"

As Saturday's dinner approached, there was a great last-minute rush to make certain that the script for the evening would strike just the right tone. Conrades was to be emcee for the main event. No one should get short shrift at the expense of anyone else. It was a nearly impossible task. At the last minute, seating assignments were shuffled yet again. When the dinner finally commenced, some 250 people packed the Grand Ballroom. Lobbying for a telecommunications bill that was pending, Congressman Markey gave a humorous speech. Cerf presented two awards, and Kahn was singled out for his lifetime of achievement. Louise Licklider, frail and elderly, stood up to receive an extended round of applause on behalf of her late husband.

The celebration held a special poignancy for Heart, now sixty-five, who had recently retired as president of BBN's Systems and Technology Division. He had been at BBN for twenty-eight years. Steve Levy, the BBN chairman, called Heart to the podium, and Heart gave a speech in which he pinpointed the reasons the ARPANET project had succeeded. "The project was an example of what can be accomplished quickly, with a really strong sophisticated leadership, adequate resources, and an avoidance of the many kinds of bureaucratic foolishness that can affect so many projects." Roberts had seen to that. Heart ended on a high note. "Only a small fraction of the technically trained population get a shot at riding a technological rocket, and then get to see that revolution change the world." The networking revolution, Heart said, would rank among a small number of the most important technological changes of the century. And that night, in that room, it looked like he might be right.

The next morning, one by one, the ARPANET pioneers said their goodbyes and checked out of the hotel. Everyone was still riding high, at least a little bit. It hadn't been a bad couple of days.

Chapter Notes

Chapter One

The description of the formation of the Advanced Research Projects Agency and its Information Processing Techniques Office is derived from personal interviews, two books written by Eisenhower's science advisor James Killian (see bibliography), magazine articles, and from an excellent and thorough history of the agency commissioned by DARPA and written by Richard J. Barber Associates in 1975. The description of Licklider's early years is based on talks given in his honor, on interviews with Louise Licklider and Bill McGill, and on an obituary written by Karl D. Kryter. The description of Licklider's introduction to computers is based on personal interviews with Wes Clark and Jack Ruina, and on Licklider's interview with the Charles Babbage Institute, as well as the Barber Associates report.

Chapter Two

The description of Paul Baran's work on distributed communications is based on personal interviews with Baran, as well as various interviews conducted by the Babbage Institute. The description of Donald Davies' early work on packet-switching is based on interviews and correspondence with Donald Davies, and on Martin Campbell-Kelly's articles and interviews. Arthur Norberg and Judy O'Neill's awesome report, "A History of the Information Processing Techniques Office of the Defense Advanced Research Projects Agency" also guided us through biographical material and through the early years of IPTO. The report served as the basis for their book *Transforming Computer Technology: Information Processing for the Pentagon, 1962–1986* (Johns Hopkins University Press, 1996).

Paul Baran and Professor Manley Irwin supplied the information concerning AT&T's lawsuits against parties thought to be depriving AT&T of revenues.

Doug Engelbart's patent for his mouse came on November 17, 1970. It is patent No. 3,541,541.

Chapter Three

The history of Bolt Beranek and Newman was based on personal interviews with Dick Bolt and Leo Beranek. The description of Lincoln Laboratory was based on interviews with Wes Clark, Frank Heart, Larry Roberts, and Len Kleinrock. The description of events surrounding the request for proposals for the Interface Message Processor was based on interviews with Jerome Elkind, Frank Heart, Dave Walden, and Severo Ornstein, as well as various interviews conducted by the Charles Babbage Institute.

Chapter Four

The description of the building of the Interface Message Processor was based on interviews with Dave Walden, Ben Barker, Severo Ornstein, Bob Kahn, Frank Heart, Alex McKenzie, and Will Crowther. We also relied on ARPA's request for proposals and on BBN's proposal.

Chapter Five

The description of UCLA's preparations for and receipt of the IMP Number One is based on interviews with Len Kleinrock, Steve Crocker, Mike Wingfield, and Vint Cerf. The description of the Network Working Group's early work in layered protocols was based on interviews with Steve Crocker, Jon Postel, and Vint Cerf. The description of the first log-in session between UCLA and SRI was based on interviews with Len Kleinrock and

Charley Kline. The description of the gridlock tests conducted in early 1970 was based on interviews with Bob Kahn, Dave Walden, and Vint Cerf.

John Melvin helped us in our unsuccessful search for whoever might have been at the other end of the initial log-in session between UCLA and SRI. Now we know who it was not. We are still eager to know who it was.

Chapter Six

The description of the early ARPANET sites was based on BBN quarterly technical reports, technical papers, and interviews with John Melvin and John Day. Alex McKenzie supplied information on the early days of the Network Operations Center. The description of the IMP's maintenance problems and subsequent resolution was based on interviews with Ben Barker, Frank Heart, Severo Ornstein, and Alex McKenzie. The description of the ICCC '72 demonstration of the ARPANET was based on interviews with Al Vezza, Bob Kahn, Steve Crocker, Len Kleinrock, Jon Postel, Alex McKenzie, and Larry Roberts. "PARRY Encounters the Doctor" was published in its entirety as an RFC and appeared in *Datamation* magazine, July 1973.

Chapter Seven

The description of Ray Tomlinson's original e-mail hack and his choice of the @ sign as a separator—and as a problem for UNIX users—was based on interviews with Tomlinson and John Vittal.

Parts of the MsgGroup archives were first sent to us by Ed Vielmetti. Einar Stefferud saved them all and deposited them at the Boston Computer Museum. Ken Harrenstien helped us straighten out some early mailing-list history. Ned Freed supplied us with comparative figures on e-mail usage.

The description of the origins of Adventure was based on interviews with Don Woods, Will Crowther, and Dave Walden. Woods's recollections of Adventure also appear in *The Unix Book of Games*, by Janice Winsor, Prentice-Hall Computer Books, 1996. Observations on page 208 about proclamations of officialness on the Net come from "How Anarchy Works," by Paulina Borsook, *Wired* magazine, October 1995. The history of the finger program came from Les Earnest.

Chapter Eight

Descriptions of the packet-radio and packet-satellite programs were based on various technical papers (see bibliography), as well as on personal interviews with Vint Cerf, Alex McKenzie, and Bob Kahn. Some material was taken from interviews conducted by the Charles Babbage Institute. The description of the evolution of TCP/IP was based on interviews with Vint Cerf, Bob Kahn, John Shoch, Alex McKenzie, and Jon Postel.

The description of the origins of Ethernet was based on interviews with Bob Metcalfe. Butler Lampson's description of Ethernet is taken from *Fumbling the Future,* by Douglas Smith and Robert C. Alexander (William Morrow, 1988), p. 97.

Ole Jacobsen's article, "The Trouble with OSI," *ConneXions,* volume 6, no. 5, May 1992, particularly the reference to double AA batteries, helped guide the section on OSI vs. TCP/IP. Peter Salus's book *Casting the Net,* (Addison-Wesley, 1995), and his article "Protocol Wars: Is OSI Finally Dead?" in *ConneXions,* volume 9, no. 8, August 1995, also helped frame the debate.

Danny Cohen gave us permission to edit slightly and reprint the poem that he read to those gathered at the Act One Symposium at UCLA in 1989.

Bibliography

Books

Alexander, Charles C. *Holding the Line: The Eisenhower Era, 1952–1961.* Bloomington: Indiana University Press, 1975.

Baran, Paul. "Packet Switching." In *Fundamentals of Digital Switching.* 2d ed. Edited by John C. McDonald. New York: Plenum Press, 1990.

Barry, John A. *Technobabble.* Cambridge: MIT Press, 1991.

Bell, C. Gordon, Alan Kotok, Thomas N. Hastings, and Richard Hill. "The Evolution of the DEC System-10." In *Computer Engineering: A DEC View of Hardware Systems Design.* Edited by C. Gordon Bell, J. Craig Mudge, and John E. McNamara. Bedford, Mass.: Digital Equipment Corporation, 1978.

Bell, C. Gordon, Gerald Butler, Robert Gray, John E. McNamara, Donald Vonada, and Ronald Wilson. "The PDP-1 and Other 18-Bit Computers." In *Computer Engineering: A DEC View of Hardware Systems Design.* Edited by C. Gordon Bell, J. Craig Mudge, and John E. McNamara. Bedford, Mass.: Digital Equipment Corporation, 1978.

Bergaust, Erik. *Wernher von Braun.* Washington, D.C.: National Space Institute, 1976.

Blanc, Robert P., and Ira W. Cotton, eds. *Computer Networking.* New York: IEEE Press, 1976.

Brendon, Piers. *Ike: His Life and Times.* New York: Harper & Row, 1986.

Brooks, John. *Telephone: The First Hundred Years.* New York: Harper & Row, 1976.

Brucker, Roger W., and Richard A. Watson. *The Longest Cave.* New York: Alfred A. Knopf, 1976.

Clarke, Arthur C., et al. *The Telephone's First Century—And Beyond: Essays on the Occasion of the 100th Anniversary of Telephone Communication.* New York: Thomas Y. Crowell Company, 1977

Computer Science, Numerical Analysis and Computing. National Physical Laboratory, Engineering Sciences Group, Research 1971. London: Her Majesty's Stationery Office, 1972.

Froehlich, Fritz E., Allen Kent, and Carolyn M. Hall, eds. "ARPANET, the Defense Data Network, and Internet." In *The Froehlich/Kent Encyclopedia of Telecommunications.* New York: Marcel Dekker, Inc., 1991.

Goldstein, Jack S. *A Different Sort of Time: The Life of Jerrold R. Zacharias.* Cambridge MIT Press, 1992.

Halberstam, David. *The Fifties.* New York: Villard Books, 1993.

Hall, Mark, and John Barry. *Sunburst: The Ascent of Sun Microsystems.* Chicago: Contemporary Books, 1990.

Hammond, William M. *Public Affairs: The Military and the Media, 1962–1968.* Washington, D.C.: Center of Military History, U.S. Army, Superintendent of Documents, U.S. Government Printing Office, 1968.

Hamner, W. Clay. "The United States Postal Service: Will It Be Ready for the Year 2000?" In *The Future of the Postal Service.* Edited by Joel L. Fleishman. New York: Praeger, 1983.

Holzmann, Gerard J., and Björn Pehrson. *The Early History of Data Network.* Los Alamitos, Calif.: IEEE Computer Society Press, 1995.

Kidder, Tracy. *The Soul of a New Machine.* Boston: Little, Brown, 1981.

Killian, James R., Jr. *Sputnik, Scientists, and Eisenhower: A Memoir of the First Special Assistant to the President for Science and Technology.* Cambridge: MIT Press, 1977.

———. *The Education of a College President: A Memoir.* Cambridge: MIT Press, 1985.

Kleinrock, Leonard. *Communication Nets: Stochastic Message Flow and Delay.* New York: McGraw-Hill, 1964.

———. *Queueing Systems.* 2 vols. New York: John Wiley & Sons, 1974–1976.

Langdon-Davies, John. *NPL: Jubilee Book of the National Physical Laboratory.* London: His Majesty's Stationery Office, 1951.

Lebow, Irwin. *Information Highways & Byways: From the Telegraph to the 21st Century.* New York: IEEE Press, 1995.

Licklider, J. C. R. "Computers and Government." In *The Computer Age: A Twenty-Year View,* edited by Michael L. Dertouzos and Joel Moses. MIT Bicentennial Series. Cambridge: MIT Press, 1979.

———. *Libraries of the Future.* Cambridge: MIT Press, 1965.

Padlipsky, M. A. *The Elements of Networking Style and Other Essays & Animadversions of the Art of Intercomputer Networking.* Englewood Cliffs, N.J.: Prentice-Hall, Inc., 1985.

Proceedings of the Fifth Data Communications Symposium. IEEE Computer Society, Snowbird, Utah, September 27–29, 1977.

Pyatt, Edward. *The National Physical Laboratory: A History.* Bristol, England: Adam Hilger Ltd., 1983.

Redmond, Kent C., and Thomas M. Smith. *The Whirlwind Project: The History of a Pioneer Computer.* Bedford, Mass.: Digital Press, 1980.

Rheingold, Howard. *The Virtual Community.* New York: Harper Perennial, 1994.

———. *Tools for Thought: The People and Ideas Behind the Next Computer Revolution.* New York: Simon & Schuster, 1988.

Roberts, Lawrence G. "The ARPANET and Computer Networks." In *A History of Personal Workstations,* edited by Adele Goldberg. Reading, Mass.: ACM Press (Addison-Wesley), 1988.

Rose, Marshall T. *The Internet Message: Closing the Book with Electronic Mail.* Englewood Cliffs, N.J.: PTR Prentice Hall, 1993.

Sherman, Kenneth. *Data Communications: A User's Guide.* Reston, Virginia: Reston Publishing Company, 1981.

Smith, Douglas K., and Robert C. Alexander. *Fumbling the Future: How Xerox Invented, then Ignored, the First Personal Computer.* New York: William Morrow, 1988.

Udall, Stewart L. *The Myths of August: A Personal Exploration of Our Tragic Cold War Affair with the Atom.* New York: Pantheon, 1994.

Wildes, Karl L., and Nilo A. Lindgren. *A Century of Electrical Engineering and Computer Science at MIT, 1882–1982.* Cambridge, Mass.: MIT Press, 1985.

Winner, Langdon. *The Whale and the Reactor: A Search for Limits in an Age of High Technology.* Chicago: University of Chicago Press, 1986.

Journal, Magazine, and Newspaper Articles

Abramson, Norman. "Development of the Alohanet." *IEEE Transactions on Information Theory*, January 1985.

Anderson, Christopher. "The Accidental Superhighway." *The Economist*, 1 July 1995.

Baran, Paul. "On Distributed Communications Networks." *IEEE Transactions on Communications Systems*, 1 March 1964.

————. "Reliable Digital Communications Systems Using Unreliable Network Repeater Nodes." RAND Corporation Mathematics Division Report No. P-1995, 27 May 1960.

Boggs, David R., John F. Shoch, Edward A. Taft, and Robert M. Metcalfe. "PUP: An Internetwork Architecture." *IEEE Transactions on Communications*, April 1980.

"Bolt Beranek Accused by Government of Contract Overcharges." Dow Jones News Service–*Wall Street Journal* combined stories, 27 October 1980.

"Bolt Beranek and Newman: Two Aides Plead Guilty to U.S. Charge." Dow Jones News Service–*Wall Street Journal* combined stories, 12 November 1980.

"Bolt Beranek, Aides Accused of Cheating U.S. on Several Jobs." *The Wall Street Journal*, 28 October 1980.

Bulkeley, William M. "Can He Turn Big Ideas into Big Sales?" *The Wall Street Journal*, 12 September 1994.

Bush, Vannevar. "As We May Think." *Atlantic Monthly*, July 1945.

Campbell-Kelly, Martin. "Data Communications at the National Physical Laboratory: 1965–1975." *Annals of the History of Computing* 9, no. 3/4, 1988.

Cerf, Vinton G., and Peter T. Kirstein. "Issues in Packet-Network Interconnection." *Proceedings of the IEEE*, November 1979.

Cerf, Vinton G., and Robert E. Kahn. "A Protocol for Packet-Network Intercommunication." *IEEE Transactions on Communications*, May 1974.

Cerf, Vinton. "PARRY Encounters the Doctor: Conversation Between a Simulated Paranoid and a Simulated Psychiatrist." *Datamation*, July 1973.

Clark, David D. "The Design Philosophy of the DARPA Internet Protocols." *Proceedings of the Association for Computing Machinery Sigcomm Symposium on Data Communications*, August 1988.

Clark, David D., Kenneth T. Pogran, and David P. Reed. "An Introduction to Local Area Networks." *Proceedings of the IEEE,* November 1979.

Comer, Douglas. "The Computer Science Research Network CSNET: A History and Status Report." *Communications of the ACM,* October 1983.

Crowther, William, and David Walden. "Current Views of Timing." Memorandum to Frank E. Heart, Cambridge, Mass., 8 July 1969.

Crowther, W. R., F. E. Heart, A. A. McKenzie, J. M. McQuillan, and D. C. Walden. "Issues in Packet Switching Networking Design." *Proceedings of the 1975 National Computer Conference,* 1975.

Denning, Peter J. "The Science of Computing: The ARPANET After Twenty Years." *American Scientist,* November-December 1989.

Denning, Peter J., Anthony Hearn, and C. William Kern. "History and Overview of CSNET. "*Proceedings of the Association for Computing Machinery Sigcomm Symposium on Data Communications,* March 1983.

"Dr. J. C. R. Licklider Receives Biennial Award at State College Meeting." *The Journal of the Acoustical Society of America,* November 1950.

Engelbart, Douglas C. "Coordinated Information Services for a Discipline- or Mission-Oriented Community." *Proceedings of the Second Annual Computer Communications Conference,* January 1972.

————. "Intellectual Implications of Multi-Access Computer Networks." *Proceedings of the Interdisciplinary Conference on Multi-Access Computer Networks,* Austin, Texas, April 1970.

Ericson, Raymond. "Philharmonic Hall Acoustics Start Rumors Flying." *The New York Times,* 4 December 1962.

Finucane, Martin. "Creators of the Internet Forerunner Gather in Boston." *Reading (Mass.) Daily Times Herald,* 12 September 1994.

Fisher, Sharon. "The Largest Computer Network: Internet Links UNIX Computers Worldwide." *InfoWorld,* 25 April 1988.

Hines, William. "Mail." *Chicago Sun-Times,* 29 March 1978.

Haughney, Joseph F. "Anatomy of a Packet-Switching Overhaul." *Data Communications,* June 1982.

Holusha, John. "Computer Tied Carter, Mondale Campaigns: The Bethesda Connection." *Washington Star,* 21 November 1976.

Jacobs, Irwin M., Richard Binder, and Estil V. Hoversten. "General Purpose Packet Satellite Networks." *Proceedings of the IEEE,* November 1978.

Jennings, Dennis M., Lawrence H. Landweber, Ira H. Fuchs, David J. Farber, and W. Richards Adrion. "Computer Networking for Scientists." *Science,* 22 February 1986.

Kahn, Robert E. "The Role of Government in the Evolution of the Internet." *Communications of the ACM,* August 1994.

Kahn, Robert E., Steven A. Gronemeyer, Jerry Burchfiel, and Ronald C. Kunzelman. "Advances in Packet Radio Technology." *Proceedings of the IEEE,* November 1978.

Kantrowitz, Barbara, and Adam Rogers. "The Birth of the Internet." *Newsweek,* 8 August 1994.

Kleinrock, Leonard. "Principles and Lessons in Packet Communications." *Proceedings of the IEEE,* November 1978.

Landweber, Lawrence H., Dennis M. Jennings, and Ira Fuchs. "Research Computer Networks and Their Interconnection." *IEEE Communications Magazine,* June 1986.

Lee, J. A. N., and Robert F. Rosin. "The CTSS Interviews." *IEEE Annals of the History of Computing* 14, no. 1, 1992.

———. "The Project MAC Interviews." *IEEE Annals of the History of Computing* 14, no. 2, 1992.

Licklider, J. C. R. "A Gridless, Wireless Rat-Shocker." *Journal of Comparative and Physiological Psychology* 44, 1951.

———. "Man-Computer Symbiosis." Reprint. *In Memoriam: J. C. R. Licklider.* Digital Equipment Corporation Systems Research Center, 7 August 1990.

Licklider, J. C. R., and Albert Vezza. "Applications of Information Networks." *Proceedings of the IEEE,* November 1978.

Licklider, J. C. R., and Robert W. Taylor. "The Computer as a Communication Device." Reprint. *In Memoriam: J. C. R. Licklider.* Digital Equipment Corporation Systems Research Center, 7 August 1990.

Markoff, John. "Up from the Computer Underground." *The New York Times,* 27 August 1993.

McKenzie, Alexander A., and B. P. Cosell, J. M. McQuillan, M. J. Thrope. "The Network Control Center for the ARPA Network." *Proceedings of the IEEE,* 1972.

Mier, Edwin E. "Defense Department Readying Network Ramparts." *Data Communications,* October 1983.

Mills, Jeffrey. "Electronic Mail." Associated Press, 4 January 1976.

———. "Electronic Mail." Associated Press, 19 June 1976.

———. "Postal Service Tests Electronic Message Service." Associated Press, 28 March 1978.

Mills, Kay. "The Public Concern: Mail." Newhouse News Service, 27 July 1976.

Mohl, Bruce A. "2 Bolt, Beranek Officials Collapse in Federal Court." *The Boston Globe,* 31 October 1980.

Pallesen, Gayle. "Consultant Firm on PBIA Faces Criminal Charges." *Palm Beach (Florida) Post,* 8 November 1980.

Pearse, Ben. "Defense Chief in the Sputnik Age." *The New York Times Magazine,* 10 November 1957.

Pool, Bob. "Inventing the Future: UCLA Scientist Who Helped Create Internet Isn't Done Yet." *Los Angeles Times,* 11 August 1994.

Quarterman, John S., and Josiah C. Hoskins. "Notable Computer Networks." *Communications of the ACM,* October 1986.

Roberts, Lawrence G. "ARPA Network Implications." *Educom,* Bulletin of the Interuniversity Communications Council, fall 1971.

Salus, Peter. "Pioneers of the Internet." *Internet World,* September 1994.

"Scanning the Issues," *IEEE Spectrum,* August 1964.

Schonberg, Harold C. "4 Acoustics Experts to Urge Revisions in Auditorium." *The New York Times,* 4 April 1963.

————. "Acoustics Again: Philharmonic Hall Has Some Defects, But Also Has a Poetry of Its Own." *The New York Times,* 9 December 1962.

Selling It. *Consumer Reports,* June 1977.

Space Agencies. "ARPA Shapes Military Space Research." *Aviation Week,* 16 June 1958.

Sterling, Bruce. "Internet." *Fantasy and Science Fiction,* February 1993.

Swartzlander, Earl. "Time-Sharing at MIT." *IEEE Annals of the History of Computing* 14, no. 1, 1992.

"Transforming BB&N: ARPANET's Architect Targets Non-Military Networks." *Data Communications,* April 1984.

Wilson, David McKay. "BBN Executives Collapse in Court." *Cambridge (Mass.) Chronicle,* 6 November 1980.

————. "Consulting Co. Admits Overcharge." *Cambridge (Mass.) Chronicle,* 30 October 1980.

Zitner, Aaron. "A Quiet Leap Forward in Cyberspace." *The Boston Globe,* 11 September 1994.

Zuckerman, Laurence. "BBN Steps Out of the Shadows and into the Limelight." *The New York Times,* 17 July 1995.

Unpublished Papers, Interviews from Secondary Sources, and Other Documents

"Act One." Symposium on the history of the ARPANET held at the University of California at Los Angeles, 17 August 1989. Transcript.

ARPA Network Information Center, Stanford Research Institute, Menlo Park, Calif. "Scenarios for Using the ARPANET." Booklet. Prepared for the International Conference on Computer Communication, Washington, D.C., October 1972.

Baran, Paul. Interview by Judy O'Neill. Charles Babbage Institute, DARPA/IPTO Oral History Collection, University of Minnesota Center for the History of Information Processing, Minneapolis, Minn., 5 March 1990.

Barlow, John Perry. "Crime and Puzzlement." Pinedale, Wyo., June 1990.

BBN Systems and Technologies Corporation. "Annual Report of the Science Development Program." Cambridge, Mass., 1988.

Bhushan, A. K. "Comments on the File Transfer Protocol." Request for Comments 385. Stanford Research Institute, Menlo Park, Calif., August 1972.

————. "The File Transfer Protocol." Request for Comments 354. Stanford Research Institute, Menlo Park, Calif., July 1972.

Bhushan, Abhay, Ken Pogran, Ray Tomlinson, and Jim White. "Standardizing Network Mail Headers." Request for Comments 561. MIT, Cambridge, Mass., 5 September 1973.

Blue, Allan. Interview by William Aspray. Charles Babbage Institute, DARPA/IPTO Oral History Collection, University of Minnesota Center for the History of Information Processing, Minneapolis, Minn., 12 June 1989.

Bolt Beranek and Newman Inc. "ARPANET Completion Report: Draft." Cambridge, Mass., September 1977.

————. "BBN Proposal No. IMP P69-IST-5: Interface Message Processors for the ARPA Computer Network." Design proposal. Submitted to the Department of the Army, Defense Supply Service, in response to RFQ No. DAHC15 69 Q 0002. Washington, D.C., 6 September 1968.

————. "BBN Report No. 1763: Initial Design for Interface Message Processors for the ARPA Computer Network." Design proposal. Submitted to the Advanced Research Projects Agency under contract no. DAHC 15-69-C-0179. Washington, D.C., 6 January 1969.

————. "BBN Report No. 1822: Interface Message Processor." Technical report. Cambridge, Mass., 1969.

————. "Interface Message Processors for the ARPA Computer Network." Quarterly technical reports. Submitted to the Advanced Research Projects Agency under contract no. DAHC 15-69-C-0179 and contract no. F08606-73-C-0027. Washington, D.C., 1969–1973.

————. "Operating Manual for Interface Message Processors: 516 IMP, 316 IMP, TIP." Revised. Submitted to the Advanced Research Projects Agency under ARPA order no. 1260, contract no. DAHC15-69-C-0179. Arlington, Va., April 1973.

————. "Report No. 4799: A History of the ARPANET: The First Decade." Submitted to the Defense Advanced Research Projects Agency. Arlington, Va., April 1981.

————. "The Four Cities Plan." Draft proposal and cost analysis for maintenance of IMPs and TIPs in Boston, Washington, Los Angeles, and San Francisco. Papers of BBN Division 6. Cambridge, Mass., April 1974.

————. Internal memoranda and papers relating to the work of Division 6. Cambridge, Mass., 1971–1972.

Carr, C. Stephen, Stephen D. Crocker, and Vinton G. Cerf. "HOST-HOST Communication Protocol in the ARPA Network." Paper presented at the Spring Joint Computer Conference of the American Federation of Information Processing Societies, 1970.

Catton, Major General, USAF, Jack. Letter to F. R. Collbohm of RAND Corporation, 11 October 1965. Referring the preliminary technical development plan for message-block network to the Defense Communications Agency.

Cerf, Vinton G. "Confessions of a Hearing-Impaired Engineer." Unpublished.

————. "PARRY Encounters the Doctor." Request for Comments 439 (NIC 13771). Network Working Group, 21 January 1973.

Cerf, Vinton G., and Jonathan B. Postel. "Specification of Internetwork Transmission Control Protocol: TCP Version 3." Information Sciences Institute, University of Southern California, January 1978.

Cerf, Vinton G. Interview by Judy O'Neill. Charles Babbage Institute, DARPA/ IPTO Oral History Collection, University of Minnesota Center for the History of Information Processing, Minneapolis, Minn., 24 April 1990.

Cerf, Vinton G., and Robert Kahn. "HOST and PROCESS Level Protocols for Internetwork Communication." Notes of the International Network Working Group 39, 13 September 1973.

Clark, Wesley. Interview by Judy O'Neill. Charles Babbage Institute, DARPA/IPTO Oral History Collection, University of Minnesota Center for the History of Information Processing, Minneapolis, Minn., 3 May 1990.

Crocker, David H. "Standard for the Format of ARPA Internet Text Messages." Request for Comments 822. Department of Electrical Engineering, University of Delaware, 13 August 1982.

Crocker, David H., John J. Vittal, Kenneth T. Pogran, and D. Austin Henderson Jr. "Standard for the Format of ARPA Network Text Messages." Request for Comments 733. The RAND Corporation, Santa Monica, Calif., 21 November 1977.

Crowther, William. Interview by Judy O'Neill. Charles Babbage Institute, DARPA/IPTO Oral History Collection, University of Minnesota Center for the History of Information Processing, Minneapolis, Minn., 12 March 1990.

Davies, Donald W. "Further Speculations on Data Transmission." Private papers. London, 16 November 1965.

———. "Proposal for a Digital Communication Network." Private papers, photocopied and widely circulated. London, June 1966.

———. "Proposal for the Development of a National Communications Service for On-Line Data Processing." Private papers. London, 15 December 1965.

———. "Remote On-line Data Processing and Its Communication Needs." Private papers. London, 10 November 1965.

Davies, Donald W. Interview by Martin Campbell-Kelly. National Physical Laboratory, U.K., 17 March 1986.

Davies, Donald W., Keith Bartlett, Roger Scantlebury, and Peter Wilkinson. "A Digital Communications Network for Computers Giving Rapid Response at Remote Terminals." Paper presented at the Association for Computing Machinery Symposium on Operating System Principles, Gatlinburg, Tenn., October 1967.

Davis, Ruth M. "Comments and Recommendations Concerning the ARPA Network." Center for Computer Sciences and Technology, U.S. National Bureau of Standards, 6 October 1971.

Digital Equipment Corporation. "Interface Message Processors for the ARPA Computer Network." Design proposal. Submitted to the Department of the Army, Defense Supply Service, in RFQ no. DAHC15 69 Q 002, 5 September 1968.

Frank, Howard. Interview by Judy O'Neill. Charles Babbage Institute, DARPA/IPTO Oral History Collection, University of Minnesota Center for the History of Information Processing, Minneapolis, Minn., 30 March 1990.

Goldstein, Paul. "The Proposed ARPANET Divestiture: Legal Questions and Economic Issues." Working Paper, Cabledata Associates, Inc., CAWP no. 101, 27 July 1973.

Hauben, Michael, and Ronda Hauben. *The Netizens Netbook* page can be found at http://www.columbia.edu/~hauben/netbook/. The Haubens' work has also appeared in the *Amateur Computerist Newsletter*, available from ftp://wuarchive.wustl.edu/doc/misc/acn/.

Heart, F. E., R. E. Kahn, S. M. Ornstein, W. R. Crowther, and D. C. Walden. "The Interface Message Processor for the ARPA Computer Network." Paper presented at the Spring Joint Computer Conference of the American Federation of Information Processing Societies, 1970.

Heart, Frank E. Interview by Judy O'Neill. Charles Babbage Institute, DARPA/IPTO Oral History Collection, University of Minnesota Center for the History of Information Processing, Minneapolis, Minn., 13 March 1990.

Herzfeld, Charles. Interview by Arthur Norberg. Charles Babbage Institute, DARPA/IPTO Oral History Collection, University of Minnesota Center for the History of Information Processing, Minneapolis, Minn., 6 August 1990.

Honeywell, Inc. "Honeywell at Bolt Beranek and Newman, Inc." Brochure. Published for the ARPA Network demonstration at the International Conference on Computer Communication, Washington, D.C., October 1972.

Information Sciences Institute, University of Southern California. "DOD Standard Transmission Control Protocol." Request for Comments 761. Prepared for the Defense Advanced Research Projects Agency, Information Processing Techniques Office, Arlington, Va., January 1980.

International Data Corporation. "ARPA Computer Network Provides Communications Technology for Computer/Computer Interaction Within Special Research Community." Industry report and market review. Newtonville, Mass., 3 March 1972.

Kahn, Robert. Interview by Judy O'Neill. Charles Babbage Institute, DARPA/IPTO Oral History Collection, University of Minnesota Center for the History of Information Processing, Minneapolis, Minn., 24 April 1990.

Kahn, Robert. Interview by William Aspray. Charles Babbage Institute, DARPA/IPTO Oral History Collection, University of Minnesota Center for the History of Information Processing, Minneapolis, Minn., 22 March 1989.

Kleinrock, Leonard. Interview by Judy O'Neill. Charles Babbage Institute, DARPA/IPTO Oral History Collection, University of Minnesota Center for the History of Information Processing, Minneapolis, Minn., 3 April 1990.

Kryter, Karl D. "Lick as a Psychoacoustician and Physioacoustician." Presentation honoring J. C. R. Licklider at the Meeting of the Acoustical Society of America, Baltimore, Md., 30 April 1991.

———. Obituary of J. C. R. Licklider, *Journal of the Acoustical Society of America*, December 1990.

Licklider, J. C. R., and Welden E. Clark. "On-Line Man-Computer Communication." Paper presented at the Spring Joint Computer Conference of the American Federation of Information Processing Societies, 1962.

Licklider, J. C. R. Interview by William Aspray. Charles Babbage Institute, DARPA/IPTO Oral History Collection, University of Minnesota Center for the History of Information Processing, Minneapolis, Minn., 28 October 1988.

Lukasik, Stephen. Interview by Judy O'Neill. Charles Babbage Institute, DARPA/IPTO Oral History Collection, University of Minnesota Center for the History of Information Processing, Minneapolis, Minn., 17 October 1991.

Marill, Thomas, and Lawrence G. Roberts. "Toward a Cooperative Network of Time-Shared Computers." Paper presented at the Fall Joint Computer Conference of the American Federation of Information Processing Societies, 1966.

McCarthy, J., S. Boilen, E. Fredkin, and J. C. R. Licklider. "A Time-Sharing Debugging System for a Small Computer." Paper presented at the Spring Joint Computer Conference of the American Federation of Information Processing Societies, 1963.

McKenzie, Alexander A. "The ARPA Network Control Center." Paper presented at the Fourth Data Communications Symposium of the Institute for Electrical and Electronics Engineers, October 1975.

McKenzie, Alexander A. Interview by Judy O'Neill. Charles Babbage Institute, DARPA/IPTO Oral History Collection, University of Minnesota

Center for the History of Information Processing, Minneapolis, Minn., 13 March 1990.

Message Group. The full text of more than 2,600 e-mail messages sent by members of the Message Group (or MsgGroup), one of the first electronic mailing lists, relating to the development of e-mail. The Computer Museum, Boston, Mass., June 1975–June 1986. Electronic document. (http://www.tcm.org/msgroup)

Metcalfe, Robert. "Some Historic Moments in Networking." Request for Comments 89. Network Working Group, 19 January 1971.

Myer, T. H., and D. A. Henderson. "Message Transmission Protocol." Request for Comments 680. Stanford Research Institute, Menlo Park, Calif., 1975.

National Research Council, Commission on Engineering and Technical Systems. "Transport Protocols for Department of Defense Data Networks." Report to the Department of Defense and the National Bureau of Standards, Board on Telecommunication and Computer Applications, 1985.

Neigus, N.J. "File Transfer Protocol." Request for Comments 542. Bolt Beranek and Newman Inc., Cambridge, Mass., 12 July 1973.

Norberg, Arthur L., and Judy E. O'Neill. "A History of the Information Processing Techniques Office of the Defense Advanced Research Projects Agency." Charles Babbage Institute, University of Minnesota, Minneapolis, Minn., 1992.

Ornstein, Severo M., F. E. Heart, W. R. Crowther, H. K. Rising, S. B. Russell, and A. Michel. "The Terminal IMP for the ARPA Network." Paper presented at the Spring Joint Computer Conference of the American Federation of Information Processing Societies, Atlantic City, N.J., May 1972.

Ornstein, Severo. Interview by Judy O'Neill. Charles Babbage Institute, DARPA/IPTO Oral History Collection, University of Minnesota Center for the History of Information Processing, Minneapolis, Minn., 6 March 1990.

Pogran, Ken, John Vittal, Dave Crowther, and Austin Henderson. "Proposed Official Standard for the Format of ARPA Network Messages." Request for Comments 724. MIT, Cambridge, Mass., 12 May 1977.

Postel, Jonathan B. "Simple Mail Transfer Protocol." Request for Comments 821. Information Sciences Institute, University of Southern California, August 1982.

————. "Specification of Internetwork Transmission Control Protocol: TCP Version 4." Information Sciences Institute, University of Southern California, September 1978.

————. "TCP and IP Bake Off." Request for Comments 1025. Network Working Group, September 1987.

Pouzin, Louis. "Network Protocols." Notes of the International Network Working Group 50, September 1973.

————. "Presentation and Major Design Aspects of the Cyclades Computer Network." Paper presented at the IEEE Third Data Communications Symposium (Data Networks: Analysis and Design), November 1973.

————. "Experimental Communication Protocol: Basic Message Frame." Notes of the International Network Working Group 48, January 1974.

————. "Interconnection of Packet Switching Networks." Notes of the International Network Working Group 42, October 1973.

————. "Network Architecture and Components." Notes of the International Network Working Group 49, August 1973.

RAND Corporation. "Development of the Distributed Adaptive Message-Block Network." Recommendation to the Air Staff, 30 August 1965.

RCA Service Company, Government Services Division. "ARPANET Study Final Report." Submitted under contract no. F08606-73-C-0018. 24 November 1972.

Richard J. Barber Associates, Inc. "The Advanced Research Projects Agency: 1958–1974." A study for the Advanced Research Projects Agency under contract no. MDA-903-74-C-0096. Washington, D.C., December 1975. Photocopy.

Roberts, Lawrence G. "Extensions of Packet Communications Technology to a Hand-Held Personal Terminal." Paper presented at the Spring Joint Computer Conference of the American Federation of Information Processing Societies, May 1972.

————. "Multiple Computer Networks and Intercomputer Communication." Paper presented at the Association for Computing Machinery Symposium on Operating System Principles, October 1967.

Roberts, Lawrence G., and Barry D. Wessler. "Computer Network Development to Achieve Resource Sharing." Paper presented at the Spring Joint Computer Conference of the American Federation of Information Processing Societies, 1970.

Roberts, Lawrence G. Interview by Arthur Norberg. Charles Babbage Institute, DARPA/IPTO Oral History Collection, University of Minnesota

Center for the History of Information Processing, Minneapolis, Minn., 4 April 1989.

Ruina, Jack. Interview by William Aspray. Charles Babbage Institute, DARPA/IPTO Oral History Collection, University of Minnesota Center for the History of Information Processing, Minneapolis, Minn., 20 April 1989.

Sutherland, Ivan. Interview by William Aspray. Charles Babbage Institute DARPA/IPTO Oral History Collection, University of Minnesota Center for the History of Information Processing, Minneapolis, Minn., 1 May 1989.

Taylor, Robert. Interview by William Aspray. Charles Babbage Institute, DARPA/IPTO Oral History Collection, University of Minnesota Center for the History of Information Processing, Minneapolis, Minn., 28 February 1989.

U.S. Postal Service. "Electronic Message Systems for the U.S. Postal Service." Report of the U.S.P.S. Support Panel, Committee on Telecommunications, Washington, D.C., January 1977.

Walden, David C. "Experiences in Building, Operating, and Using the ARPA Network." Paper presented at the Second USA-Japan Computer Conference, Tokyo, Japan, August 1975.

Walden, David. Interview by Judy O'Neill. Charles Babbage Institute, DARPA/IPTO Oral History Collection, University of Minnesota Center for the History of Information Processing, Minneapolis, Minn., 6 February 1990.

Walker, Stephen T. "Completion Report: ARPA Network Development." Defense Advanced Research Projects Agency, Information Processing Techniques Office, Washington, D.C., 4 January 1978.

Weik, Martin H. "A Third Survey of Domestic Electronic Digital Computing Systems." Ballistic Research Laboratories, report no. 1115, March 1961.

White, Jim. "Proposed Mail Protocol." Request for Comments 524. Stanford Research Institute, Menlo Park, Calif., 13 June 1973.

Zimmermann, H., and M. Elie. "Proposed Standard Host-Host Protocol for Heterogeneous Computer Networks: Transport Protocol." Notes of the International Network Working Group 43, December 1973.

Electronic Archives

Charles Babbage Institute, Center for the History of Information Processing, University of Minnesota. Large archival collection relating to the
history of computing. More information can be obtained via the CBI
Web site at http://cbi.itdean.umn.edu/cbi/welcome.html or via e-mail
addressed to bruce@fs1.itdean.umn.edu.

Computer Museum, Boston, Massachusetts. Large collection relating to
the history of computing, including the archives of the Message Group
concerning the early development of e-mail. The archive is available via
the homepage at http://www.tcm.org/msgroup.

Information Sciences Institute, University of Southern California. Collection includes up-to-date indexes and tests of Internet standards, protocols, Requests for Comments (RFCs), and various other technical notes
available via the ISI Web site: http://www.isi.edu. Some of the earlier
RFCs are not available electronically, but are archived off-line in meticulous fashion by RFC editor Jon Postel. A searchable archive is main-
tained at http://info.internet.isi.edu:80/in-notes/rfc.

Ohio State University, Department of Computer and Information Science.
The CIS Web Server offers access to RFCs and various other technical
and historical documents related to the Internet via http://www.cis.ohio-
state.edu:80/hypertext/information/rfc.html.

Acknowledgments

This book grew out of an idea that originated with engineers at Bolt Beranek and Newman. Memories were growing fuzzy in late 1993, when we first started thinking about doing a book, and Frank Heart and others were interested in having BBN's considerable role in the creation of the original ARPANET recorded. Not only did the company open its archives to us and cooperate in every way but it helped fund the project as well, while agreeing to exercise no control over the content of the book. Marian Bremer, then BBN's head librarian, made the initial phone call that led to the book. Cary Lu and John Markoff urged us to take on the project.

Helen Samuels and the folks at MIT archives were immensely helpful, as was Kevin Corbitt, assistant archivist at the Charles Babbage Institute, Center for the History of Information Processing, at the University of Minnesota. We are grateful to John Day, Larry Roberts, Al Vezza, and John Shoch for digging around in old boxes for us. Deborah Melone and Bob Menk sent photographs and archives from BBN. Kevin Kelly and Martha Baer at *Wired* magazine got us focused on the history of e-mail. Noel Chiappa, good-natured tutor, spent hours on the telephone explaining, among other technical points, how routing tables and RFNMs work.

The following people allowed us to interview them at length: Wes Clark, Vint Cerf, Bob Kahn, Severo Ornstein, Bob Taylor, Larry Roberts, Jon Postel, Frank Heart, Alex McKenzie, Dave Walden, Ben Barker, Donald Davies, Paul Baran, Len Kleinrock, Steve Lukasik, Steve Crocker, and Bob Metcalfe. Louise Licklider, Bill McGill, John Swets, and Karl Kryter shared their memories of J. C. R. Licklider with us, and Mitch Waldrop helped fill in some blanks. Phil Patton entrusted us with his copy of the Barber Associates study, for which we are grateful. Brian Reid, Gary Chapman, Kevin Buckley, Dave Farber, and Colonel Clair Shirey let us pick their brains on various relevant topics. Marsha Longshore of IEEE sent technical articles our way, and Earl Swartzlander lent us his copies of the IEEE computer history annals. Steve Wolff helped us understand the often labyrinthine events that took place in the 1980s, particularly concerning NSF's role in the development of the Internet.

The manuscript was read in whole or in part in various stages of completion by Vint Cerf, Lyman Chapin, Steve Crocker, Peter Denning, Frank Heart, Bob Kahn, John Kelley, Larry Landweber, Steven Levy, Hank Long, Paul McJones, Alex McKenzie, Peter Preuss, Larry Roberts, Einar Stefferud, Bob Taylor, John Vittal, Dave Walden, and Susan Zacharias. Everett Hafner, perfectionist and workhorse, kept us honest. The manuscript benefited tremendously from the keen mind and careful pen of Richard Lyon. Responsibility for errors, of course, rests with us.

Jon Coifman, our ace research assistant, helped immensely with the final stages of the manuscript preparation, and Andrea Perry was a careful proofreader. Julian Darley helped type in changes. Denise Bugg transcribed many tapes. Pete Lewis saved the day with his Wacom Pen Tablet. Sigrid Cerf supplied us with colorful stories and much sage advice. Matt Pallakoff, who wrote Retrieve It!, helped shave hours off our work weeks. And thanks to John Aielli, who knows why.

Zoë Mark Lyon, though busy with her own book, took time out of her schedule every single day to bolster our spirits and make us laugh. Denny Lyon, Amy Goodwin, Kelly McRee, Ellen Lyon, and Jeremy Lyon gamely took on extra child care. Sherry Turkle, Sarah Hafner, Teresa Carpenter, Terry Evers, Robert Wallich, Tony Bianco, and Carol Flake lent a sympathetic ear. Ladd Hanson and Mark McFarland helped with technical troubles. George Hackett and Bob Berdahl were long-suffering bosses, against their better judgment. Ann Walther, Lindsey Lane, and Tom Ferguson (keeper of the postage meter) came to the rescue more than once. Paulina Borsook offered her customary invaluable insights.

During our travels, Chris Paine, Katherine Magraw, Holly Myers, Kirk Neely, Lisa Van Dusen, Candace Thille, Julie Graham, Debbie Yager, Katherine and Irving Gottsegen, Jane and Frank Heart, Barry Muhlfelder, Jane Anderson, and Eric Ponteri put a roof over our heads.

As usual, literary agents John Brockman and Katinka Matson knew there was a book there. Bob Bender, our marvelous editor at Simon & Schuster, knew what that book should be. His wondrous assistant, Johanna Li, never let us down.

—Katie Hafner
katieh@ zilker.net

—Matthew Lyon
m_lyon@ utxvms.cc.utexas.edu

Index